EMOTION
Theory, Research, and Experience

Volume 5
Emotion, Psychopathology, and Psychotherapy

EMOTION
Theory, Research, and Experience

EDITED BY

Robert Plutchik
Albert Einstein College of Medicine
Bronx, New York

Henry Kellerman
Postgraduate Center for Mental Health
New York, New York

EMOTION
Theory, Research, and Experience

Volume 5

Emotion, Psychopathology, and Psychotherapy

Edited by

Robert Plutchik

Albert Einstein College of Medicine
Bronx, New York

Henry Kellerman

Postgraduate Center for Mental Health
New York, New York

ACADEMIC PRESS, INC.
Harcourt Brace Jovanovich, Publishers
San Diego   New York   Berkeley   Boston
London   Sydney   Tokyo   Toronto

Copyright © 1990 by Academic Press, Inc.
All Rights Reserved.
No part of this publication may be reproduced or transmitted in any form or
by any means, electronic or mechanical, including photocopy, recording, or
any information storage and retrieval system, without permission in writing
from the publisher.

Academic Press, Inc.
San Diego, California 92101

United Kingdom Edition published by
Academic Press Limited
24–28 Oval Road, London NW1 7DX

Library of Congress Cataloging-in-Publication Data

Emotion, psychopathology, and psychotherapy / edited by Robert
    Plutchik and Henry Kellerman.
        p.   cm. — (Emotion ; v. 5)
    Includes bibliographies and index.
    ISBN   0-12-558705-8   (alk. paper)
    1. Emotions. 2. Affect (Psychology) 3. Psychotherapy.
4. Psychology, Pathological.   I. Plutchik, Robert. II. Kellerman,
Henry. III. Series: Emotion, theory, research, and experience ; v.
5.
    [DNLM: 1. Affective Disorders. 2. Affective Symptoms.
3. Emotions. 4. Psychotherapy.   W1 EM668 v. 5 / WM 171 E54]
BF561.E48   vol. 5
[RC489.E45]
152.4 s—dc20
[616.89]
DNLM/DLC
for Library of Congress   89-6848
                                                                 CIP

Printed in the United States of America
89   90   91   92   9   8   7   6   5   4   3   2   1

CONTENTS

Part I   EVOLUTIONARY FOCUS

Chapter 1
Emotions and Psychotherapy: A Psychoevolutionary Perspective   3

Robert Plutchik

Chapter 2
Anger: An Evolutionary View   43

Michael T. McGuire and Alfonso Troisi

Chapter 3
Emotional-Change Processes in Psychotherapy   59

Leslie S. Greenberg and Jeremy D. Safran

Part II PSYCHOANALYTIC FOCUS

Chapter 4
Emotion and the Organization of Primary Process   89

Henry Kellerman

Chapter 5
New Perspectives in Psychoanalytic Affect Theory   115

Otto F. Kernberg

Chapter 6
Emotion, Time, and the Self   133

Jacob A. Arlow

Chapter 7
The Changing Role of Emotion in Group Psychotherapy   147

K. Roy MacKenzie

Part III COGNITIVE, BEHAVIORAL, AND DYNAMIC FOCUS

Chapter 8
Cognitive Approaches to Psychotherapy: Theory and Therapy   177

Michael S. Greenberg and Aaron T. Beck

Chapter 9
Emotions: A Multimodal Therapy Perspective   195

Arnold A. Lazarus and Clifford N. Lazarus

Chapter 10
Interpersonal Analysis of the Cathartic Model   209

Lorna Smith Benjamin

Chapter 11
Emotion and Rules of Living   231

Richard L. Wessler and Sheenah Hankin-Wessler

CONTRIBUTORS

Numbers in parentheses indicate the pages on which the authors' contributions begin.

JACOB A. ARLOW (133), Department of Psychiatry, New York University College of Medicine, New York, New York 10016

AARON T. BECK (177), Department of Psychiatry, University of Pennsylvania, Philadelphia, Pennsylvania

LORNA SMITH BENJAMIN (209), Department of Psychology, University of Utah, Salt Lake City, Utah 84112

LESLIE S. GREENBERG (59), Department of Psychology, York University, North York, Ontario M3J 1P3, Canada

MICHAEL S. GREENBERG (177), Florida Center for Cognitive Therapy, Clearwater, Florida 34621

SHEENAH HANKIN-WESSLER (231), Cognitive Psychotherapy Associates, New York, New York 10728

HENRY KELLERMAN (89), Postgraduate Center for Mental Health, New York, New York 10016

OTTO F. KERNBERG (115), Department of Psychiatry, Cornell Medical College and New York Hospital, New York, New York 10021

ARNOLD A. LAZARUS (195), Graduate School of Applied and Professional Psychology, Rutgers University, New Brunswick, New Jersey 08903

CLIFFORD N. LAZARUS (195), Department of Psychology, Rutgers University, New Brunswick, New Jersey 08903

K. ROY MACKENZIE (147), Department of Psychiatry, University of Texas Health Science Center at Houston, Department of Psychiatry and Behavioral Sciences, Houston, Texas 77725

MICHAEL T. MCGUIRE (43), Department of Psychiatry, School of Medicine, University of California at Los Angeles, Los Angeles, California 90024

ROBERT PLUTCHIK (3), Department of Psychiatry, Albert Einstein College of Medicine, Bronx, New York 10461

JEREMY D. SAFRAN (59), Cognitive Therapy Unit, Clarke Institute of Psychiatry, Department of Psychiatry, University of Toronto, Toronto, Ontario M5T IR8, Canada

ALFONSO TROISI (43), Cattedra di Clinica Psichiatrica, 11 Universita di Roma, Rome 00162, Italy

RICHARD L. WESSLER (231), Department of Psychology, Pace University, Pleasantville, New York 10570

PREFACE

The publication of this volume, *Emotion, Psychopathology, and Psychotherapy*, completes the five-volume edition of the series, *Emotion: Theory, Research, and Experience*. The first volume of the series on *Theories of Emotion* was published in 1980, followed by Volume 2, *Emotions in Early Development*, published in 1983. The third volume, *Biological Foundations of Emotion*, appeared in 1986. Volume 4, *The Measurement of Emotions*, was published in 1989.

Emotion as a distinct scientific and clinical area of study as well as an organizing concept in the field of psychology had been, until the 1970s, largely relegated to peripheral status in the overall psychological literature. This position was especially evident with respect to the meager treatment afforded the coverage of emotion in psychology texts. Despite this limited focus on emotions, theorists and researchers continued to generate important new ideas about the domain and continued to map its overall clinical and biological structure.

In the ensuing decade, papers and books on emotions and their relations to a wide variety of theoretical and clinical concerns have proliferated. During this period of expanding interest in the field of emotion, a significant sampling of the seminal ideas that have been produced appears throughout the five-volume series *Emotion: Theory, Research, and Experience*. The series has helped focus attention on emotion as a distinct discipline and has related it to many other domains of discourse. The study of emotion has dramatically expanded from a concern with a few limited traditional areas to a major research arena that has attracted theoreticians, clinicians, and experimenters from the fields of psychology, psychoanalysis, psychiatry, psychopharmacology, neuro-physiology, sociobiology, genetics, and anthropology. Theoretical work is being generated along with empirical data concerning a multitude of variables directly relevant to the influence and operation of the emotions. We believe that the present five-volume work represents a major compendium of original sources that reveal the known parameters of the study of emotion.

INTRODUCTION

In order to understand the nature of emotions, several complementary approaches need to be used. One approach is concerned with the development of theories and models; a second is concerned with the accumulation of empirical data. The third approach attempts to explore the vicissitudes of emotion and how emotions can be changed.

The previous volumes of this series have largely focused on theory and research; in the present volume the contributors are concerned with the formulation of models of emotion psychopathology and psychotherapy. The chapters focus on the experience of emotion, the dysregulation of emotion, and methods for changing emotion.

Each author in the present volume was asked to address a number of key questions relevant to the themes of emotions and psychopathology, the experience of emotional dysfunction, and the strategies needed to effect change. Specifically, they were asked to describe the role that emotions play in psychopathology and in psychotherapy. They were asked to consider issues such as the following: how emotion concepts enlighten us with regard to diagnoses of psychopathology; various aspects of personality, defenses, dreams, and cognitions; and important clinical notions such as object relations, character structure, and the development of the self.

The various contributions are grouped into three parts. The first part contains theoretical work that links emotions to psychopathology and psychotherapy on the basis of a number of concepts that are derived from a consideration of evolutionary biology. The second part contains theoretical work that reflects the psychoanalytic tradition in the understanding of these links. These first two parts, reflecting the evolutionary and psychoanalytic points of view, can be seen as blueprints that set out strategies that might guide specific psychotherapeutic interventions. They also help define the nature of psychopathology. In the third part, a series of chapters are presented in which the authors emphasize the role of cognitive constructions of reality and how psychotherapy can influence affects through transformations of cognitions.

THE EVOLUTIONARY FOCUS

In the first chapter, Plutchik describes his psychoevolutionary theory of emotions and its relation to a number of important ideas taken from evolutionary biology, particularly the notion of evolutionary compromises and deception. He suggests that emotional behavior is the proximate basis for the ultimate outcome of increased inclusive fitness. He introduces the idea that all individuals need to deal with the key issues of dominance hierarchies, territorial imperatives, identity formation, and genetic representation in succeeding generations. These ideas are used to describe conflict areas that are the typical basis for therapeutic efforts. Plutchik also describes five fundamental processes that are involved in emotional change.

In Chapter 2, McGuire and Troisi present a theory of the vicissitudes of the emotion of anger from an evolutionary point of view. The authors describe the functions of anger and its effects in changing the behavior of individuals. The intensity and duration of anger are considered to be major variables as determinants of change. They believe that a change in an individual's physiology is also a necessary aspect of the change process. Anger is claimed to have many functions. These include asserting one's authority, gaining revenge, destroying an object, and changing the behavior of an object. These functions are discussed in cost-benefit terms referred to as the economic vocabulary of evolutionary theory.

In Chapter 3, Greenberg and Safran describe emotion as a biologically adaptive system that presents people with information about their reactions to situations and organizes them for action. The authors present six emotional change processes that are applied in the therapy setting. These include creation of meaning, acknowledgment of emotional experience, and arousal of emotions. Emotions are considered to be adaptive organizers of information. The authors believe that pathological symptoms in individuals can be reduced through the restructuring of emotional schemata, modifying dysfunctional and emotional responses, and disconfirming certain relationship expectations. Emotions not only are an inner experience but also serve as a bridge to the environment by organizing individuals for action in the world.

In Chapter 4, Kellerman introduces a series of contributions dealing with psychoanalytic approaches to understanding emotions. Kellerman relates the concept of primary process — severe psychopathology — to various aspects of personality, diagnoses, cognitive orientations, defensive structures, dreams and nightmares, and secondary process. These correlations are derived from a theory of emotion and suggest that there are a small number of personality types that are systematically related to primary processes. This formulation also proposes that various object-relations concepts are connected with the organization of primary process and other aspects of personality.

In Chapter 5, Kernberg sets forth a psychoanalytic theory of drives and object relations that are linked through the development of affects in early life. In this chapter, Kernberg conceives of affects as related to drives, which in turn are considered as motivational systems. These motivational systems contain libidinal and aggressive components that appear clinically as signal states. Kernberg also describes how early object relations determine the cognitive aspects of emotions. Overall, an attempt is made to link drives, instincts, and affects from a psychoanalytic viewpoint.

Arlow, in Chapter 6, presents an analysis of the individual's sense of time and how this sense of time is utilized for defensive purposes in the personality. The analysis describes how the sense of time affects both the sense of self and the experience of emotions. Arlow proposes that emotions contain a temporal dimension that connects past, present, and future. The time element of emotion is connected to psychophysiological needs, gratification of needs, and relief of tension. Time distortion is related to psychopathological manifestations and defense operations, that is, the alleviation of guilt and depersonalization experiences.

The concluding chapter in this part, Chapter 7 by MacKenzie, considers the role of emotion in group psychotherapy. Interpersonal patterns of group processes are examined with respect to their emotional meaning. Emotion is related to therapeutic change factors and to group dimensions such as cohesion. Group stages and role functions are considered with reference to basic emotion dimensions. Five stages of group development are related to corresponding emotion dimensions and role types. Emotions are believed to reflect central motives that drive the group to resolve its problems.

The third part of the book deals with emotional change from the point of view of cognitive, dynamic, and behavioral therapies. In Chapter 8, Greenberg and Beck describe maladaptive cognitive schemas that have strong impact upon affect and behavior. Psychological disorders are identified on the basis of ideation associated with depressive or anxiety schemas. The authors propose that in cognitive psychotherapy individuals identify and examine their own biased conclusions concerning the self and reality. Depressive disorders contain themes of failure, worthlessness, incompetence, and rejection, whereas anxiety disorders contain themes of threat, danger, and uncertainty. Individuals are assisted to develop methods, both cognitive and behavioral, to modify these themes and thus to manage, reduce, or eliminate depression and anxiety.

In Chapter 9, Lazarus and Lazarus focus on the role of emotion in producing change in psychotherapy. They emphasize the point that emotion and cognition are inextricable. They believe that appropriate treatment of affective disorders requires the correction of irrational beliefs, deviant behaviors, unpleasant feelings, and intrusive images. The authors describe an assessment profile of each of a series of factors that are considered in their therapy. Their multimodel position is that assessments of behavior, sensation, imagery, cognition, and interpersonal relationships are the salient variables that need to be addressed in attempting to change psychopathological manifestations of emotion.

The assumptions underlying the cathartic model are examined by Benjamin in Chapter 10. It is frequently claimed that identification and expression of emotion is a valuable technique in the psychotherapeutic endeavor. In this chapter, Benjamin tries to demonstrate that catharsis does not always have beneficial effects. She distinguishes three possible effects of the expression of emotion: helpfulness, irrelevance, and harm. She offers a theoretical framework for anticipating whether catharsis, that is, the expression of emotion in any given instance, is likely to be constructive, irrelevant, or harmful. Benjamin describes a series of therapist–patient interactions illustrating these various effects. She provides strategies for the management of anger that also apply to other emotions as well.

In Chapter 11, Wessler and Hankin-Wessler relate emotions to rules of living. These rules of living are a set of mores and folkways regarding how people do or should conduct themselves. Wessler and Hankin-Wessler specifically relate rules of living to the emotions of depression, anxiety, and hostility; the rules mediate affect and action. The authors propose techniques for discovering these rules and suggest implications for psychotherapy that help clients learn how to manage their own emotions. Of special importance are techniques for helping clients become aware of security maneuvers and learned affect states. These techniques include imagery, self-disclosure, and role playing.

Overall, these various contributions provide a panorama of methods that clinicians and others have found helpful for changing emotions. The methods can be seen not only to reflect different theoretical models of personality and selfhood but also, by implication, to define the nature of psychopathology. A central conclusion that stems from these concepts is that theories of emotion, to be viable, need to have implications for change and remediation. As has often been stated in the various chapters of this series, emotions are adaptive processes that normally function to increase the likelihood of accurate communication as well as survival. When these functions fail we need to know what to do. The contributors of the present volume provide a set of theories or models for understanding emotion and psychopathology as well as therapeutic strategies. Future research and practice will be based upon many of the ideas found here.

Part I

EVOLUTIONARY FOCUS

Chapter 1

EMOTIONS AND PSYCHOTHERAPY:
A PSYCHOEVOLUTIONARY PERSPECTIVE

ROBERT PLUTCHIK

ABSTRACT

After examining the six basic postulates of the author's psychoevolutionary theory of emotion, certain key ideas of evolutionary biology are described. Of special relevance to issues of psychotherapy are the ideas of evolutionary compromises and deception. The hypothesis is proposed that emotional behavior is the proximate basis for the ultimate outcome of increased inclusive fitness. In describing specific clinical implications of the theory, the concept of four types of existential issues is introduced. These issues are hierarchy, territoriality, identity, and temporality. This classification leads to a list of conflict areas that include many of the problems individuals describe when seeking psychotherapy. The classification also implies the existence of five fundamental strategies that guide the process of psychotherapy. These are assessment, historical reconstruction, functional analysis, goal setting, and skill acquisition. A model of therapeutic communication is proposed and is followed by a description of nine general tactics of psychotherapy. It is concluded that psychotherapy is a process of self-evaluation, goal setting, problem solving, reinterpretation, and skill acquisition, a view that is consistent with a broad evolutionary perspective on human life.

Psychotherapy patients describe their personal problems in several interrelated ways. They may experience certain emotions too often or too strongly, emotions such as depression, anxiety, or anger. The same may be said about other emotions such as disgust (in the form of blame or hostility), trust (in the form of

EMOTION
Theory, Research, and Experience
Volume 5

excessive gullability) and joy (in the form of mania). The client would like such emotions reduced in intensity or frequency.

In contrast, patients may experience certain emotions too weakly or too infrequently. They may complain that they cannot cry, or show affection or love, or get angry, or be assertive. In such cases, the client would like to increase the frequency or intensity of these emotions.

Sometimes patients describe their problems in interpersonal terms. They experience difficulty in getting along with other people, their spouses, lovers, parents, children, friends, employers, or coworkers. When such complaints are examined closely it becomes evident that emotions are at the heart of them. Parents make the patients feel guilty, bosses make them feel resentful, children disappoint them, and lovers make them anxious. The interpersonal relations apparently trigger emotional reactions that the individual finds difficult to handle. It thus becomes evident why patients are said to suffer from "emotional disorders" or to be "emotionally disturbed or upset."

Psychotherapy, therefore, is, or should be, concerned with emotions, their *nature, initiation, control,* and *change.* Success in these areas can lead to desirable changes in interpersonal relations as well as to feelings of satisfactory experience and expression of emotions. This also implies that any theory of emotion that claims to be a general one should have something to say about these issues, should have some implications for psychotherapy.

The purpose of the present chapter is to examine these issues. It will provide a brief overview of the author's psychoevolutionary theory of emotion developed over the past two decades. It will also describe some important ideas in evolutionary biology that have some relevance for emotions and will then make some detailed observations on the implications of these ideas for the practice of psychotherapy.

THE PSYCHOEVOLUTIONARY THEORY
OF EMOTIONS: AN OVERVIEW

The theory was first described in a paper in 1958 (Plutchik, 1958). It was elaborated in a book (Plutchik, 1962) and further extended in a series of papers and books (Conte & Plutchik, 1981; Plutchik, 1970, 1980a, 1980b, 1983a, 1983b, 1984a, 1984b, 1989; Plutchik, Kellerman, & Conte, 1979; Plutchik & Platman, 1977). It has been used to help reveal the infrastructure of group processes and personality interaction (Kellerman, 1979), the nature of nightmares (Kellerman, 1987), and the affective structure of Rorschach categories (Kellerman, 1989). It has·at least six fundamental postulates; these are listed in Table 1.1.

The first postulate, that emotions are communication and survival mecha-

TABLE 1.1

Basic Propositions of a Psychoevolutionary Theory of Emotions

1. Emotions are communications and survival mechanisms based on evolutionary adaptations.
2. Emotions have a genetic basis.
3. Emotions are hypothetical constructs based on various classes of evidence.
4. Emotions are complex chains of events with stabilizing feedback loops that produce some kind of behavioral homeostasis.
5. The relation among emotions can be represented by a three-dimensional structural model.
6. Emotions are related to a number of derivative conceptual domains.

nisms, is a direct reflection of the Darwinian, ethological tradition. Darwin (1872/1965) pointed out that emotions have two functions for all animals. First, they increase the chances of individual survival through appropriate reactions to emergency events in the environment (by flight, for example). Second, they act as signals of intentions of future action through display behaviors of various kinds (Enquist, 1985).

Evolutionary theory assumes that the natural environment creates survival problems for all organisms that must be successfully dealt with if they are to survive. These problems include, for example, differentially responding to prey and predators, food and mates, and caregivers and care solicitors. Emotions can be conceptualized as basic adaptive patterns that can be identified at all phylogenetic levels that deal with these basic survival issues. Emotions are the ultraconservative evolutionary behavioral adaptations (such as amino acids, DNA, and genes) that have been successful in increasing the chances of survival of organisms. They have therefore been maintained in functionally equivalent forms through all phylogenetic levels (Plutchik, 1962, 1970, 1980a, 1980b).

The second postulate, that emotions have a genetic basis, stems directly from the psychoevolutionary context. Darwin (1872/1965) first suggested at least four types of evidence one can use for establishing a genetic basis for emotions. First, he noted that some emotional expressions appear in similar form in many lower animals (for example, the apparent increase in body size during rage or agonistic interactions due to erection of body hair or feathers, changes in postures, or expansion of air pouches). Second, some emotional expressions appear in infants in the same form as in adults (smiling and frowning, for example). Third, some emotional expressions are shown in identical ways by those born blind as by those who are normally sighted (pouting and laughter, for example). And fourth, some emotional expressions appear in similar form in widely separated races and groups of humans (Eibl-Eibesfeldt, 1975; Ekman & Friesen, 1971).

Recent genetic studies comparing monozygotic and dizygotic twins, cross-adoption studies, and other methods have revealed hereditary contributions to such temperamental (emotional) qualities as aggressiveness (Fuller, 1986; Wimer & Wimer, 1985), timidity or fearfulness (Goddard & Beilharz, 1985), assertiveness (Loehlin, Horn, & Williams, 1981), and shyness (Stevenson-Hinde & Simpson, 1982), as well as many others.

Genetic theory indicates that individuals do not inherit behavior per se but only the structural and physiological mechanisms that mediate behavior. Genes influence theshholds of sensitivity, perceptual inclinations, cellular structures, and biochemical events. They determine epigenetic rules that act as filters limiting the kind of information allowed into the system and how that information is to be processed. For example, most animals appear to have auditory detectors "tuned" to signals that are of special significance for their survival (Lumsden & Wilson, 1981). Most, but not all, emotional expressions are based on genetic templates or schemata that determine the generality of emotional development and reactions to probable events in the environment (Plutchik, 1983a).

The third basic postulate of the psychoevolutionary theory of emotion is that emotions are hypothetical constructs or inferences based on various classes of evidence. The kinds of evidence we use to infer the existence of emotions include (1) knowledge of stimulus conditions, (2) knowledge of an organism's behavior in a variety of settings, (3) knowledge of what species typical behavior is, (4) knowledge of how an organism's peers react to it, and (5) knowledge of the effect of an individual's behavior on others (Plutchik, 1980a). One of the more important reasons that emotional states are difficult to define unequivocally is that more than one emotion can occur at the same time. Any given overt display of emotion can reflect such complex states as approach and avoidance, attack and flight, sex and aggression, or fear and pleasure.

The fourth basic postulate of the theory is that emotions are complex chains of events with stabilizing loops that tend to produce some kind of behavioral homeostasis. Figure 1.1 illustrates this idea. Emotions are triggered by various events. These events must be cognitively evaluated as being of significance to the well-being or integrity of the individual. If such a determination is made, various feelings as well as a pattern of physiological changes will result. These physiological changes have the character of anticipatory reactions associated with various types of exertions or impulses, such as the urge to explore, to attack, to retreat, or to mate. Depending on the relative strengths of these various impulses, a final vectorial resultant will occur in the form of overt action that is designed to have an effect on the stimulus that triggered this chain of events in the first place. For example, distress signals by a puppy or the crying of an infant will increase the probability that the mother or a mother-substitute will arrive on the scene. The overall effect of this complex feedback system is to reduce the threat or to

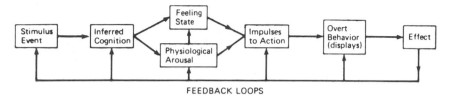

FIGURE 1.1. The complex chain of events defining an emotion.

change the emergency situation in such a way as to achieve a temporary behavioral homeostatic balance.

The fifth postulate of the theory suggests that the relations among emotions can be represented by a three-dimensional structural model shaped like a cone. The vertical dimension represents the intensity of emotions, the circle defines degree of similarity of emotions, and polarity is represented by the opposite emotions on the circle. This postulate also includes the idea that some emotions are primary and others are derivatives or blends, in the same sense that some colors are primary and others are mixed. A number of studies have been published showing that the language of emotions can be represented by means of a circle or circumplex (Fisher, Heise, Bohrnstedt, & Lucke, 1985; Conte & Plutchik, 1981; Plutchik, 1980a; Russell, 1989; Wiggins & Broughton, 1985).

The concept of primary and derived emotions leads to the sixth basic postulate of the theory, which states that emotions are related to a number of derivative conceptual domains. This idea has been explored in a number of different ways. For example, it has been shown that the language of mixed emotions is identical to the language of personality traits. Hostility has been judged to be composed of anger and disgust, sociability is a blend of joy and acceptance, and guilt is a combination of pleasure plus fear. Emotional components have been identified for hundreds of personality traits. In addition, there is now clear-cut evidence that personality traits also exhibit a circumplex structure just as do emotions (Conte & Plutchik, 1981; Russell, 1989; Wiggins & Broughton, 1985).

The idea of derivatives can be extended further. Diagnostic terms such as "depressed," "manic," and "paranoid" can be conceived as extreme expressions of such basic emotions as sadness, joy, and disgust. Several studies have also revealed that the language of diagnosis also shares a circumplex structure with emotions (Plutchik & Platman, 1977; Schaefer & Plutchik, 1966).

Carrying the notion of derivatives still another step, our research has shown that the language of ego defenses can also be conceptualized as being related to emotions. For example, displacement can be conceptualized as an unconscious way to deal with anger that cannot be directly expressed without punishment. Similarly, projection can be conceptualized as an unconscious way to deal with a

feeling of disgust for (or rejection of) oneself by attributing this feeling to
outsiders. Parallels of this sort have been drawn for each of the primary emotions
and are described in detail in Kellerman (1979) and Plutchik et al. (1979). The
concept of derivatives is illustrated more fully in Table 1.2 where the conceptual
links between affects, behavior, functions, personality traits, diagnoses, and ego
defenses are shown. Also added is the domain of coping styles, which can be
hypothesized to be the conscious derivatives of the unconscious ego-defenses.
Thus, fault finding corresponds to projection, reversal to reaction-formation, and
mapping to intellectualization. Other derivative domains have also been proposed (Plutchik, 1984b, 1989).

The psychoevolutionary theory of emotion has been useful in a number of
ways. It has provided a general approach to emotions that is relevant to lower
animals as well as to humans. It is parsimonious in that the same set of assumptions has relevance and explanatory value for a number of conceptual domains
(affects, personality, defenses, diagnoses). It has predicted some new observations that have been empirically confirmed (the circumplex structure of affects,
personality traits, diagnoses, and defenses). It has also provided some new
insights into specific issues such as the relations between emotions and motivations (Plutchik, 1980a), emotions and cognitions (Plutchik, 1977, 1985), emotions and imagery (Plutchik, 1984a), emotions and temperament (Plutchik,
1971, 1985), emotions and empathy (Plutchik, 1987), emotions and dreams
(Kellerman, 1987), and emotions and primary processes (Kellerman, this volume, Chap. 4). And also of great importance, it has provided a theoretical
rationale for the construction of a number of new test instruments designed to
measure affects (Plutchik, 1966, 1971, 1989), personality (Plutchik & Kellerman, 1974), ego defenses (Plutchik et al., 1979), and coping styles (Buckley,
Conte, Plutchik, Wild, & Karasu, 1984; Wilder & Plutchik, 1982).

The various ideas that have been outlined above clearly draw on aspects of
genetics and evolutionary theory. They imply that emotions represent fundamental adaptive mechanisms that can be identified at all evolutionary levels, and that
there are genetic underpinings to emotional states. The following section provides an overview of some important ideas from evolutionary theory. In the last
major section an attempt will be made to integrate these two sets of ideas,
emotion theory and evolutionary theory, and to suggest some implications for
psychotherapy.

EVOLUTIONARY THEORY: AN OVERVIEW

If we accept an evolutionary framework for looking at human behavior we
recognize that most transactions with the environment (both human and non-
human) are in the service of survival. There are, however, two senses in which

TABLE 1.2
EMOTIONS AND THEIR DERIVATIVES

Subjective language	Behavioral language	Functional language	Trait language	Diagnostic language	Ego-defense language	Coping-style language
Fear	Escape	Protection	Timid	Passive	Repression	Suppression
Anger	Attack	Destruction	Quarrelsome	Antisocial	Displacement	Substitution
Joy	Mate	Reproduction	Sociable	Manic	Reaction-formation	Reversal
Sadness	Cry	Reintegration	Gloomy	Depressed	Compensation	Replacement
Acceptance	Groom	Incorporation	Trusting	Histrionic	Denial	Minimization
Disgust	Vomit	Rejection	Hostile	Paranoid	Projection	Fault finding
Expectation	Map	Exploration	Demanding	Obsessive–Compulsive	Intellectualization	Mapping
Surprise	Stop	Orientation	Indecisive	Borderline	Regression	Help seeking

the term survival is used. In the more familiar sense, the term refers to survival of the individual as a total organism over a length of time that is characteristic of the species (one's life span). In the biological sense, survival means genetic representation in succeeding generations, what the sociobiologists call inclusive fitness. The two are clearly not the same. Some individuals will give up their lives to save that of their offspring.

These two types of survival create different problems for the individual, and the differences are reflected by some of the different concerns of ethologists and sociobiologists. Ethologists have tended to focus their attention on variables that influence important interpersonal behaviors such as displacements, intention movements, rituals, appeasement gestures, fragmentations, and displays. All of these patterns influence the probability of individual survival. In contrast, sociobiologists have been largely concerned with concepts that are related to gene distributions in different populations, concepts such as reciprocal altruism, parental investment, courtship strategies, evolutionarily stable strategies, and inclusive fitness. Although the two sets of concepts are interrelated, there are some differences that deal with the issue of proximate versus ultimate causation.

PROXIMATE AND ULTIMATE CAUSATION

There are several ways one might explain the phenomenon of changes in apparent size that many animals show when dealing with an aggressive encounter. Many animals exhibit threat postures that involve standing erect (as, for example, in canines and rodents) and raising the neck hairs. The manes of lions erect, fish expand their fins, birds extend their wings and fluff their feathers, while lizards and some frogs have inflatable pouches.

One level of explanation for such behavior attempts to trace the stimulus conditions that precipitate the increase in apparent size and to identify the hormonal and neurophysiological changes that are associated with it. Another level of explanation uses sociobiologic concepts such as "resource holding power." Since size is a cue used by an animal to assess the ability of another animal to successfully defend a territory, the selection of mechanisms that increase apparent size has occurred during the course of evolution in widely dispersed species. The capacity to use size cues to defend resources is thus related to inclusive fitness (G. A. Parker, 1974). Although there is a difference of focus when considering individual survival versus genetic survival, it is obvious that they are interrelated and not mutually exclusive.

It is important to emphasize that evolution does not pit genetics against environment as determinants of behavior. All behaviors are based on genetic programs that interact with environmental events. Strictly speaking, it is wrong to say that a behavior is learned or that it is innate, since every behavior must develop in an environment and its development must inevitably be influenced by genetic factors. The evidence is overwhelming that organisms, including humans, do not come into the world as a tabula rasa upon which any program of social behavior can be imposed by proper manipulation. "Organisms have an inherited biological nature, shaped by natural selection, that predisposes them to develop behaviorally along lines that have been successful in the past" (Fuller, 1986, p. 437). Although some social scientists have been skeptical of this viewpoint, Fuller (1986) points out that "any mammalian group that does not match its social organization to its reproductive physiology and the duration of the dependency of its offspring is bound to become extinct" (p. 437).

STABLE AND LABILE TRAITS

Hinde (1966) introduced the idea that some characteristics (anatomical, physiological, or behavioral) are "environmentally stable" and others are "environmentally labile." Examples of stable characteristics are the color of eyes, the body temperature of warm-blooded animals, and the nest-building behavior of most birds. Labile characteristics are illustrated by flute-playing skills in humans and the dancing behavior of circus bears. These terms represent extremes on a theoretical continuum; however, even very stable characteristics can be influenced by marked environmental changes that are outside the range that is usual for a given species. In humans, the learning of a specific language is clearly the result of particular experiences and can vary greatly from one individual to another. However, the age at which humans begin to learn language is similar and quite environmentally stable in all human groups. Thus, the capacity to learn language is under strong genetic control, although the specific words of a language are not.

An interesting analysis of how certain aspects of language are influenced by genetic factors is given by Bornstein (1973). He reviewed the cross-cultural literature on color vision and color naming. Of 98 societies whose languages were examined for color names, it was found that 100% of them had names for black and white (or dark and light), 91% had a name for red, 74% had a name for yellow and/or green, and 55% had a name for blue (Berlin & Kay, 1969). In many societies no distinction is made between green and blue or blue and black.

As one examines color-naming systems around the world, the degree of confusion between these primary colors appears to be ordered with increasing skin pigmentation according to the degree of proximity to the equator. The hypothesis Bornstein (1973) proposes is that increased exposure to ultraviolet radiation has led to an increased density of yellow pigmentation at the cornea, the lens, and the pigment epithelium. This results in a decrease in spectral sensitivity to short wavelengths and in a confusion between short wavelength stimuli (blue and green or blue and black) in color naming. The conclusion reached is that dense ocular pigmentation (which has been shown to be subject to genetic inheritance) has a direct effect on the color vocabulary of a given culture.

Another example of a genetic effect on behavior can be found in the studies of bipolar illness in the Amish, a relatively genetically isolated farming community found mostly in Pennsylvania. In this community extensive family records have been maintained for over 200 years. Through a review of such records certain family lines were found to be associated with a high risk of depressive illness. Examination of tissues from living individuals descended from these families who were currently suffering from manic–depressive illness has now demonstrated a gene abnormality on Chromosome 11 (Egeland et al., 1987).

EXAMPLES OF ENVIRONMENTALLY STABLE TRAITS

In lower animals it is easy to recognize very stable, species-typical behavior patterns. These include such things as migratory behavior, communication and defense behaviors, and parenting and weaning behaviors, to name just a few. In higher animals, variability of behavior is more marked and more subject to influences by environmental sources of stimulation.

The trainability of animals and the importance of learning in shaping their repertoires has led some social scientists to denigrate the role of genetic programs in higher animals, particularly in humans. But all animals, including humans, have a characteristic, genetically influenced ethogram, that is, a set of behaviors that are typical of humans as a species and that distinguish them from all chimpanzees, gorillas, dogs, and lions. An example of the human ethogram as seen in infants has been reported by Young and Decarie (1977). They report that the 8 to 12-month-old human infant shows certain characteristic facial and verbal expressions that include closed-mouth smile, grimace, yawn, blink, sigh, babble, coo, squeal, laugh, wail, and pout. Similarly, the ethogram of chimpanzees include such sounds as pant-hoot, grunt, scream, bark, cough, wraaa, lip smack, roar, growl, and whine (Marler & Tenaza, 1977). The human infant ethogram has over 100 different behaviors or expressions (Plutchik, 1983a).

Even personality traits, which are believed by many social scientists to be highly malleable (environmentally labile), have been shown to be under varying degrees of genetic control. Breed differences in dogs have been shown to be associated with characteristic temperamental differences as well as sex differences, and to be quite stable over time (Plutchik, 1971). Such temperamental differences are directly related to the types of functions, such as hunting, tracking, working, or fighting, that dogs were bred for. McGuire and Fairbanks (1977) have pointed out that "breeding studies, particularly with dogs, have shown that virtually any personality type is under enough genetic control to respond to selection within a few generations. Genetic differences are manifested in increased learning ability, increased plasticity, greater tolerance to stress, as well as the reverse of these tendencies'' (p. 29). A large-scale study of 850 pairs of human same-sex twins has also demonstrated that monozygotic twins are consistently more alike than dizygotic twins on every personality domain that has been measured. This is especially convincing in view of the fact that parents report similar treatment of co-twins regardless of whether they are identical or fraternal (Loehlin & Nichols, 1978).

IS THERE A HUMAN ADULT ETHOGRAM?

Evolutionary biologists have speculated about the question of whether there is a universal human adult ethogram. Wilson (1975) has suggested the following list: aggressive dominance systems, males dominant over females, scaled intensity of social signals, prolonged maternal care, an extended juvenile period of socialization, and a matrilineal social organization. To these characteristics, Tiger and Fox (1971) have added organization into groups for joint action, competition for status within groups, and sexual and mother–infant bonding.

Other specific human characteristics that might be included in an adult ethogram relate to sex differences. Cross-cultural reviews of several hundred societies have revealed that men are more sexually active, more dominant, less nurturant, and less emotionally expressive than women. Almost universally, women performed child-rearing roles. Noncontact play was more typically female, while rough-and-tumble play was more typically male. Warfare was carried out exclusively by adult men (Henry & Stephens, 1977).

In hunter–gatherer societies, men are typically involved in hunting, and women and children in gathering. A review of many such societies has demonstrated a high correlation between the relative importance of hunting—particularly of big game—and the extent of sexual division of labor (Hayden, 1981).

A factor that influences the nature of behavior patterns in males and females is the relative difference in their comparative size and strength. Such dimorphism has been found to be correlated with a number of patterns, such as (1) high levels of aggressive conflict between males and competition for females, (2) weak or absent pair bonds, (3) little or no paternal care of offspring, (4) high promiscuity of males and the presence of large harems, (5) the presence of natural weapons such as large incisors for threat displays, and (6) mortality rates that are higher among males than females (Brown, 1975). Differential reproductive success among males of differing strength, power, and status led to the physical ability of males to dominate females (Alexander, 1987).

Another aspect of sex differences concerns marital patterns. Although monogamy is considered by many people to be the desirable norm, the fact is that "the vast majority of human societies were and still are polygamous, with the number of wives per husband generally correlated with the latter's social status" (Barash, 1982, p. 245; Chagnon, 1988).

It thus appears that there is some evidence for a generalized human adult ethogram. There appear to be widespread behavior patterns that are found in many diverse human groups. These patterns presumably developed as cumulative effects of differential reproduction in environments that no longer exist or that exist to a limited degree. In evolutionary terms, humans have evolved to retain their genetic materials by creating descendants and by assisting individuals who share some degree of genetic relatedness (nepotism).

EVOLUTIONARY COMPROMISES

A fundamental premise of evolutionary thinking is that each individual has a unique set of reproductive and life interests. This idea stems directly from the fact of sexual reproduction and the uniqueness resulting from random combinations of genetic materials. When Darwin considered the causal forces that promoted natural selection, he referred to parasites, predators, diseases, food shortages, and relative reproductive failure. In modern times most of these forces have been greatly minimized by humans as guiding factors in evolution. The most pervasive remaining force is group versus group, within-species competition in the form of war or genocide. This fact has led to many of the evolutionary adaptations seen in humans. In a fundamental sense, every organism can be described as a set of compromises resulting from the composite effects of countless conflicting directions of natural selection.

One of the evolutionary consequences of intergroup competition and aggression is the development of hierarchical relations among the members of a group. Such hierarchies create a social dominance–submission ladder that serves to control within-group aggression and that makes group defense more effective. Intergroup competition also leads to highly cooperative relations among group members, reflected in such traits as loyalty and patriotism. Hierarchies as well as cooperation increase the effectiveness of group defense. It appears that "within group amity serves between group enmity" (Alexander, 1987, p. 195).

Another consequence of competition and the need for stability within increasingly large social groups is the gradual equalizing of reproductive opportunities. This is expressed through the general spread of monogamy around the world, a fact that greatly limits the power of particular families and promotes reciprocity. Large social groups are maintained by reciprocity rather than nepotism (Alexander, 1987). Alexander also suggests that the function of moral systems is to provide the unity needed to enable a group to compete successfully with other human groups.

DECEPTION

Another aspect of evolutionary thinking that has implications for understanding psychopathology and psychotherapy concerns the role of deception. One of the consequences of intergroup aggression is the development of threat features that act to dramatize and exaggerate an individual's capabilities. These features include facial hair patterns such as tufts, ruffs, or manes in lower animals, and beards and eyebrows in humans. In species in which biting is a part of aggression (as is the case with primates), tooth displays are often used to intimidate an adversary. In many such species, jaw muscles are exaggerated with a face ruff or beard. These displays and threat patterns are used by animals in the service of gaining advantage through deception.

Other examples of deception concern the odors that people have that are normally increased at sexual maturity and tend to become stronger with age. Most mammals, including humans, exude a strong odor during times of conflict. Despite these normal patterns, humans mimic prepubertal juveniles as much as possible by shaving their faces, underarms, and legs and by deodorizing and powdering their skin. The probable aim of these actions is to reduce conflict within a crowded society of strangers. This suggests that society can never be a completely truthful organization.

There is another side to the deception that occurs in organized groups. From an evolutionary viewpoint, in a situation of sexual competition, an individual without resources should mimic someone who has resources, status, and power. In an effort to serve one's own individual interests, there is some advantage in keeping some of those interests secret as well as in suggesting that one has more power than the competitor thinks. When two individuals compete for mates or territory, expressive behaviors are used as tricks to help win.

A surprising implication of this view, developed extensively by Alexander (1987), is that deception of others tends to be associated with deception of self. Deception enables individuals to get other people to see them as they wish to be seen, so that the individual's interests can be better served. It is important to emphasize that self-deception is not necessarily a pathological trait. Self-deception may have evolved as a way to deceive others. An individual who erroneously describes himself as "generous" may be using this self-image to achieve benefits from others. The ability to present oneself in socially desirable ways and to believe in the self-image has powerful reinforcing value; it is related both to popularity and reproductive success.

Alexander points out, however, that it may not always be in our own interest to make unconscious deceptions conscious simply because conscious deception is socially more unacceptable than unconscious deception. An individual who is perceived by others to be unconsciously deceptive may be forgiven; one who is perceived as a conscious deceiver will be thought of as a liar and a cheat. And if deception is in fact an offshoot of natural selection, then there must be continual selection for individuals becoming both better at fooling others and better at perceiving deception in others.

Some of the conclusions that Alexander (1987) reaches concerning the implications of evolutionary biology are as follows: (1) Evolution (natural selection) prepares individuals to live in a world that has existed over countless generations. However, individuals can live contrary to what their evolutionary background has prepared them to do; (2) Evolutionary knowledge can only provide information about the ultimate causes of current conditions, and what average expectable behavior might be in certain environments; (3) Humans "have an evolved tendency to favor relatives, invest in reciprocators, and portray themselves favorably to potential reciprocators" (Alexander, 1987, p. 194). There is an evolutionary basis for altruism, sympathy, loyalty, and cooperation as well as an evolutionary basis for competition, fear, and aggression.

EMOTIONS AND EVOLUTIONARY BIOLOGY

The preceding overview of evolutionary biology has used terms that are part of the domain of emotion, but there has been relatively little detailed discussion of their connections. The present section reviews the literature relating emotions to evolutionary biology.

Trivers (1971) has described the emotional implications of reciprocal altruism, that is, cooperation between unrelated members of the same or different species. He points out that altruistic behavior is understandable in an evolutionary context. If one risks one's life for a close relative, any offspring left by the relative will contain some of one's own genes. However, altruistic behavior directed toward unrelated individuals is more difficult to understand. To account for such behavior, Trivers (1971) assumes that altruistic behavior toward others makes sense only if they are willing to show altruistic behavior in return. Such mutual concern is highly adaptive and is likely to increase the inclusive fitness of both parties. The major problem that occurs in this context is that some people are "cheaters" and will accept altruistic behavior but not express it. The existence of cheaters in turn leads to an increased ability to assess or evaluate others as a counterstrategy. In addition, the emotions of "moralistic anger," "gratitude," "sympathy," "guilt," "trust," and "suspicion" are assumed by Trivers to have evolved, in part, as a result of natural selection for reciprocal altruism.

To explicate these ideas, Trivers (1971) suggests, for example, that "moralistic anger" evolved as a way to avoid victimization and to increase the chances that one's own altruism will be reciprocated. The emotion of "gratitude" is assumed to be a motivator to reciprocate acts of altruism from others. "Guilt" is interpreted as an unpleasant emotion that tends to discourage the individual from exploiting others.

Trivers (1972) has also suggested that "coyness" is a characteristic feminine trait because of the relative difference in parental investment in offspring. Because the female incurs a lager parental investment once she gets pregnant, she tries to gain assurance before mating that the male will assist her in raising her young. The courtship ritual involves the presentation of mixed signals ("teasing") until an assessment has been made about the likely degree of commitment of the male. In contrast, for a male to commit himself to the long process of child rearing, his interest is to make sure that he does not raise another male's offspring. To guard against such a threat to his inclusive fitness, the male tends to be aggressive toward rivals. This is the probable basis for the fact that jealousy is the most frequent cause of murder within a group in most cultures of the world (Freedman, 1974).

Evolutionary biologists have also made some comments on several other emotions. Almost all animals have inhibitions against killing members of their own species. These inhibitions are expressed in the form of rituals, for example, appeasement rituals, greeting rituals, combat rituals, and defeat rituals. Such rituals are found in humans as well as in lower animals. Eibl-Eibesfeldt (1975) assumes that the subjective emotion of "pity" is a correlate of some of these rituals, just as "fear" is a correlate of others. He also suggests that gregarious mammals become apathetic when they are kept alone; they suffer from "loneliness." Most important of all is the fact that all animals exhibit different and often opposing emotions. The same individuals that are capable of sociability, altruism, and love are also capable of jealousy, hatred, and aggression. None of these reactions are more (or less) "natural" than the others, but all reflect aspects of the human ethogram.

In one of the few sociobiological papers dealing primarily with the subject of emotion, Weinrich (1980) points out that (1) every emotion must have an evolutionary history; and (2) as evolutionary adaptations based on natural selection, emotions are all fundamentally "positive" in that they are ways that help individuals increase their reproductive success.

COGNITIONS IN THE CONTEXT OF EVOLUTION

The existence of emotion implies evaluation (R. S. Lazarus, Kanner, & Folkman, 1980). However, evaluations are not always conscious or reportable. They are more like "cognitive maps" or "hypotheses" whose existence can only be inferred from various kinds of evidence. Such inferred evaluations may be quite primitive, as Zajonc (1980) suggests, or may be complex and based on extensive experience. They may sometimes be in error, but on the average, most evaluations must be reasonably accurate if an individual is to survive.

Cognitive capacities in lower animals and in humans have evolved with the evolution of the brain. The main function of a large brain and a highly developed cognitive system is to ensure survival. Survival is ensured by increasing the ability of the organism to predict the future. Cognition provides a model of the environment and codes information in a neural code. The predictions that are made are clearly in the service of biological needs such as hunger, sex, and nurturance.

Most organisms come into the world genetically equipped with a cognitive system that is precoded for response to certain events (Breland & Breland, 1966). For most organisms there are special stimuli in their environment that tend to release characteristic species-typical responses. Such releasing stimuli function to promote group cohesion, initiate courtship behavior, initiate greeting or submissive behavior, warn conspecifics, or serve as threat signals. Many young animals are protected from aggression by adults because of their infantile appearance (Eibl-Eibesfeldt, 1975). For a given type of environment many organisms (such as insects and most birds) "know," without the need for a learning period, which events are dangerous or safe, what signals indicate a mate or a nonmate, and what foods are edible. In higher organisms (mammals and primates) there are fewer innate responses to particular stimuli. Instead, there is a genetically based "curiosity" that impels the animal to explore its environment and gradually to develop an internal "map" of it. The successful exploration of a large home range requires the ability to remember features of the terrain, food areas, prey, and predators. Cognitive abilities thus contribute directly to inclusive fitness. What is available is a cognitive system—sensory mechanisms, memory stores, coordinating circuits, and so on—whose parameters have to be established by learning experiences of various kinds. In exactly the same way, the capacity for speech and conceptual thought is innate; only the symbols themselves must be learned.

G. A. Parker (1974) has pointed out that fighting behavior functions to assess the relative resource-holding power of the combatants. This means that cognitive capacities must be sufficiently developed to be able to identify displays, threats, and attacks and to judge comparative fighting ability. In species where strong dominance–submission hierarchies exist, there is considerable value for future reproductive success in being able to recognize one's relative position in the hierarchy, and in being able to choose the best time for challenging and over-throwing an aging dominant animal. This requires the cognitive capacity to assess the existing strengths and weaknesses of all parties to the conflict, and the ability to predict the outcome of a fight with some degree of accuracy.

Similarly, the fact that reciprocal altruism gives cheaters a possible advantage suggests that there must be strong selective pressures for the cognitive capacity to identify cheaters and to recognize trustworthiness in others. The appropriateness of an emotional response can determine whether the individual lives or dies. The whole cognitive process evolved over millions of years in order to make the evaluation of stimulus events more correct and the predictions more precise so that the emotional behavior that finally resulted would be adaptively related to the stimulus events. *Emotional behavior, therefore, is the proximate basis for the ultimate outcome of increased inclusive fitness.* This same idea has been expressed by Barash (1982). He points out that "the major biological function of male–female pair-bonding is the production of successful offspring. Love, companionship and sexual satisfaction are proximate means for achieving this ultimate end" (p. 295). Similarly, Alexander (1987) suggests that happiness is "a proximate mechanism that leads us to perform and repeat acts that in the environments of history, at least would have led to greater reproductive success. . . . Humans should always experience pleasure when they gain in status or increase their control of resources . . . and they should experience some converse feeling when they lose status or resource control" (p. 26).

SUMMARY AND CONCLUSIONS

The first half of this chapter was primarily concerned with identifying points of contact between evolutionary biological concepts and emotion concepts. Examination of the literature demonstrated that biology has had relatively little to say about emotions except in the context of altruism theory. However, even in that context the analyses have been primarily analogical and stated in the language of ultimate causation, for example, "spite" characterized as an emotion associated with an interaction that decreases the inclusive fitness of both initiator and recipient. Such analyses, interesting as they are, ignore the immediate quality of most emotional experiences. It is fair to add, however, that evolutionary biology has had a good deal to say about dominance and territoriality, both of which are certainly related to such emotions as anger, fear, acceptance, and rejection.

An important idea tying the two domains together is the view that all emotions are evolutionary adaptations and, as such, are fundamentally "positive" in the sense that they all tend to contribute to survival and thus increase the chances of reproductive success. Biology also finds congenial the idea that emotions involve communication acts that affect the behavioral interactions between animals.

Another important idea, consistent with biologic thinking, is that emotions can be grouped into a few basic patterns (types) that can be identified at almost all phylogenetic levels and in almost all species. This notion of types, or what I prefer to call "emotion prototypes," reflects the idea that the environments of all organisms have much in common and thus create similar functional needs in different individuals. All organisms need to take in energy supplies from the environment and to deal with issues of reproduction, predation, and elimination of wastes or unpalatable objects. Emotions are adaptive mechanisms that help carry out these tasks successfully. In a sense, emotions can be thought of as the proximate events that serve the ultimate goal of inclusive fitness.

In order for these various functions cited above to be carried out successfully, the organism must be able to make reasonably correct discriminations and evaluations of its social and physical environment. It needs to be able to make predictions about weather, food, the environment, and the relative resource holding power of other individuals. It needs to be able to distinguish cheaters from trustworthy individuals, estimate relative social rank of other member of its group, and distinguish between those who belong to the group and those who do not. The ability to interpret the motives of others is also an important skill for social organisms. These various discriminations and evaluations represent the cognitive functions needed for survival.

Another important idea about emotions that relates to evaluation is the view that emotions are forms of behavioral homeostasis. In other words, emotions are activated in an individual when issues of survival are raised in fact or by implication (e.g., threats, attacks, poisons, or potential mates). The effect of the emotional state is to create an interaction between the individual and the event (or stimulus) that precipitated the emotion in the first place. This interaction usually functions to reduce the disequilibrium and to reestablish a state of comparative rest.

Another important emotion idea that biologists should find congenial is the concept that an emotion should not be defined solely as a subjective feeling state. Such a narrow definition is one factor that makes it difficult for biologists to use the concept of emotion in their work with animals. However, if one recognizes that an emotion is a complex chain of loosely connected events that begins with a stimulus and includes feelings, physiological changes, impulses to action, and specific goal-directed behavior, one can see the application of these ideas to all species.

Finally, one of the most important overlapping ideas is the concept of derivatives. This term is used in three different senses. It can mean that certain human behaviors stem from behaviors seen in lower animals, for example, the sneer of the human, may be said to be derived from the snarl of the wolf. It can also mean that certain behaviors seen in adults are derivatives of certain behaviors seen in infants. An example might be the feeding and babyish behaviors sometimes seen between adult lovers. A third meaning of the concept is the idea that certain conceptual domains are derivative of other more primitive events or concepts. For example, there is good evidence that personality traits and certain diagnostic terms can be thought of as derivatives of basic emotions. One can also argue that basic emotions are derivatives of more basic ecological selection pressures related to resources, territory, and power, thus suggesting a connection between the literature on dominance and territoriality and the literature on emotions (Plutchik,

1983a). It may even be possible to argue that social institutions such as religion, science, and warfare are evolutionary adaptations used to control certain basic emotions (Plutchik, 1984b).

CLINICAL IMPLICATIONS OF A
PSYCHOEVOLUTIONARY APPROACH
TO EMOTIONS

Evolutionary considerations suggest that most organisms must deal with certain fundamental problems related to their survival. Social animals must find their place in a hierarchy or rank order and deal with threats to the positions obtained. They must handle territorial conflicts over what part of the environment belongs to them. They must identify the group members that are part of their own species so they can interact with them, and they must somehow come to terms with the limited length of an individual life. These four areas of concern are fundamental in the sense that they all relate in some way to issues of inclusive fitness and the likelihood of sexual reproduction and maintenance of one's genes in future generations. I refer to those issues as the problem of hierarchy, territoriality, identity, and temporality (Plutchik, 1980a, 1980b, 1983a, 1983b). The following sections provide brief descriptions of those problems along with some hypotheses about their connections to emotions.

Hierarchy

The concept of hierarchy refers to the vertical dimension of social life. This is seen almost universally as dominance hierarchies both in lower animals and in humans. In general, the major expressions of high hierarchical positions are first access to food, to shelter, to comforts, and to sex, that is, the resources needed for both personal and genetic survival.

The vertical organization of social life is reflected in the age relations among people, in the usual relations between the sexes, in economic and military organizations, and in social classes. Generally speaking, hierarchical organizations reflect the fact that some people know more than other people, that some people are stronger or more skillful than others, and that all people vary in affective dispositions. All individuals must face these realities and come to terms with them whether or not they want to and whether or not they are aware of them.

Of great importance is the fact that an individual's attempt to cope with hierarchical issues implies competition, status conflict, and power struggles. People near the top of a hierarchy tend to feel dominant, self-confident, and bossy and assertive, while those near the bottom feel submissive and anxious

(Buirski, Plutchik, & Kellerman, 1978). Depression appears to be related, in part, to perceived downward mobility within a particular hierarchy (Plutchik & Landau, 1973).

Haley (1980) has demonstrated the importance of understanding hierarchical relations in the context of family therapy. He points out that all organizations, including the family, are hierarchical in form, with some members having more authority, power, and status than others. Clinical experience with adolescents revealed that psychopathology was the result of a malfunctioning organization, and it implied that the task of the therapist is to help change the organization so that the parents, rather than their offspring, are in charge.

Territoriality

The second universal conflict area for all individuals concerns the problem of territoriality. In every species, each organism must learn what aspects of the environment and of the self "belong" to it. From an evolutionary point of view territories define an area or space of potential nourishment necessary for survival, or an area that is safe from attack or predation. Territories may be defined explicitly by scent markings, tree scratches, or boundary lines, or implicitly by the distance one organism allows another to approach before aggression is initiated. Crowding usually generates territorial crises.

Individuals attempting to cope with territorial issues are concerned with feelings of possessiveness, jealousy, and envy. Those who are in possession of some aspect of the environment (including other people) feel in control. In contrast, individuals whose boundaries have been penetrated (or whose possessions have been taken) feel despair and lack of control. From the point of view of my model of the emotions, I assume that the feelings of control–dyscontrol are basic to the territorial crisis.

Identity

The third major problem that all organisms encounter is the problem of identity. In simplest terms, this refers to the basic question of who we are, or alternately, what group or groups we belong to. The issue of identity is a fundamental existential crisis for all organisms because isolated individuals neither propagate nor survive.

In lower organisms, genetic coding mechanisms enable an individual to recognize other individuals of the same species. In humans, however, group memberships are very complex because of the variety of categories one can use to define an identity. The most important criteria of group membership are undoubtedly sex, race, age, religion, occupation, and geography. The fact that these often conflict with one another is one of the reasons for the identity crisis. Adolescents are particularly prone to a crisis of sexual identity, while older people are more likely to have to confront religious or occupational crises of identity. Hogan (1982) has emphasized the survival value of status and popularity. These concepts are basically synonyms for the ideas of hierarchy and identity.

Certain emotions are closely tied to the sense of identity. For those who are part of our group, who share our identity, we feel a sense of belonging, of acceptance. We share language, customs, rituals, jokes, and play. We allow hugging, kissing, and, under certain conditions, sexual behavior. The emotion associated with a lack of identity is rejection or disgust. Prejudice against strangers is universal and reflects the sense of danger to survival connected with individuals who are not members of our group. In order to feel comfortable about rejecting someone we often try to disconnect that person from our group—to dehumanize by certain verbal labels, for example. Acceptance and liking versus rejection and hate are the emotional poles connected with the struggle to identify.

Temporality

The fourth universal problem encountered by all organisms is the problem of temporality. This word refers to the limited span of life, part of which is spent in infancy, childhood, and adolescence learning fundamental skills about social living. From an evolutionary point of view, the purpose of the acquisition of skills is to enable the individual to survive as long as possible and to become a successful reproducing adult member of a group.

The reality of death creates the inevitability of loss and separation for those who are living. There is a need for social solutions to the problem of loss, since individuals without support from other members of their social group do not survive well or long. During the course of evolution several solutions have evolved for the problem of loss or separation. One solution is the development of distress signals, which serve as the functional equivalent of cries for help. The second evolutionary solution for the problem of loss is the evolution of sympathetic or nurturing responses in other members of the social group. It might even be argued that altruism is an extreme form of the nurturing response.

In humans, the problem of the limited span of existence has affected the evolution of a series of social institutions that function to deal with death and loss. These include mourning rituals; birth, death, and reunion myths; preparation for an afterlife; and certain aspects of religion.

Emotions also relate to these basic experiences of loss and separation. Sadness is a cry for help that functions as an attempt to reintegrate the individual with a lost person or a substitute. If the signal of a need for help and nurturance works

TABLE 1.3

Derivatives of the Existential Crises

Hierarchy	Identity	Territoriality	Temporality
Being assertive	Making friends	Keeping a job	Dealing with illness
Being dominant	Courting someone	Having an unambiguous personal space	Dealing with death
Being submissive	Falling in love	Having a sense of boundary	Getting or providing social supports
Seeking fame	Marrying	Accumulating possessions	Showing altruism
Seeking wealth	Organizing a family	Feelings of envy and jealousy	Showing compassion
Feelings of anger and fear	Becoming part of a community	Feelings of control and loss of control	Showing empathy
	Feelings of nationalism		Feelings of gain or loss, joy or sadness
	Feelings of acceptance and rejection		

only partly, it may produce a persistent, long-term distress signal that we call depression. If the cry for help actually works and brings help, it produces an opposite emotion, the emotion of joy. Joy stems from the experience of rejoining or of possession.

From the point of view of existential crises, it thus becomes possible to make inferences from emotions to the existential issues with which individuals are most concerned. For example, people who are very competitive are probably very much concerned with their place in the ladder of life, that is, with hierarchical issues. Someone who is an obsessive collector and envious of other people's possessions is probably concerned with territorial issues. Someone who is preoccupied with issues of family closeness and loyalty is probably concerned with identity conflicts. And someone who is an avid and anxious reader of the obituary columns is probably concerned with issues of temporality. Obviously, any single concern can be interpreted in more than one way.

DERIVATIVES OF THE EXISTENTIAL CRISES

If we go down a step in the level of abstraction, we recognize that there are many experiences in life that relate directly or indirectly to the existential issues. For example, if we take the problem of hierarchy, we can see that such issues as being assertive, being dominant or in control, being submissive or being controlled, and seeking fame and wealth are all related to one another, and all are tied to or derived from the question of finding one's place in the ladder of life. Similarly, issues concerned with keeping a job, buying a car or a house, and establishing a personal sense of space or boundaries are all connected to or derived from territorial problems.

Table 1.3 summarizes a set of hypotheses about important problems in life that are related to the four basic existential crises. I assume that issues of assertiveness are related to hierarchical problems, that one's personal space is related to territorial problems, that courtship and love are related to identity issues, and that feelings about illness and death are related to the problem of temporality. These connections exist whether or not we are aware of them.

Figure 1.2 summarizes these proposed relations. It assumes that the basic motivation is survival both of one's genes (as expressed in terms of representation in future generations) and of one's physical body. In the struggle for survival, organisms have to deal with problems of hierarchy, territoriality, identity, and temporality. These life issues tend to generate certain basic emotions, fear and anger in the case of hierarchical issues, acceptance and rejection in connection with identity issues, and others. The problem remains of how individuals deal with these various existential crises.

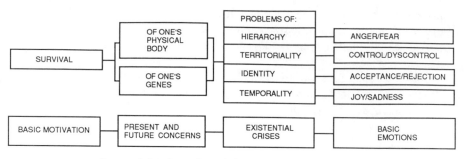

FIGURE 1.2. A psychoevolutionary model—general issues.

COPING WITH CONFLICTS AND PROBLEMS

All the problems listed are related to whether and how we survive as individuals, and to whether we leave our genes to future generations. All living things are fragile and exist in a delicate and precarious balance between challenge and response. Geology reveals that there are more species whose only traces are found in sedimentary rocks than there are species in existence today. If individual humans are to survive, they need to function effectively in the real world. This means that they need to cope successfully both with the world of things (e.g., houses, cars, electric stoves, or weather) and with the world of people. For most of us it is the world of people that creates the most problems.

The list of conflict areas derived from the existential crises that is presented in Table 1.3 covers a great many of the problems that individuals describe when seeking psychotherapy. Problems in lack of assertiveness, feelings of being controlled by others, difficulties in showing affection and finding love, and depression and anxiety connected with personal losses are very common. How one tries to deal with these kinds of problems is the subject of countless publications and the basis for the different schools of psychotherapy.

An illustration of this point may be seen in a questionnaire study of a sample of psychoanalytically oriented psychiatrists and a sample of behavior therapists (Plutchik, Conte, & Karasu, 1988). The therapists were asked to describe their conception of mental illness, their modes of treatment, and their conceptions of successful change. It was found that the psychodynamic therapists assumed that pathology involves unconscious sexual drives while the behavior therapists did not. The dynamic therapists also assumed that the goal of therapy is to resolve underlying conflicts and to understand the effects of childhood experiences on current life situations. The way to do this is to deal primarily with a patient's subjective historical past. In contrast, the behavior therapists interpreted their task as the shaping of client behavior through information and rewards.

Of special interest is the fact that there were some important points of agreement. Both types of therapists believe that the prime concerns of psychotherapy are to deal with maladaptive behavior, cognitive distortions, and anxiety, and that the overall goal of therapy is to remove symptoms and reduce anxiety. Both believe that the basis of change is the reassessment of faulty attitudes, and that the mode of operation involves dealing with the objective present as well as current perceptions through shared dialogue.

Thus, it appears that two of the most diverse therapies in existence today share many goals and tend to differ primarily in their methods and in their theories. This overlap may help us understand why the various metanalyses of controlled psychotherapy studies have revealed that all are effective, as compared to no therapy, and to roughly the same degree (Smith, Glass, & Miller, 1980).

WHAT TO CHANGE

Fundamentally, it appears that the way to deal with conflicts and problems is to do two things: change attitudes and increase skills. The differences among therapies consist in the specific attitudes and skills with which they concern themselves. Behavior therapy and assertiveness training, for example, are largely concerned with teaching such skills as systematic desensitization, relaxation, and confrontation. In contrast, psychoanalysis is mostly concerned with changing attitudes about the meaning of one's own current behaviors, largely by relating them to certain family interactions of the patient's childhood. Rational–emotive therapy is quite explicit about its aim of changing an individual's implicit philosophy (attitudes). Eclectic therapies attempt to manipulate both attitudes and skills.

Although there may be a difference of opinion about exactly what skills to develop or to encourage, there are some skills about which there is probably little disagreement. Based on the social-skills literature, Table 1.4 provides a preliminary listing of important skills necessary for effective functioning in the real world. These include job skills, conversational skills, courtship skills, sexual skills, negotiating skills, and parenting skills, among others. Although there are probably few if any who would disagree on the need for such skills in living, they may believe that assistance in the acquisition of such skills is not the task of the psychotherapist. The question of who does what is a moot point so long as we can agree that such skills, however obtained, are crucial for successful adaptation to the world of people.

Putting these ideas in a different context, they imply that psychotherapy should be concerned with the existential issues described above. Psychotherapy deals with problems of dominance and dependence; feelings of control or loss of control; issues of individuation, friendship, and marriage; and problems surrounding illness, loss, and death. Some problems are dealt with by changing

TABLE 1.4
BASIC SKILLS NEEDED FOR EFFECTIVE FUNCTIONING

Job skills
Conversational skills
Handling money
Making friends
Sizing people up
Coping with emotions
Courtship skills
Sexual skills
Negotiating skills
Parenting skills

one's behavior; others can be dealt with only by changing how one interprets the world or by changing what one believes about the world.

THE STRATEGY OF CHANGE: FIVE BASIC QUESTIONS

Psychotherapy implicitly or explicitly deals with one or more of five fundamental questions. These are:

1. Who am I?
2. How did I get to be me?
3. What rewards do I get out of being me?
4. What do I want to become (or change to)?
5. How can I reach this goal?

These questions imply certain therapeutic activities. The question "Who am I?" implies a need for *assessment*. "How did I get to be me?" implies *historical reconstruction*. "What rewards do I get out of being me?" implies a *functional analysis*. "What do I want to become?" implies *goal setting*. And "How can I reach this goal?" implies *skill acquisition*.

In traditional hospital psychiatry, assessment means making a diagnosis, doing a mental status, and determining family background, medical history, and dynamic conflicts. In psychoanalytic outpatient practice, assessment is more likely to mean a set of judgments about personality styles, ego functions, ego defenses, and probable fixations in childhood. Sometimes projective test measures are added to the evaluations.

In contrast, A. A. Lazarus (1976) has proposed his BASIC I.D. acronym as a guide to assessment. This means measuring or evaluating the clients behavior, affects, sensations, imagery, cognitions, interpersonal relations, and need for drugs. Other important areas of assessment include an individual's social supports, interpersonal conflicts, sense of personal control, willingness to take risks, skills or competencies, and close and loving attachments. All assessments are basically ways of determining how well an individual is functioning at present in terms of survival of self and in terms of inclusive fitness. This is true whether or not this is the avowed aim of the assessment. Assessments are particularly important because of the strong tendency on the part of individuals to deceive others as well as themselves, a point made in the earlier discussion on evolutionary principles. The problem is very much the same as what Freud once described: How can the therapist and the patient discover things about the patient that the patient does not know? This problem is the basis for the complex technology of assessment procedures that has been developed (Plutchik & Conte, 1985).

The second basic question is concerned with historical reconstruction, that is, the recognition of early experiences, traumas, identifications, and fantasies that presumably have a bearing on an individual's present life-style. Therapists with a psychoanalytic orientation are especially likely to focus considerable attention on the past. The assumption is made that if a patient can discover the supposed historical roots of a particular problem and the current transferential relationship is identified, then the problem is likely to disappear.

However, the assumption that there is a limited, identifiable set of environmental events that are the source of a later problem is very likely to be incorrect. In light of the evolutionary considerations described earlier, there must surely be genetic potentials of many kinds that play a role in the development of an individual's personality and life problems. To the extent that this is true, no historical reconstruction can be complete. And in a complex, open system such as a human being, none but the most limited of causal connections are possible between the events of childhood and adult behavior.

The third basic question—"What rewards do I get out of being me?"—also has bearing on the second question. There is considerable experience to suggest that individuals maintain their traits over time because of current experiences or events that serve to reinforce them. For example, some individuals are aggressive because it intimidates others and results in the intimidator getting his way. Other illustrations would be people who sulk because sulking gets them something they want, or people who develop agoraphobia as a way of keeping a spouse or parent in close attendance.

The fourth basic question is concerned with the issue of goals. In order to get somewhere, we need to know where we want to go. One of the special qualities of human beings is their great capacity to fantasize about the future and about events that have not yet happened. This process is like setting the goal of a self-correcting instrument. When the goal is clear, appropriate mechanisms often "kick in" to accomplish it. The problem, however, is that one's goals are often not clear and individuals are blinded by self-deception or by the need to get approval for goals considered desirable by others. Psychotherapy must therefore explore the patient's goals in some detail.

The fifth basic question is concerned with the issue of competence. If you know where you want to go, do you have the skills to enable you to get there? In recent years, a considerable literature has developed that suggests that social-skills training is very efficacious in producing therapeutic changes (Liberman, Mueser, & Wallace, 1986). Social-skills training is concerned with such fundamental skills as having a conversation, making friends, sizing people up, courtship, sex, negotiating, and parenting. From a broad psychoevolutionary point of view, however, the development of such skills is essential to accomplishing most life goals as well as to increasing inclusive fitness.

Some of these questions bear an interesting relation to Hogan's (1982) concept of the three principal end products of personality development. These are self-images, reference groups, and self-presentational skills. Self-images evidently relate to the question "Who am I?", reference groups refer to identity formation ("What rewards do I get out of being me?"), and self-presentational skills deal with issues of competence ("How can I reach my goals?").

In summary, it is possible that these five basic questions can serve as the underlying strategy of psychotherapeutic interaction. They represent guiding principles that justify and explain the highly variable day-to-day interactions that take place.

THE SPECIAL NATURE
OF THERAPEUTIC COMMUNICATION

Evolutionary biologists have devoted considerable attention to the subject of communication (Hahn & Simmel, 1976; Wilson, 1975). An important conclusion is that communicative displays in animals are usually the result of more than one behavioral impulse in conflict. Attack and retreat, affinity and sexuality, care giving, and exploration all interact to produce the graded facial, vocal, and postural signals that determine appropriate social interactions. Evidence exists, based on studies of animals, children born deaf-and-blind, and preliterate and isolated groups of humans, that some facial expressions, such as rage, startle, fear, and pleasure, are universal and probably have an innate basis. However, it is also evident that in human beings, with highly developed facial musculature, a large number of facial expressions can be voluntarily created and given arbitrary meanings akin to those of the words of a language. In ordinary interactions between humans, there is a subtle interplay of expressions between those innate display signals that are characteristic of humans and those conventional expressions that people learn in order to convey information rapidly. Anthropologists have also suggested that language activities have been selected during evolution as a means of social manipulation in the context of subsistence activities (S. T. Parker, 1985) and that they function to increase the smooth flow of social interactions.

Clear and explicit communications obviously provide reproductive advantages in connection with courtship, sexual behavior, care of the young, food acquisition, and defense. They also are important in conveying threat and dominant or submissive status. Such signals tend to reduce or prevent physical encounters and thus the risk of injury or death.

Language has two aspects; it provides both digital and analog coding (Sebeok, 1963). Digital coding (the use of discrete words to convey information) is believed to be a late phylogenetic development. Analog coding refers to the graded signals varying in intensity or frequency that convey information about emotional states. For example, crows have been reported to possess at least four distinct cries. Two of them have been identified as assembly calls and dispersal calls. Once contact has been established, the number of caws emitted will vary from one to five depending on the degree of excitement. In humans, words can convey one message while intensity of expression conveys another. However, since it is evident that content and intensity cannot be separated, all communications convey *both* information and emotion.

Since psychotherapy relies primarily on person-to-person communications for its effects, it is not surprising that considerable attention has been devoted to trying to understand the nature of therapeutic communication. For example, Scheflen (1963) has suggested that the transmission of new information is only one function of the therapeutic interaction. Another is the reduction of ambiguity in spoken language by means of stress patterns, gaze patterns, paralanguage, and kinesics (e.g., hand movements, head nods, and dress and decor props). A third function of communication signals is to regulate or monitor the pace of the interaction as well as deviant individual behaviors.

An example of this third function is given by Scheflen (1963). In a session involving a schizophrenic girl, her mother, and two psychotherapists, every few minutes the young woman would cross her legs seductively and expose her thigh to one of the physicians. Immediately afterward she would move closer to him. On each such occasion the mother made a characteristic gesture, sweeping the side of her index finger across her nostrils. Each time the mother wiped her nose, the daughter uncrossed her legs and returned them to a more "ladylike" position. Examples of interactions between the patient and therapist are also given. Scheflen concludes that there is reciprocal communication between the people involved in a therapy relationship that serves to regulate their actions. Other examples of studies of the "grammar" of psychotherapy are given in Cobb and Lieberman (1987) and in Liberman and Cobb (1987). Research on the "microstructure" of therapy is found in Ivey and Simek-Downing (1980).

SOCIAL CONVERSATION VERSUS
THERAPEUTIC COMMUNICATION

An important question that can be asked about psychotherapy concerns the nature of the dialogue between patient and therapist. In what ways is therapy dialogue special? In what ways is it different from ordinary conversation? In order to understand the nature of therapeutic communication it may be helpful to compare and contrast it with what can loosely be called "normal social conversation." Although it is unlikely that there are sharp lines of distinction between these two modes of interaction, there are differences of focus and of emphasis. These differences can be grouped under a number of categories.

The *goal* of social conversation is to socialize, to have fun, and to share experiences. The *focus* is generally on positive emotions such as cooperation, curiosity, and pleasure. Its *setting* is informal and open-ended and the conversation can occur anywhere. It is not much concerned with *self-disclosure* except at a relatively superficial level, and its direction of interaction is *bidirectional*. The *content* is largely concerned with the external world (e.g., world events, news, gossip, and work), and participants usually feel free to express their *values*.

In contrast, the *goal* of therapy is usually to discover the meaning of the patient's current and past behavior and to explore feelings. The *focus* is on painful emotions such as depression, anxiety, resentment, shame, and hate. The *setting* is formal and spatially and temporally limited, and self-disclosure is limited almost exclusively to the client (patient). The *direction of interaction* is mostly the inner subjective world of the client. During the interaction the therapist generally avoids expressing personal *values*. Most important, the *purpose* of social conversation is to maintain a relationship that can continue indefinitely, while the purpose of the therapeutic interaction is to produce a desired change so that the relationship can end. These differences and a number of others are listed in Table 1.5.

These suggested differences between social conversation and therapeutic conversation are part of the *tactics* of psychotherapy. The following section will describe a number of other therapeutic tactics that relate to a psychoevolutionary conception of emotions.

SOME TACTICS OF PSYCHOTHERAPY

1. The theory of emotion described here assumes that cognitive evaluations of stimulus events determine the nature of the affective state that is aroused. It is a common experience in therapy that clients are often not aware of their own interpretations of the events that occur in their lives and that trigger emotions.

Attribute	Social conversation	Therapeutic communication
1. Goal	To socialize, to have fun, to exchange ideas	To discover meanings in current and past behavior, to explore feelings
2. Emotions	Focus on positive emotions such as cooperation, joy, curiosity, and pleasure	Focus on painful emotions such as depression, anxiety, resentment, revenge, shame, and hate
3. Roles	Friend to friend	Teacher to student, parent to child, expert to novice, professional to client
4. Purpose	To maintain a relationship that can continue indefinitely	To produce a desired change so that the relationship can end
5. Power	Mutual influences on one another	Influencing the patient (client) in a desired way
6. Modeling	No interest in being someone other than oneself	Therapist presents a model of acceptance, concern, and professionalism
7. Setting	Informal, open-ended, anywhere	Formal, serious, the office of the therapist only
8. Structure	No time limits and no financial arrangements	Limited time of contact and fee-for-service
9. Topics	Concern with world events, news, gossip, work	Concern with personal life experiences only
10. Intimacy	Sometimes deep, often superficial	Deep, concerning sexual as well as nonsexual material
11. Self-disclosure	Relatively little; when it occurs both parties contribute	Almost exclusively limited to the client (patient)
12. Direction of interaction	Mostly bidirectional	Mostly from client (patient) to therapist
13. Focus	Each participant competes to become the focus of attention	Focus of attention is almost exclusively on patient (client)
14. Amount of communication	Roughly equal	Much more from patient
15. Nature of reality	Concern with the real world out there	Concern with the inner, subjective world of the patient
16. Revelation	Both participants free to reveal themselves as they wish	Patient expected to reveal himself; therapist never or rarely
17. Values	Each participant expresses values, opinions, attitudes	Therapist avoids expressing personal values
18. Meaning	Participants deal with manifest content	Therapist concerned with hidden meaning of communications
19. Theory	Changes of topic often random and unplanned	Therapist has a theory of human nature to guide interactions
20. Sexuality	Can be a prelude to sexual or aggressive encounters	Therapists largely immune to sexual or aggressive provocation

This implies that a specific therapeutic task is the identification by patients of their own particular cognitions that trigger the unpleasant affects experienced as symptoms. As a corollary of this idea, one way of dealing with stressful life events is by consciously redefining (i.e., reinterpreting) the stimulus or by putting it into a new context.

Example: A woman felt angry, resentful, and depressed because of an abusive alcoholic husband. When she began to think of him as sick rather than as cruel, she felt less angry and sad and more compassionate. Other examples of reinterpreting the stimulus would be to consider a difficult child as "only going through a stage," or difficult older parents as "senile and unable to help themselves," rather than as "thoughtless" or "selfish." Such reinterpretations are only part of the complex process of psychotherapy.

2. The theory proposes that all emotions are either one of the eight basic ones, or mixed states. It further assumes that the basic emotions seldom, if ever, occur in pure form, and if they do, only transiently. Most emotions, therefore, are mixed emotions or blends. A further assumption is that the blending of emotions always produces some level of conflict. Several personality tests based on these assumptions have been developed, and empirical research supports the idea that different personality traits indirectly express different levels of conflict (Conte & Plutchik, 1981; Plutchik & Kellerman, 1974). The therapeutic principle this leads to is this: *Most emotional states are mixtures implying conflicts. To understand the nature of the conflict we need to identify the components.*

Example: A client said she felt guilty about leaving her husband and getting her own apartment. Previous research suggests that guilt is a mixture of fear and pleasure. It was possible to explore these components of her guilt. She was in conflict over her fear of not being able to make it on her own (i.e., continued dependence) and her pleasure at the thought of making it (i.e., being independent). She was in conflict over the fear of breaking up her family versus the joy of consolidating or remaking her family. She was in conflict over the fear that her husband would interfere and stop her from leaving and her pleasure at the thought of saying no to him. Examining these components separately enabled her to evaluate the relative importance of each one in the process of making a reasoned decision for her life.

3. The concept that an emotion is a complex chain of events containing both feeling states and impulses to action does not necessarily mean that each component of the chain is equally distinct or accessible to consciousness. Studies by Davitz (1969), for example, have shown that the feeling of an emotion is often vague, confused, and obscure and that the same emotion can be described by a large number of different words and phrases. For example, depression has been described by college students as feeling "empty, drained, hollow, undercharged, heavy, tired, sleepy, unmotivated, helpless, insignificant, incompetent, self-pitying, sorry, and suffocating."

In contrast, the impulse to action in any given emotion is somewhat clearer, probably because there are fewer relevant actions possible. The following principle is implied here: *The subjective feeling states of emotion (that is, the labels we give them) are usually more ambiguous and obscure than the impulses to action. Therefore, always examine impulses to action.*

Example: A client was talking about a brother who had committed suicide. Her answer to the question of "How did you feel about it?" was that she did not know, but when she was asked what she felt like doing, she immediately replied, "I felt like crying but couldn't because I really felt like killing him myself for what he did to our mother."

4. The fact that most emotions that people experience are mixed emotions implies that diverse impulses to action exist. This means that life is filled with feelings of ambivalence. When a client describes an emotional situation, the therapist should assume that only part of the story has been told. No one is ever certain what the "real truth" is. Ambivalences are particularly evident if individuals report that they are doing something that they do not want to do. Therefore, the basic principle is the following: *Always look for ambivalences.*

Example: A relatively young man inherited his father's business after the father died suddenly of a heart attack. The son knew nothing about the business, having been trained to go into one of the professions. He developed anxiety about making decisions and began to rely increasingly on the foreman who in turn treated him like a "kid." The young man began to hate the foreman, but in therapy he gradually revealed his ambivalence based upon the foreman's undoubted skill and decisiveness. Once the ambivalence was clarified and related to some obvious transferential issues, the new owner of the business could set up a reasonable relation to his foreman.

5. Clients often report that they are reluctant or unable to do something that they want to do (e.g., eat alone in a fancy restaurant, visit a nudist colony for a day, or learn parachute jumping). Conversely, they often say that they do things they really do not want to do (e.g., visit people they do not like, allow themselves to be taken advantage of, or buy something they do not need or want). Close examination of such situations invariably reveals that some kind of fear is always present: fear or rejection, fear of humiliation, fear of criticism, or fear of looking foolish. Fear is the great inhibitor of action. The therapeutic principle is the following: *When a client appears stuck on one theme, or is reluctant to examine alternative ideas or actions, look for the fear.*

Example: An older woman had recently moved into a new house. After a few weeks she called her son and asked him to come over and move some furniture for her. The son refused saying he was busy and that he would help her some other time. The woman hung up the phone and shortly thereafter developed a painful constriction in her throat and began to cry. As she explored this incident in therapy, she realized that she expected help from her son, was embarrassed by his refusal to help, and was afraid to demand his help. The impulse to criticize her son was inhibited by fear of rejection; this fear and the experience of humiliation apparently resulted in a constriction of her throat.

6. We take it for granted that everyone is unique; talents differ, educations differ, goals differ. What we do not appreciate as clearly is that the very words we commonly use have different connotations and meanings for different people. One client described himself as "sick." When he was asked what the opposite of "sick" was, he said "free" (rather than the more obvious word "well"). It turned out that his sickness was his inability to free himself from an unhappy marriage. Another client came into the group bristling with anger. She had been brooding for a week that someone in the group had described her as "stubborn." It appeared that "stubborn" meant to her "bad" and "mean," and the opposite of stubborn was "nice" and "friendly." The implied therapeutic principle is the following: *The labels people give to their feelings and emotions may have idiosyncratic meanings that need to be explored.*

7. One of the things we mean by the term "emotional maladjustment" is that there is a kind of emotional skewness in an individual, that is, that one or two emotions are strong, or troublesome, or at the center of the individual's existence. Depression, for example, implies that feelings of sadness are the dominant theme and the major way of relating to other people. Someone who is hostile uses anger as the keynote emotion that becomes expressed in a large number of different situations.

The theory of emotion that I have proposed implies that all emotions have potential survival value for the individual. Joy is an expression of pleasurable contact that may be associated with the propagation of one's genes. But fear is just as adaptive as joy in that it mobilizes the individual to avoid threat or conflict. Similarly, anger is an adaptive emotion in the sense that it mobilizes the individual to cope with a barrier to the satisfaction of one's needs. The same general argument can be made for each basic emotion; they all are adaptive and serve survival needs. From this point of view, an individual who appears to experience primarily only one emotion is maladjusted. Ideally, *the capacity to experience and express a wide range of emotion is a sign of successful adaptation, or good mental health.*

Example: A client described himself as coping with most problems by seeking help. This coping style was an expression of his feeling small, helpless, needy, and sad. Exploration of this imbalance in his affect states, and of the many ways that it was expressed in his life, gradually led him to an awareness of his limited range of feelings and to a gradual expansion of that range.

8. When something goes wrong many people have a strong urge to find an explanation, a scapegoat, or a person to blame. They try to account for their unhappiness, depression, anxiety, or anger by relating it to a dull job, a demanding boss, or an unfaithful wife. Sometimes they may blame their neighborhood, their parents, or their siblings.

Such attitudes, to the extent that they exist, are expressions of the feeling that the individuals have lost some degree of control over their lives and that evil forces are manipulating them. Such attitudes are also expressions of the belief that events directly determine our emotions, when in fact it is our *interpretation of events* that determine what we feel, and to that extent our world of emotions is created by our cognitions.

This is true also of our past. Everyone's past is complex, ambiguous, and impossible to define precisely. Recognizing that our cognitions determine our emotional world implies that our cognitions also determine our conception of our own past. So-called bad pasts can be reinterpreted in more benign ways just as our conceptions of an unsatisfactory job can be reinterpreted to make it less stressful or boring. These changes can be brought about by learning to use new coping styles as a result of the therapeutic interaction. The therapeutic principle is the following: *Reduce the influence of the environment and disconnect from the past by using appropriate coping styles.*

Example: One member of a therapy group is 70 years old. She is married to a former alcoholic who is insensitive, withdrawn, and sometimes demanding. Her experiences in group therapy gradually helped her change her coping styles so that she began to handle problems differently. She decreased her ruminations about her unhappy childhood and her husband's faults. She began to do more things that please her (such as travel). She uses the coping styles of minimization (i.e., *not* seeing every incident as catastrophic) a lot more than she formerly did. She feels that she is largely responsible for her life now and is not controlled by her past unhappiness.

CONCLUSION

Psychotherapy helps an individual achieve the goal of symptom reduction and self-growth by engaging in a complex interpersonal exchange of ideas and emotions. Three types of skills need to be acquired by the client if therapy is to be maximally successful. The first is to learn communication skills designed to decrease interpersonal conflicts. The second is to learn how to assess the balance of motives or emotions associated with one's conflicts with other people. The third is to learn a variety of coping skills and to use them flexibly. These skills can be learned or developed during the therapeutic process. Other life skills connected with work, courtship, love, and parenting also can be acquired through the therapeutic encounter. Conceptualizing psychotherapy as self-evaluation, goal setting, problem solving, skill acquisition, and reinterpretation is consistent with a broad evolutionary perspective on human life.

REFERENCES

Alexander, R. D. (1987). *The biology of moral systems.* New York: Aldine de Gruyter.

Barash, D. P. (1982). *Sociobiology and behavior.* New York: Elsevier.

Berlin, B., & Kay, P. (1969). *Basic color terms: Their universality and evolution.* Berkeley: University of California Press.

Bornstein, M. H. (1973). Color vision and color naming: A psychophysiological hypothesis of cultural difference. *Psychological Bulletin, 80,* 257–285.

Breland, K., & Breland, M. (1966). *Animal behavior.* New York: Macmillan.

Brown, J. L. (1975). *The evolution of behavior.* New York: Norton.

Buckley, P., Conte, H. R., Plutchik, R., Wild, K. V., & Karasu, T. B. (1984). Psychodynamic variables as predictors of psychotherapy outcome. *American Journal of Psychiatry, 141,* 742–748.

Buirski, P., Plutchik, R., & Kellerman, H. (1978). Sex differences, dominance, and personality in the chimpanzee. *Animal Behaviour, 26,* 123–129.

Chagnon, N. A. (1988). Life histories, blood revenge, and warfare in a tribal population. *Science, 239,* 985–993.

Cobb, J. P., & Lieberman, S. (1987). The grammar of psychotherapy: A descriptive account. *British Journal of Psychiatry, 151,* 589–594.

Conte, H. R., & Plutchik, R. (1981). A circumplex model for interpersonal traits. *Journal of Personality and Social Psychology, 2,* 823–830.

Darwin, C. (1965). *The expression of the emotions in man and animals.* Chicago, IL: University of Chicago Press. (Original work published 1872).

Davitz, J. R. (1969). *The language of emotions.* New York: McGraw-Hill.

Egeland, J. A., Gerhard, D. S., Pauls, D. L., Sussex, J. N., Kidd, K. K., Allen, C. R., Hostetter, A. M., & Housman, D. E. (1987). Bipolar affective disorders linked to DNA markers on chromosome 11. *Nature (London), 325,* 783–787.

Eibl-Eibesfeldt, I. (1971). *Love and hate.* New York: Holt, Rinehart & Winston.

Eibl-Eibesfeldt, I. (1975). *Ethology: The biology of behavior* (2nd ed.). New York: Holt.

Ekman, P., & Friesen, W. V. (1971). Constants across cultures in the face and emotion. *Journal of Personality and Social Psychology, 17,* 124–129.

Enquist, M. (1985). Communication during aggressive interactions with particular reference to variation in choice of behavior. *Animal Behaviour, 33,* 1152–1161.

Fisher, G. A., Heise, D. R., Bohrnstedt, G. W., & Lucke, J. Z. (1985). Evidence for extending the circumplex model of personality trait language to self-reported moods. *Journal of Personality and Social Psychology, 49,* 233–242.

Freedman, D. G. (1974). *Human infancy: An ethological perspective.* Hillsdale, NJ: Erlbaum.

Fuller, J. L. (1986). Genetics and emotions. In R. Plutchik & H. Kellerman (Eds.), *Emotion: Theory, research, and experience: Vol. 3. Biological foundations of emotion.* Orlando, FL: Academic Press.

Goddard, M. E., & Beilharz, R. G. (1985). A multivariate analysis of the genetics of fearfulness in potential guide dogs. *Behavior Genetics, 15,* 69–89.

Hahn, M. E., & Simmel, E. C. (Eds.). (1976). *Communicative behavior and evolution.* New York: Academic Press.

Haley, J. (1980). *Leaving home: The therapy of disturbed young people.* New York: McGraw-Hill.

Hayden, B. (1981). Subsistence and ecological adaptations of modern hunter/gatherers. In R. S. O. Harding & G. Teleki (Eds.), *Omniverous primates: Gathering and hunting in human evolution.* New York: Columbia University Press.

Henry, J. P., & Stephen, P. M. (1977). *Stress, health and the social environment: A sociobiologic approach to medicine.* New York: Springer-Verlag.

Hinde, R. A. (1966). *Animal behavior: A synthesis of ethology and comparative psychology.* New York: McGraw-Hill.

Hogan, R. (1982). A socioanalytic theory of personality. In *Nebraska symposium on motivation.* Lincoln: University of Nebraska Press.

Ivey, A. E., & Simek-Downing, L. (1980). *Counseling and psychotherapy: Skills, theories and practices.* Englewood Cliffs, NJ: Prentice-Hall.

Kellerman, H. (1970). *Group therapy and personality: Intersecting structures.* New York: Grune & Stratton.

Kellerman, H. (1987). Nightmares and the structure of personality. In H. Kellerman (Ed.), *The nightmare: Psychological and biological formulations.* New York: Columbia University Press.

Kellerman, H. (1989). Projective measures of emotion. In R. Plutchik & H. Kellerman (Eds.), *Emotion: Theory, research, and experience: Vol. 4. The measurement of emotions.* San Diego, CA: Academic Press.

Lazarus, A. A. (1976). *Multimodel behavior therapy.* New York: Springer.

Lazarus, R. S., Kanner, A. D., & Folkman, S. (1980). Emotions: A cognitive-phenomenological analysis. In R. Plutchik & H. Kellerman (Eds.), *Emotion: Theory, research, and experience: Vol. 1. Theories of emotion.* New York: Academic Press.

Lieberman, R. P., Mueser, K. T., & Wallace, C. J. (1986). Social skills training for schizophrenic individuals at risk for relapse. *American Journal of Psychiatry, 143,* 523–526.

Lieberman, S., & Cobb, J. P. (1987). The grammar of psychotherapy. Interactograms: Three self-monitoring instruments for audiotape feedback. *British Journal of Psychiatry, 151,* 594–601.

Loehlin, J. C., Horn, J. M., & Williams, L. (1981). Personality resemblance in adoptive familes. *Behavior Genetics, 11,* 309–330.

Loehlin, J. C., & Nichols, R. C. (1978). *Heredity, environment and personality: A study of 850 sets of twins.* Austin: University of Texas Press.

Lumsden, C. J., & Wilson, E. O. (1981). *Genes, mind and culture: The coevolutionary process.* Cambridge, MA: Harvard University Press.

Marler, P., & Tenaza, R. (1977). Signaling behavior of apes with special reference to vocalization. In T. A. Sebeok (Ed.), *How animals communicate.* Bloomington: Indiana University Press.

McGuire, M. T., & Fairbanks, L. A. (1977). Ethology: Psychiatry's bridge to behavior. In M. T. McGuire & L. A. Fairbanks (Eds.), *Ethological psychiatry.* New York: Grune & Stratton.

Parker, G. A. (1974). Assessment strategy and the evolution of fighting behavior. *Journal of Theoretical Biology, 47,* 223–243.

Parker, S. T. (1985). A social technological model for the evolution of language. *Current Anthropology, 26,* 617–639.

Plutchik, R. (1958). Outlines of a new theory of emotion. *Transactions of the New York Academy of Sciences, 20,* 394–403.

Plutchik, R. (1962). *The emotions: Facts, theories and a new model.* New York: Random House.

Plutchik, R. (1966). Multiple rating scales for the measurement of affective states. *Journal of Clinical Psychology, 22,* 423–425.

Plutchik, R. (1970). Emotions, evolution, and adaptive processes. In M. B. Arnold (Ed.), *Feelings and emotions.* New York: Academic Press.

Plutchik, R. (1971). Individual and breed differences in approach and withdrawal in dogs. *Behaviour, 40,* 302–311.

Plutchik, R. (1977). Cognitions in the service of emotions. In D. K. Candland, J. P. Fell, E. Kean, A. I. Leshner, R. Plutchik, & R. M. Tharpy (Eds.), *Emotion.* Monterey, CA: Brooks/Cole.

Plutchik, R. (1980a). *Emotions: A psychoevolutionary synthesis.* New York: Harper & Row.

Plutchik, R. (1980b). A psychoevolutionary theory of emotion. In R. Plutchik & H. Kellerman (Eds.), *Emotion: Theory, research, and experience: Vol. 1. Theories of emotion.* New York: Academic Press.

Plutchik, R. (1983a). Emotions in early development: A psychoevolutionary approach. In R. Plutchik & H. Kellerman (Eds.), *Emotion: Theory, research, and experience: Vol. 2. Emotions in early development*. New York: Academic Press.

Plutchik, R. (1983b). Universal problems of adaptation: Hierarchy, territoriality, identity, and temporality. In J. B. Calhoun (Ed.), *Environment and population: Problems of adaptation*. New York: Praeger.

Plutchik, R. (1984a). Emotions and imagery. *Journal of Mental Imagery, 8,* 105–112.

Plutchik, R. (1984b). Emotions: A general psychoevolutionary theory. In K. R. Scherer & P. Ekman (Eds.), *Approaches to emotion*. Hillsdale, NJ: Erlbaum.

Plutchik, R. (1985, August). *Emotion and temperament*. Paper presented at the symposium on "Biology and temperament" at the meeting of the American Psychological Association, Los Angeles, CA.

Plutchik, R. (1987). Evolutionary bases of empathy. In N. Eisenberg & J. Strayer (Eds.), *Empathy and its development*. New York: Cambridge University Press.

Plutchik, R. (1989). Measuring emotions and their derivatives. In R. Plutchik & H. Kellerman (Eds.), *Emotion: Theory, research, and experience: Vol. 4. The measurement of emotions*. San Diego, CA: Academic Press.

Plutchik, R., & Conte, H. R. (1985). Quantitative assessment of personality disorders. In R. Michels, J. O. Cavenar, Jr., H. K. H. Brodie et al. (Eds.), *Psychiatry* (Vol. 1). Philadelphia, PA: Lippincott.

Plutchik, R., Conte, H. R., & Karasu, T. B., (1988). Psychodynamic and behavioral therapy: A survey and discussion of integrative models. *Integrative Psychiatry, 6,* 22–26.

Plutchik, R., & Kellerman, H. (1974). *Manual of the Emotions Profile Index*. Los Angeles, CA: Western Psychological Services.

Plutchik, R., Kellerman, H., & Conte, H. R. (1979). A structural theory of ego defenses. In C. E. Izard (Ed.), *Emotions, personality and psychopathology*. New York: Plenum.

Plutchik, R., & Landau, H. (1973). Perceived dominance and emotional states in small groups. *Psychotherapy: Theory, Research and Practice, 10,* 341–342.

Plutchik, R., & Platman, S. R. (1977). Personality connotations of psychiatric diagnoses. *Journal of Nervous and Mental Disease, 165,* 418–422.

Russell, J. A. (1989). Verbal measures of emotion. In R. Plutchik & H. Kellerman (Ed.), *Emotion: Theory, research, and experience: Vol. 4. The measurement of emotions*. San Diego, CA: Academic Press.

Schaefer, E. S., & Plutchik, R. (1966). Interrelationships of emotions, traits, and diagnostic constructs. *Psychological Reports, 18,* 399–410.

Scheflen, A. E. (1963). Communication and regulation in psychotherapy. *Psychiatry, 26,* 126–136.

Sebeok, T. A. (1963). The informational model of language: Analogue and digital coding in animal and human communication. In P. L. Garvin (Ed.), *Natural language and the computer*. New York: McGraw-Hill.

Smith, M. L., Glass, G. V., & Miller, T. I. (1980). *The benefits of psychotherapy*. Baltimore, MD: Johns Hopkins University Press.

Stevenson-Hinde, J., & Simpson, A. E. (1982). Temperament and relationships. In R. Porter & G. M. Collins (Eds.), *Temperamental differences in infants and young children*. London: Pitman.

Tiger, L., & Fox, R. (1971). *The imperial animal*. New York: Holt.

Trivers, R. L. (1971). The evolution of reciprocal altruism. *Quarterly Review of Biology, 46,* 35–57.

Trivers, R. L. (1972). Parental investment and sexual selection. In B. Campbell (Ed.), *Sexual selection and the descent of man*. Chicago, IL: Aldine.

Weinrich, J. D. (1980). Toward a sociobiological theory of the emotions. In R. Plutchik & H. Kellerman Eds.), *Emotion: Theory, research, and experience: Vol. 1. Theories of emotion*. New York: Academic Press.

Wiggins, J. S., & Broughton, R. (1985). The interpersonal circle: A structural model for the integration of personality research. *Perspectives in Personality*, **1**, 1–47.

Wilder, J. F., & Plutchik, R. (1982). Preparing the professional: Building prevention into training. In W. S. Paine (Ed.), *Job stress and burnout*. Beverly Hills, CA: Sage.

Wilson, E. O. (1975). *Sociobiology: The new synthesis*. Boston, MA: Harvard University Press.

Wimer, R. E., & Wimer, C. C. (1985). Animal behavior genetics: A search for the biological foundations of behavior. *Annual Review of Psychology*, **36**, 171–218.

Young, G., & Decarie, T. G. (1977). An ethology-based catalogue of facial and vocal behavior in infancy. *Animal Behaviour*, **25**, 95–107.

Zajonc, R. B. (1980). Feeling and thinking: Preferences need no inferences. *American Psychologist*, **35**, 151–175.

Chapter 2

ANGER: AN EVOLUTIONARY VIEW

MICHAEL T. McGUIRE AND ALFONSO TROISI

ABSTRACT

An evolutionary interpretation of anger is developed with emphasis on its function in changing behavior in the recipient of anger. Intensity and duration of anger, as well as the recipient's responses, are viewed as critical variables to be explained. Mechanisms of behavioral change in the recipient are discussed. Alteration of the recipient's physiology is viewed as a critical step in the process of change. The analysis places equal emphasis on the person who is angry and the recipient, one implication of which is that both parties have limited behavioral options. A final section discusses possible effects of psychiatric disorders on the expression of anger and its functional effectiveness.

INTRODUCTION

Anger is a frequently experienced emotion often associated with feelings of displeasure primarily about someone else's behavior (Averill, 1979, 1982). For every person who is angry, there is a different probability that the anger will be overtly expressed. When it is expressed, forms differ across persons and situations. In effect, anger is never twice the same. The more closely anger is studied, the more obvious it becomes that anger is not simply a primitive and uncontrolled emotion but a complex interaction between feelings, behaviors, and consequences (Averill, 1982; McKenna, 1983; Plutchik, 1980) in which both the

43

person angered and the recipient of anger are actors that influence the outcome (Maynard Smith & Price, 1973).

Anyone who has studied anger will be impressed by the extensive research and literature on the subject. A case in point concerns the possible causes of anger. The list is long (e.g., disappointment in the behavior of another, frustration with ongoing activities, loss of self-esteem, property damage, and injury and pain; see, for example, Averill, 1979, 1982). The length of the list immediately suggests that any attempt to discuss anger as a general phenomenon must consider numerous variables. There have been repeated attempts to categorize anger (e.g., interpersonal, territorial, and instrumental; see, for example, Blanchard & Blanchard, 1984; Moyer, 1968) in efforts to bring conceptual order and understanding to experiential, clinical, and research data. Yet, in our view, a critical and, in many ways, a self-evident function—the use of anger to change the behavior of another—has not received sufficient or deserved attention. This paper focuses primarily on this function and the features of anger that we believe influences its effectiveness in changing the behavior of another.

Our analysis will be limited to a single situation, one in which (1) persons A and B have agreed to engage in a particular behavior, (2) B does not behave as agreed, and (3) A becomes angry and expresses this anger to B. For example, B agrees to help A move furniture that A cannot move alone; without warning or explanation, B refuses to help A; and A becomes angry and expresses this anger to B. Situations of this type are not uncommon nor is the associated anger trivial. Averill (1982), for example, reports that the most frequent cause of anger is dissatisfaction with another's behavior.

ANGER—AN EVOLUTIONARY VIEW

From an evolutionary perspective, anger may be thought of as one of the emotional correlates of attack aggression (Blanchard & Blanchard, 1984). Attack aggression (as separate from, say, defensive aggression) can be viewed as a continuum, bracketed by mild irritation and overt destructive behavior. For most of this paper, the term anger will refer to situations approximately at the middle of the continuum. Anger involving physical contact will not be considered nor will we discuss everyday situations resulting in passing irritations or frustrations.

Just as there are many possible contributing factors to anger, so too are there many possible functions, including asserting one's authority, gaining revenge, destroying another, or changing the behavior of another (see Averill, 1979, 1982; Blanchard & Blanchard, 1984; Brian, 1984). Each of these functions can be discussed in cost–benefit terms, the economic vocabulary of evolutionary theory. For example, A attempts to change B's behavior so that B's behavior is more beneficial and less costly to A (which does not preclude the possibility that B's behavioral change also may become more beneficial and less costly to B): A and B may agree to divide work responsibilities at a job in which they will be paid when work is completed. If B fails to do his or her share, A will not be reimbursed. A, therefore, may become angry with B in order to alter B's behavior so that A has to work less (reduced cost) to get paid (benefit).

In evolutionary thinking, costs and benefits are important concepts because they facilitate making connections between behavior and inclusive fitness, which is, essentially, the degree to which one's genes are replicated in successive generations. In effect, and other things being equal, repeated interactions in which benefits exceed costs are taken to imply a greater probability of achieving genetic replication than the reverse situation (costs > benefits). This equation remains undemonstrated among humans primarily because of the infeasibility of doing extensive cross-generational research. Nevertheless, the logic is well founded and examples that might disprove the cost–benefit approach have not been compelling.

Several evolutionary ideas underlie the interpretation developed here. First, it is likely that anger and aggression have been favored products of selection. In the past, as in the present, they often successfully serve to protect individuals who are angry, as well as their kin, friends, and resources. Selection, however, is unlikely to have favored uncontrolled anger. Rather, it should favor individuals whose cognitive–analytic skills permit them to assess when and to what degree anger (and aggression) should be expressed (McKenna, 1983). Second, persons engage in reciprocal relationships because they anticipate that such relationships will yield benefits equal to or in excess of costs (Trivers, 1971). It is in part because expected benefits are not forthcoming that people become angry with one another. Third, anger incurs specific physiological costs (e.g., energy and time expenditures) both to the person who is angry and to the recipient of anger. Being angry leads to changes in numerous physiological systems, resulting in, for example, elevations in blood pressure, pulse rate, testosterone levels, adrenal activity; changes in epinephrine function, glucose metabolism, and alterations in autonomic nervous system activity (see Brain, 1984, for a recent review; and Schwartz, Weinberger, & Singer, 1981, for comparisons of selected physiological consequences of anger, fear, and happiness). The fact that physiological changes can be documented does not mean that anger is uniformly unpleasurable. Interviews with persons who frequently are angry suggest that when the intensity of anger is increasing it is sometimes experienced as pleasurable (M. T. McGuire, unpublished data).

A number of anatomical systems also have been implicated in anger, including the hypothalamus, midbrain central grey area, amygdala, and the central and anterior portions of the septum (for discussions, see Adams, 1979; Blanchard & Blanchard, 1984; Brain, 1984). Likewise, a number of neurotransmitter systems appear to be involved, including norepinephrine, epinephrine, dopamine, and serotonin (see, for example, Raleigh & McGuire, 1980). Findings from physiological studies often are difficult to interpret, however. This difficulty is owing to the fact that anger (defensive anger excluded) is seldom immediate. It builds slowly. And once it builds, it may continue in duration from hours to days (Averill, 1982). At other times anger is intermittent, although its focus remains constant (Averill, 1982). Different neurotransmitter systems are implicated at different points over the course of different types of anger. For example, serotonin function changes slowly and is not thought to be an important factor in the early moments of anger, although pre-anger function may influence the probability of anger (Raleigh & McGuire, 1980). On the other hand, dopamine, norepinephrine, and epinephrine functions change rapidly and are more likely to be important early-moment contributors. Each of these possible changes involve physiological costs and, in many instances, these costs are associated with the experience of displeasure. The number of implicated anatomical areas, their different ages (in evolutionary terms), and the interactions between physiological and behavioral systems, when taken together, suggest that anger is an evolutionarily old and complex emotion.

Available experiential and laboratory data are compatible with the following views: for the angered person, the greater the intensity of anger (other things being constant), the greater the physiological costs (e.g., energy and metabolite expenditures and time of physiological recovery); and the greater the duration of anger (other things being constant), the greater the physiological costs and possibly also other costs. The term "other costs" has two meanings: the angered person, because of the constricted focus of attention, may overlook possible alternative beneficial options; and, the act of being angered often results in the angered person becoming socially unattractive, which can result in reduced social options.

Costs also occur in the recipient of anger. Experientially, the recipient may be frightened, guilty, self-righteous, or irritated. If the angered person's anger persists, the recipient also may become angry. Surprisingly, few studies have focused on the physiological effects of anger on recipients. Thus, while precise relationships between increased intensity, extended duration, and physiological costs are still to be determined among recipients, it is our view that two points are likely to be established by further research: physiological costs of anger rapidly accumulate and costs significantly influence outcome.

The likelihood that physiological costs accumulate rapidly sets important constraints on the behavior of the person who is angry. Person A should behave in ways calculated to bring about the desired change in B at the least cost to A. Thus A is likely to utilize different behavioral strategies—be angry in different ways—depending on which of B's behaviors A wishes to change and the importance of such changes to A. In addition, A's choice of strategies will be influenced by factors such as A's physiological state at the time he or she becomes angry (see, for example, McGuire & Troisi, in press), known or postulated characteristics of B, the history of A's and B's relationship, and the importance to A of continuing a relationship with B. Each of these variables will influence A's anger. An interaction between the physiological costs to B of A's anger and the probability of B changing behavior also is expected. That B has the option to reject A's anger and to walk away (discontinue the relationship) not only serves as a constraint on A but also represents a behavioral option that B may exploit during a bout of anger.

A number of other constraints are likely to be applicable given different situations. For example, to bring about an anger-induced behavioral change in B, A's anger must be communicated in ways that B understands. A, therefore, must not only behave in ways that have the desired effect on B but also make repeated assessments of B's responses to determine if B is changing in the desired way. Similar reasoning applies to the relevance of anger. To be effective, A's anger must be viewed by B as relevant to B's behavior. While there may be temporary physiological costs to the recipient of irrelevant anger (A is angry at B for something C did), such anger is unlikely to result in either extended physiological costs or behavioral change among recipients. Although different in kind, constraints also apply to the recipient. For example, to reject A (walk away) may result in increased indirect costs to B, such as the loss of future benefits by continuing a relationship with A or the direct costs involved in B's development of new relationships. At times, potential indirect costs can be sufficient to lead B to change behavior, irrespective of the relevance of A's anger.

Points developed in the preceding paragraph have been discussed from other evolutionary perspectives, often referred to as evolutionary stable strategies or ESS (see, for example, Maynard-Smith & Price, 1973). ESS theory postulates that animals of the same species are likely to have evolved such that engaging in limited destructive interactions will be optimal for individual reproductive success. The implication is that there are evolved constraints on behavior and that an understanding of anger requires a recognition of these constraints and their functional translations.

The preceding and far-from-complete discussion hints at the complexity of anger as it might be viewed from an evolutionary perspective. Clearly, limiting the number of areas to be discussed is essential. Until the section in which anger among persons with psychiatric disorders is discussed, we will make the following assumptions: we are discussing adults who are *not* cognitively or emotionally compromised; A's angry behavior (postures, statement, voice changes, etc.) is understood by B; B's failure to behave as expected (the event initiating A's anger) is undertaken with B's awareness of not behaving as A expects as well as with the knowledge that A will be angry; and A and B are well known to each other and have engaged previously in reciprocal interactions that have been more beneficial than costly. In effect, we are discussing a situation (B not appearing as promised to help A move furniture) in which some degree of anger by A toward B would be considered normal and justified.

INTERACTION OF SELECTED VARIABLES

In the following analysis, anger intensity and anger duration are independent variables, and the probability of B changing his own behavior in a way desired by A is the dependent variable. Figure 2.1 depicts the postulated relationship between the intensity of A's anger and the probability of B changing behavior in ways desired by A. The intensity of A's anger will be influenced by the following kinds of costs: A's prior benefits minus costs in the relationship with B (e.g., if A is in a positive cost–benefit balance—B owes A—the intensity of A's anger is likely to be less than if the reverse is true); the immediate costs to A of B not acting as expected; and the indirect costs to A if B rejects A's anger and walks away. For Figure 2.1 it is assumed that the duration of anger is constant and that B previously has not acted in a similar manner toward A.

Figure 2.1 can be viewed from the standpoint of either A or B. An inverted U curve depicts B's possible responses to the increasing intensity of A's anger. B, not having behaved as expected, will have calculated both the consequences to A and the probable intensity of A's anger. Because estimates of others always are somewhat inaccurate (e.g., B cannot know the full range of costs to A), B can be expected to calculate upper (Point X) and lower (Point Q) limits to the intensity of A's anger. Assuming that A and B calculate the same curve, maximum anger by A (Point X) is most likely to change B's behavior. However, if the intensity of A's anger is greater than that expected by B (to the right of Point X), the probability of B changing behavior declines rapidly due to the cumulative physiological costs to B. If A does not show any anger (Point Q), the probability that B will change behavior (given the assumptions stated earlier) is greater than zero because of B's awareness of not having behaved as A expected and the likelihood that B will attempt to compensate A. At Point Z, the probability of B acting as A desires becomes less than if A had shown no anger at all.

Clinical evidence suggests that cross-person variance for Figure 2.1 may be considerable. Just as some people seldom get angry, others get angry and remain so for extended periods. Thus, Figure 2.1 is limited to the conditions discussed for the figure and not applicable to all possible situations of anger.

In reality, A and B are unlikely to calculate the same curve. From either A's or B's perspective, it is B's curve that is most critical, however, because if B fails to change behavior, A has accrued costs without achieving benefits.

There are of course many factors that could lead to a modification of Figure

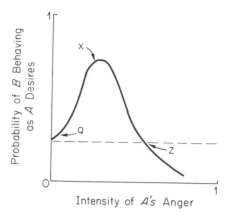

FIGURE 2.1. Intensity of A's anger versus the probability of B changing behavior. Anger becomes more intense as a function of increasing loudness of voice, rigidity of posture, rate of speech (usually), autonomic nervous signs (e.g., redness of face), and decreasing willingness to listen to the recipient. Note that the probability of B behaving as A desires never reaches 1.

2.1. For example, the history of the relationship between A and B should affect the shape of the curve. If the relationship is long-standing and consistently beneficial to both A and B, the intensity of A's anger is likely to be less than it would be in a relationship with a shorter and a less beneficial history. In the former situation, A would wish to bring about changes in B's behavior while not risking a discontinuation of the relationship. A also will wish to contain personal costs. From B's perspective, B has the opportunity to reduce both personal costs and A's costs by communicating to A that he or she (B) will change behavior.

Figure 2.2 shows the postulated relationship between the duration of A's anger and the probability of B changing behavior in ways A desires. For Figure 2.2 it is assumed that the intensity of anger is moderate (a point halfway between Q and X in Figure 2.1) and constant.

Figure 2.2 shows a relationship similar to but in important ways different from Figure 2.1: both the rate of rise and of decline of the two curves differ, and the highest probability of A changing B's behavior is less than the highest probability depicted in Figure 2.1. As in Figure 2.1, Figure 2.2 will differ depending on whether it is viewed from A's or from B's perspective (see Averill, 1982, for a discussion of studies dealing with the duration of anger). A clear implication of Figure 2.2 is that a short period of anger is less likely to be effective in changing B's behavior than a more extended period. This effect is predicted because the physiological costs of a short period of medium-intensity anger by A are relatively small to B. Further, B may interpret a short period of anger as an indication that the costs to A of B not having behaved as expected are less than B calculated. Compared to Figure 2.1, A has a longer period within which his

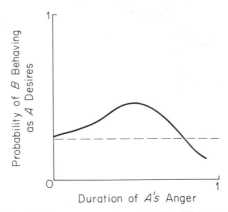

FIGURE 2.2.   Duration of A's anger versus the probability of B behaving as A desires. Continuous anger is revealed through some combination of at least the following: facial expressions (e.g., angry glances and refusal to smile), reduced interaction, remindful comments to the recipient, failure to respond and/or be empathetic, and refusal to accept apologies. Note that the probability of B behaving as A desires never reaches 1 and that the highest probability of B changing behavior is less than for the optimal intensity of anger in Figure 2.1.

anger can be expressed and still maintain a reasonable probability that his anger will be effective. B's calculation of A's curve should influence B's behavior. For example, if B calculates that A will be angry for a long period, B has the option of shortening the duration of A's anger by behaving as A desires. To do so reduces B's physiological costs. This choice may represent B's optimal strategy if B has a strong desire to continue a relationship with A. Beyond the midpoint of the curve, the probability of B behaving as A desires decreases because the cumulative costs of A's anger now become excessive relative to B's estimate of the costs to A of B not behaving as A expected.

Figure 2.3 presents the postulated effectiveness of three intensities of anger as a function of duration (assuming the three intensities remain constant). The figure summarizes points from Figures 2.1 and 2.2.

In Figure 2.3 the probability of A changing B's behavior is greatest with intense anger, provided that A limits the time frame of the intensity. For low-intensity anger, the probability of B changing behavior is relatively small, and thus low-intensity anger may be a counterproductive strategy because the costs to A are likely to exceed those to B. For medium-intensity anger, the probability of B acting as A desires is less than for the optimal expression of intense anger, but there is greater leeway in duration than there is with intense anger. An advantage to A of medium-intensity anger is that A is left with greater room for error in estimating B's physiological state and calculated curve.

Thus far we have focused on the duration and intensity of A's anger and their

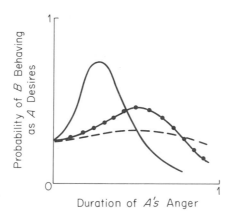

FIGURE 2.3. Probability of B changing behavior versus different durations and intensities of A's anger. Intense (—) = high-intensity anger as described for Figure 2.1. Medium (●—●) = medium-intensity anger, which includes all the observable elements described in Figure 2.1 but with each expressed as a percentage of the maximum possible. Low (---) = low-intensity anger, which most often includes subtle postural changes and alterations in normal interaction responses to recipient.

interaction with B's behavior. The discussion has assumed that B's behavior is important to A and that anger often is an effective way of altering behavior that jeopardizes relationships. Examples of this situation occur frequently when two persons have a long-standing relationship and one person changes such that previous ways of interacting now are irritable to the other person. Failure of the other person to recognize that changes have occurred and continuation of the same way of acting often lead to anger on the part of the changed person and behavioral adjustments by the other. Within limits, therefore, anger can solidify social relationships (see, for example, Averill, 1979; Blanchard & Blanchard, 1984; Bowlby, 1980; Kummer, 1968; Plutchik, 1980).

A number of the preceding points could be discussed from other perspectives. For example, A's anger may be viewed as an attempt to alter B's *behavior center* (MacKay, 1972). In effect, B's behavior can be thought of as governed by a set of rules that A wishes to change. Experience suggests that assessments of the behavioral rules of others are both difficult and time consuming. Moreover, assessments are seldom exact, most probably because rules change. Experience also suggests that bringing about lasting changes in others' behavioral rules is difficult and time consuming. Certainly evidence from everyday discussions between, for example, parent and child, or employers and employees, would support this view. Talk alone (e.g., advice or suggestions) is only occasionally effective. Judiciously used anger, therefore, can be a relatively effective means of achieving one's ends.

ANGER AND PSYCHIATRIC DISORDERS

Several introductory points will set the perspective for this section. First, in what follows we will not focus on those disorders (e.g., impulse disorders of adolescence) in which repeated irrational outbursts of anger are a striking characteristic. High-intensity anger and aggression are only occasional occurrences, even among persons suffering from psychiatric disorders (see, for example, Craig, 1982; Tardiff & Koenigsberg, 1985; Tardiff & Sweillam, 1982). Rather, our focus is on situations of mild psychopathology (e.g., neuroses) in which persons are either more or less angry than expected. Second, most people are familiar with culturally acceptable ranges relating to the intensity and duration of anger given particular situations. (That these ranges differ from culture to culture points to the importance of assessing cultural variables when studying anger.) For example, most people living in the United States would consider it unreasonable to be scolded for 15 minutes because of a 5-minute tardiness to an appointment. Third, anger that occurs outside culturally acceptable ranges is usually categorized as atypical or irrational and generally is counterproductive in bringing about long-term behavioral change (although short-term changes sometimes occur).

Given Figures 2.1–3, there are several types of anger that fall outside culturally acceptable ranges: more or less intense than expected, more or less extended than expected, and displaced (e.g., anger for which there is no obvious justification). Combinations of course exist and while the three categories may be logically distinct, it is unlikely that unambiguous examples falling into any single category are ever observed. The first two categories will be considered here. Figures 2.4 and 2.5 depict situations of more or less intense and more or less extended anger from the perspective of B, who will make judgments concerning whether A's anger fits within culturally acceptable ranges given the fact that B has failed to behave in an agreed-upon way. Unless otherwise stated, A is the person suffering from a psychiatric disorder; the figures should be read from B's perspective.

Figure 2.4 depicts situations in which the intensity of A's anger either exceeds or is less than what B expects and the probability that B will view the anger (or lack of) as irrational. B's range of expectations will be determined by culturally acceptable ranges modified by B's assessment of the costs to A of B's behavior. Note that B is differentially responsive to more intense anger. B has several possible responses to anger that is more intense than expected: to act as A desires (if possible), to interact with A to try to reduce the anger (a possibly costly interaction to B), to simply wait out the anger (a possibly costly interaction to B), and to categorize A's anger as irrational (a possibly low-cost decision for B). For less intense than expected anger, B's choices are to act as A desires (a possibly costly choice to B), to interact with A to try to get him or her to express the anger

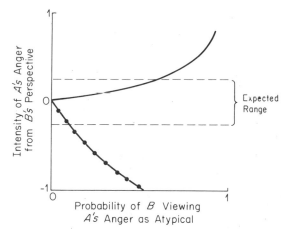

FIGURE 2.4.   Intensity of A's anger either exceeds or is less than the expected level. Note that the probability of B viewing A's anger as irrational, when the intensity of A's anger is less than expected, does not exceed .5. Even then, it is necessary that A literally not express anger. The less-than-expected curve is postulated to apply only to situations in which a significant degree of anger is expected by B. If B expects only a passing comment by A, A's failure to say anything is not likely to suggest that A's behavior is atypical.

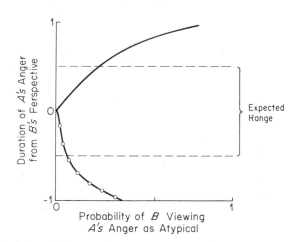

FIGURE 2.5.   Duration of A's anger either exceeds or is less than the expected level. Because of A's options with respect to duration of anger (see Figure 2.2), either extreme extensions or relatively short periods of anger are required to suggest to B that A's anger is irrational. As in Figure 2.4, a certain degree of expected anger by A is essential for the minus percentage curve to be relevant. Also, the minus percentage curve is unlikely to extend beyond .5 for reasons similar to those mentioned in Figure 2.4.

(a possibly costly interaction to B), to wait until A's anger emerges (a possibly costly activity to B), and to categorize A's anger as irrational (a possibly low-cost decision for B).

How B behaves will be influenced by prior history (e.g., the frequency with which A gets angry and the cost consequences of A's anger to B), B's physiological state (e.g., degree of B's fatigue), and the importance to B of continuing a relationship with A. Assuming that B acts in self-interest, a low-cost alternative is to classify A's anger as irrational, which of course reduces the probability that B will change behavior and increases the probability that A will remain angry.

Viewed psychologically, when A's anger exceeds normal ranges, it is likely that A is excessively dependent on B's behavior, certainly more than the situation of helping someone move furniture would normally suggest. One might pursue this line of reasoning by trying to identify the psychological factors that contribute to A's behavior. For example, A may suffer from low self-esteem and may equate B acting as expected as an indication of A's worth. A's overly intense anger might thus be explained as follows: B's expected behavior has potential benefits to A that exceed those usually associated with such situations. On the other hand, less than expected anger by A would occur if A overcalculated the effects of the anger on B.

If A's anger is within culturally acceptable ranges, and B suffers from psychopathology, there is an increased probability that A's anger will be misinterpreted. Clinically, a frequently observed response of persons with psychiatric disorders is that of overreaction. This response can be explained as follows: B already is in a negative physiological cost–benefit balance and A's anger increases B's physiological costs, which in turn hastens either a misreading of A's anger, withdrawal, or intense anger towards A. An implication of this interpretation is that normal anger in one person can have physiologically destabilizing effects on another person whose physiology already is altered. (It is likely that at certain times psychotherapy techniques have a similar effect. For example, a patient may be angry at a therapist because the therapist refuses to change behavior and interact more frequently. If the therapist does not alter his or her behavior in response to the patient's anger, the anger may increase. This would result not only in major physiological costs to the patient but also the narrowing of a patient's focus specifically on the therapist).

Figure 2.5 depicts situations in which A's anger either exceeds B's expectations of reasonable duration or is significantly shorter in duration than B's expectations. These possibilities are plotted against the probability that B will view A's expression of anger as atypical and thus not change behavior. Note that relative to Figure 2.4 the normal ranges are extended. B, therefore, is less likely to assess A's anger as irrational unless extreme deviations from the expected are encountered. Note also that extended duration can approach 100% probability whereas short duration does not. B's alternatives in both extended- and short-duration situations are similar to those discussed in relationship to Figure 2.4.

What we have said on the subject of psychopathology and anger is far from complete. We have emphasized the association between psychopathology and misreading others' behavior, which of course often occurs among persons who do not suffer from psychopathology. A more complete discussion is precluded primarily because, in our view, the interactions between anger and disorder type differ significantly. For example, people with obsessive–compulsive disorder often are angry for long periods while persons suffering from bipolar illness–manic type often show few indications of anger.

MECHANISMS

The subject of mechanisms has a long and often confused history. In large part the confusion is the result of the multiple uses of the term. Here we will briefly discuss an evolutionary approach to mechanisms in focusing on why B's behavior changes as a consequence of A's anger.

Historically, when the term "mechanism" is used to explain changes in behavior, the terms "environmentally influenced" or "internally influenced" can be substituted without loss of meaning or precision. This point is particularly true in learning theory or psychodynamic explanations. This situation can be contrasted to the use of the term in physiological explanations, for example, in the presence of enzyme X, substrate C is converted to amino acid Y. Here the essential ingredients and conditions can be specified, and substitution of a more general term for a more specific term results in loss of precision (e.g., enzyme for enzyme X). In our view, if substitution can occur without loss of precision, one is not describing a mechanism (although one may be describing a process).

Do the above criteria ever apply to psychological–behavioral explanations? From an evolutionary perspective, it is likely that there are a large number of highly evolved and specific psychological and behavioral mechanisms. Thus, in principle, the answer to the question above is yes. The problem becomes one of identifying ingredients and applying the substitution rule.

There is clear experimental evidence that behaving (or not behaving) in specific ways has significant, specific, physiological effects on others. Much of the mother–infant separation data can be so interpreted. However, the same points apply to adult animals and humans, and effects have been measured in the prolactin, cortisol, serotonin, norepinephrine, epinephrine, and dopamine systems, to name but a few (see McGuire & Troisi, in press, for a recent review). In effect, the specific behavior of another cannot be removed from the equation, and substitution of other terms results in a loss of precision. For example, submissive behavior in response to a dominance display is an essential condition for dominant male vervets to maintain high peripheral-serotonin levels. There are of course numerous physiological events in between the submissive display and elevated serotonin levels. Thus, the sequence of events initiated by this mechanism is not completely understood. But that is not to say that submissive behaviors are not an essential ingredient in the mechanism (see, for example, McGuire & Troisi, 1987).

How do the preceding points apply to the effect of A's anger on B? The psychological–behavioral events involved seem clear. First, A anticipates moving furniture. Anticipation is associated with a specific physiological state, which, if the furniture is moved as expected, is associated with a normalization of A's physiological state. If the furniture is not moved, the state continues, displeasure develops, and eventually A becomes angry. Displeasure, in this example, is the continuation of a physiological state in which an essential ingredient (the behavior of B) necessary to alter A's physiological state is absent. A's anger at B may represent an intensification of the physiological state or anger may be behavior that discontinues the physiological state and starts the process of normalization for A. We favor the latter view.

From B's perspective, essentially the same sequence of events occurs, although the physiological systems involved may differ. B anticipates A's anger and the anticipation is associated with a specific physiological state. Experientially, the state is unpleasant and it is this unpleasantness that is likely to be a critical ingredient in B's subsequent behavioral change.

DISCUSSION

We have considered the emotion anger in an evolutionary context. A clear implication of the analysis is that it shifts the perspective away from the behavior of one individual to that of the participants and to the functional implications of anger. From an evolutionary perspective, anger can be viewed as one method of changing the behavior of another. There are, however, important behavioral constraints that must be addressed if the angered person wishes to optimize his effectiveness. In situations where one party suffers from a psychiatric disorder, the critical issues appear to be those of an altered physiological state and a misreading of others' behavior.

REFERENCES

Adams, D. B.(1979). Brain mechanisms for offense, defense, and submission. *Behavioral Brain Science,* **2,** 201–241.

Averill, J. R. (1979). Anger. In *Nebraska Symposium on Motivaton, 1978* (Vol. 26, pp. 1–80). Lincoln: University of Nebraska Press.

Averill, J. R. (1982). *Anger and aggression—An essay on emotion.* New York: Springer-Verlag, 1982.

Blanchard D. C., & Blanchard, R. J. (1984). Affect and aggression: An animal model applied to human behavior. *Advances in the Study of Aggression,* **1,** 1–67.

Bowlby, J. (1980). *Attachment and loss: Vol. 3. Loss: Sadness and depression.* London: Hogarth Press.

Brain, P. F. (1984). Biological explanations of human aggression and the resulting therapies offered by such approaches: A critical evaulation. *Advances in the Study of Aggression,* **1,** 63–102.

Craig, T. J. (1982). An epidemiologic study of problems associated with violence among psychiatric inpatients. *American Journal of Psychiatry,* **139,** 1262–1266.

Kummer, H. (1968). Social organization of Hamadryas baboons. *Bibliotheca Primatologica,* **6.**

MacKay, D. M. (1972). A formal analysis of communicative processes. In R. A. Hinde (Ed.), *Nonverbal communication* (pp. 3–25). London & New York: Cambridge University Press.

Maynard Smith, J., & Price, G. R. (1973). The logic of animal conflict. *Nature, (London)* **246,** 15–18.

McGuire, M. T., & Troisi, A. (1987). Regulation-deregulation theory and psychiatric disorders. *Ethology ad Sociobiology,* **8,** 95–255.

McKenna, J. J. (1983). Primate aggression and evolution: An overview of sociobiological and anthropological perspectives. *Bulletin of the American Academy of Law,* **11,** 105–130.

Moyer, K. E. (1968). Kinds of aggression and their physiological basis. *Communications in Behavioral Biology, Part A,* **1,** 65–87.

Plutchik, R. (1980). A general psychoevolutionary theory of emotion. In R. Plutchik & S. Kellerman (Eds.), *Emotion: Theory, research, and experience: Vol. 1. Theories of emotion* (pp. 3–33). New York: Academic Press.

Plutchik, R. (1984). Emotions: A general psychoevolutionary throry. In K. R. Scherer & P. Ekman (Eds.), *Approaches to emotion* (pp. 197–219). Hillside, NJ: Erlbaum.

Raleigh, M. J., & McGuire, M. T. (1980). Biosociopharmacology. *Journal of the McLean Hospital,* **2,** 73–84.

Schwartz, G. A., Weinberger, D. A., & Singer, J. A. (1981). Cardiovascular differentiation of happiness, sadness, anger, and fear following imagery and exercise. *Psychosomatic Medicine,* **43,** 343–364.

Tardiff, K., & Koenigsberg, H. W. (1985). Assaultive behavior among psychiatric outpatients. *American Journal of Psychiatry,* **142,** 960–963.

Tardiff, K., & Sweillam, A. (1982). Assultive behavior among chronic inpatients. *American Journal of Psychiatry,* **139,** 212–215.

Trivers, R. L. (1971). The evolution of reciprocal altruism. *Quantitative Review of Biology,* **46,** 35–57.

Chapter 3

EMOTIONAL-CHANGE PROCESSES IN PSYCHOTHERAPY

LESLIE S. GREENBERG AND JEREMY D. SAFRAN

ABSTRACT

Emotion is viewed as a biologically adaptive system that presents people with information about their reactions to situations and that organises them for action. The emotion system integrates information across a variety of information-processing domains and, as such, is the most complex, integrative information-processing system humans possess, providing a constant readout of the person's current state. Emotions and feelings are therefore of central importance in psychotherapy. They need to be brought to awareness in therapy to help improve patients' orientation to the environment and to help them mobilize for action. The importance of affective assessment in therapy is stressed in order to provide the clinician with a framework for intervention and, more specifically, to guide the clinician concerning when to access, bypass, or modify particular emotions. Six therapeutic affective-change processes—acknowledging, creation of meaning, arousal, taking responsibility, modifying, and expression—are discussed as well as the role of emotion in anxiety and depression. The chapter includes a discussion of three types of change events in which a number of affective-change processes operate. In the allowing and accepting of emotion event, patients overcome the avoidance of painful feelings and acknowledge and take responsibility for their feelings. In events involving the completion of interrupted expression, emotion is aroused and expressed and the emotional network is restructured. In the third and final event, accessing core beliefs, emotion is aroused in order to access core organizing beliefs and make them amenable to change.

EMOTION
Theory, Research, and Experience
Volume 5

Inspection of the role of emotion in psychotherapeutic-change episodes (Greenberg & Safran, 1987b) has shown that emotion is involved in change in a variety of ways. Emotional processing in therapy is not a single, unified change process. Rather it is a complex process involving different information-processing activities at different times, and resulting in different types of change. For example, two different processes, *acknowledging* painful feelings that were previously avoided and *owning* disclaimed-action tendencies associated with emotions, are basic emotional-change processes common to a number of therapeutic approaches. Additional processes such as *restructuring* emotional schemas that contain representations of self, other, and the situation, *modifying* dysfunctional emotional responses to specific stimuli, and *disconfirming* certain relationship expectations through the expression of emotion in relationships are other more specific processes. Any attempt to explain the functioning of emotion in pathology and in treatment must be sensitive to the complexity and the diversity of ways in which emotion can play a role in dysfunction and change.

EMOTION AS ADAPTIVE

A variety of theoretical views (Arnold, 1960, 1970; Izard, 1977; Plutchik, 1980) and empirical findings (Buck, 1985; Eckman, 1973; Izard, 1979; Leventhal & Tomarken, 1986) are converging to support the view that emotion basically serves a biologically adaptive function in the interactive, interpersonal world of human functioning.

Arnold (1960) has defined emotion as a felt action tendency, "an intuitive appraisal of the situation that initiates an action tendency that is felt as emotion" (p. 177). Emotion, therefore, is not a biological drive but a felt action tendency that is not a motive in its own right. A motive is an action impulse that results from emotion in conjunction with a cognitive process. The emotion establishes a disposition to act in a certain way, while further cognitive processing determines whether or not this disposition will be acted upon.

Plutchik (1980) views emotions as adaptive devices that have played a role in individual survival at all evolutionary levels, and Izard (1977) views emotion as the principal motivational system. Even though Arnold, Plutchik, and Izard each accord a different role to cognition, all see emotion as providing a motivational impetus to the organism. To ignore the potentially motivating aspect of emotion in therapy and in therapeutic change is to rob the client of a powerful medium for change.

Theorists disagree on which core emotions are biologically given, but there appears to be at least some general agreement as to the biologically inherited nature of emotions that produce action tendencies toward or away from an object (the capacity to sense something as good or bad for us), tendencies to bond and to seek contact and comfort, and experiences of pleasure and displeasure. Arnold adds to these the experience of anger at being restrained, an emotion that clearly has adaptive value.

Plutchik lists 8 basic emotions: fear, anger, joy, disgust, startle, curiosity, sorrow, and acceptance. Izard defines 10: fear, anger, joy, disgust, surprise, interest, distress, contempt, shame, and guilt. These authors appear to agree on the first 6 or 7 as basic emotions. Most authors consider fear, anger, joy, and sorrow as fundamental emotions.

As stated, both Plutchik and Izard see these basic emotions as fundamentally biologically adaptive. To claim that fundamental emotions are inherently adaptive, however, does not mean that emotion can never be inappropriate or that intense emotions cannot be involved in motivating maladaptive functioning. What it does mean is that in a specific situation, particularly generic situations common to human experience, a given fundamental emotion experienced with appropriate intensity can facilitate adaptive action. The ability to experience and to express one's primary affective response in a situation provides optimal conditions for dealing appropriately with the situation, completing one's transactions with the environment, and moving on to further interactions.

In certain circumstances, perhaps as a function of extreme deprivation, learning history, or unnatural circumstance, human beings may have fundamental emotion responses that are maladaptive. This is not the case, however, with the majority of people and situations involving therapy that deals with nonpsychotic and nonpsychopathic problems.

How this evolutionary, ecologically adaptive emotion system becomes dysfunctional or plays a role in dysfunction has great significance for understanding how to bring about therapeutic change. Conversely, the study of the role of emotion in psychotherapeutic change provides us with an important perspective on how emotion functions in psychopathology.

EMOTION AS SYNTHESIS

Central to our theoretical argument is the idea that the experience of emotion is the end product of a set of parallel, automatic, or unconscious information-processing activities. We argue (Greenberg & Safran, 1987b), based on a constructive theory of emotional processing (Leventhal, 1979, 1982, 1984), that emotion is a conscious experience. This experience comes into consciousness by a tacit synthesis of subsidiary information. As Leventhal (1979, 1980) and Lang (1983, 1984) have suggested, emotion is constituted by a number of different types or levels of information processing that are all integrated preattentively to emerge into awareness as the holistic emotional experience. Emotion supplies a synthesis of expressive motor responses, autonomic responses, images and memories of important events, and conceptual processing. It is thus a complex readout of automatic parallel processing in which we are constantly engaged.

Recent network analyses of emotion, such as those (Lang, 1983; Leventhal, 1979) that view emotions as constituted by associative linkages between expressive motor, autonomic, memorial, imaginal, and conceptual components, suggest that eliciting any one of the components or some of their features can evoke other parts of the network. In this view, activation of one of the components automatically spreads to the other components of the network, increasing their probability of becoming conscious or producing a conscious emotional experience. This potential ''unconscious'' evocation of parts of the network becomes important in the practice of therapy. A central goal of affectively oriented therapy becomes one of evoking those organized cognitive–affective associative structures, which strongly influence emotional experience, in order to either motivate change or to restructure the affective schemas themselves.

This understanding of affective processing in psychotherapy begins to lend credence to certain styles of emotionally focused therapeutic intervention that have appeared to many, because of their nonlinearity, as nonrational and, at worst, irrational. The nonlinear processes of emotionally oriented therapy simply reflect the structure of the phenomena being worked with. In order for emotion to be experienced and for emotional restructuring to take place, the emotional structures governing emotional experience need to be evoked. Evocation of schemas is not a conceptual or a linear causal process but rather a stochastic one.

AFFECTIVE ASSESSMENT

As we have suggested above, emotional experience involves a complex synthesis of a number of levels of information processing of both internal and external information. The conscious experience of emotion is, in fact, a product of the preattentive synthesis of subsidiary components. Emotion is thus constructive and involves drawing on a form of tacit knowing that informs us about what events mean to us as biological organisms. Emotion is not simply an experience inside but rather serves a connecting function with the environment by organizing us for action in the world.

Emotions play a role in providing us with information about the readiness of our biological machinery to interact with specific events in the environment, and in integrating abstract cortical functions with perceptual motor reflexes, so that we can sense, think, act, and feel in an integrated fashion. In addition, emotions are intrinsically involved in memory; they help to code our experience of the world and to access certain episodic memories. Emotions are thus a form of meaning and have particular significance for the person experiencing and expressing them. Their meaning has three key aspects. They say something about our current organismic state in terms of its moment-to-moment readiness to deal with the environment, they say something about the environment, and they say something about our past experience in similar situations. Any breakdown in a system of this significance thus leaves the organism vulnerable. How then does the emotion system go wrong?

Problems in functioning arise when the integration between different levels of emotional processing breaks down and what we feel, think, and do are not congruent. A common problem occurs when the conceptual level contains injunctions against material in schematic emotional memory or against certain expressive motor responses, causing conflict. For example, a person may have learned rules such as "anger is bad" and yet feel angry at a parent or partner for having abandoned or betrayed him or her in the past. The resentment is stored in schematic emotion memory (Leventhal, 1979) but is not welcomed in awareness.

Equivalently, an immediate expressive motor response (Leventhal, 1979) associated with fear may be disallowed or inhibited by face-saving conceptual rules. Another common dysfunction in the emotion-processing system is automatic cuing out of awareness, of schematic emotional memories, without these memories being fully processed consciously. Thus a particular set of circumstances such as being called to one's bosses office may automatically evoke schemas related to fear of authority figures without one being aware of this internal process. This automatic processing can lead to inexplicable, problematic feelings. Finally schematic memories can be repositories of negative emotional associations and response sequences, which, when hooked, lead to dysfunctional behavior in the world, such as fear of harmless stimuli and anger in response to intimacy.

As previously indicated, the fact that the emotion system plays an adaptive role in human functioning does not mean that all emotional states are adaptive. In many forms of psychopathology, it is the dysfunctional emotional states such as rage (as in certain borderline states) and hopelessness (as in depression) that stand out as problematic. It is thus important for the clinician to be able to assess whether a particular emotional state is adaptive or dysfunctional. In order to encompass the variety of different types of emotional expression and experience that are dealt with in psychotherapy, we have suggested (Greenberg & Safran, 1987b, 1984) that for purposes of assessment certain heuristic distinctions be made at least between the following four broad categories of emotional expression:

1. *Biologically adaptive primary affective responses.* These provide information to the organism about their responses to situations. Emotions such as anger at violation, sadness at loss, and fear in response to danger provide adaptive action tendencies to help organize appropriate behavior. These are emotions to be accessed, intensified, and used as aids to problem solving.

2. *Secondary reactive emotional responses.* These are not necessarily adaptive and are not the organism's direct response to the environment. Rather, they are either secondary to some underlying, more primary generating process, reactions to the frustration of primary emotional responses, or complex derivatives of the primary response. Defensive or reactive responses such as crying when angry or expressing anger when afraid are secondary emotional responses to underlying emotional processes. Fear in response to anticipated danger or hopelessness in response to negative expectations are secondary emotional responses to underlying cognitive processes. Hatred, vengeance, and murderous rage are derivatives of anger in which the anger itself is transformed by complex mediating processes into a desire to annihilate. Secondary responses of the types referred to above are not to be focused on or intensified in therapy but rather are to be bypassed or explored in order to access underlying processes and deal with the dysfunctional mediating processes. Secondary emotions are recognizable in part because they are readily available to awareness and often are part of the presenting problem.

3. *Instrumental emotional responses.* These are emotional behavior patterns that people have learned to use to influence others. These are emotions that are expressed in order to achieve some intended effect such as crying to evoke sympathy or expressing anger to dominate. Instrumental expressions of this type are not information about responses to situations but attempts to influence. In therapy these expressions are best bypassed, confronted, or interpreted, rather than explored or differentiated, to access adaptive information.

4. *Learned maladaptive primary responses.* These include fear of harmless stimuli, anger in response to caring, or disgust at dependence and are direct, immediate responses to the environment with very little, if any, intermediate conceptual processing involved. Although the emotional response system generally plays an adaptive role in human functioning, maladaptive responses can be learned as a result of trauma or strongly negative environmental contingencies in childhood. These maladaptive emotional responses, then, need to be accessed in therapy for purposes of modification rather than of orientation.

We are thus suggesting the need for a differentiated affective assessment to aid the clinician in discriminating when affective experience is adaptive and when it is not. This will allow differential intervention designed to either access, bypass, or modify different affective statues for different therapeutic purposes. Primary affective responses are potential allies in the therapeutic-change process and need to be reliably identified and used as such in therapy.

PRIMARY EMOTION IN CHANGE

Primary emotions, when accessed, can facilitate problem solving. Anger facilitates aggressively protective solutions to threat; fear facilitates avoidance or "flight" solutions to threat; and sadness facilitates reparative solutions to loss.

Emotional openness and physical closeness seem to be positive aspects of human functioning associated with attachment (Bowlby, 1969), and all humans seem to require some form of contact and comfort (Harlow, 1958). In therapy, accessing the need for security, the desire to be close, or the need to be held facilitates resolution of problems of isolation and alienation. Acknowledging pain facilitates appropriate fight or flight responses. Accessing primary emotions can also be helpful in modifying those emotional expressions that we have earlier defined as secondary, instrumental, and maladaptive (Greenberg & Safran, 1987b, 1989).

People have, however, learned to avoid their emotions and often need permission to feel. Certain socialization processes, insensitive to distinctions between biologically adaptive, secondary, and instrumental emotions, have taught us to control all our emotions and have labeled certain adaptive emotional experiences and expressions as weak and out of control. In addition to this socialized restriction of emotion, the organism has learned to cope with certain painful experiences by developing intricate psychological strategies to avoid the pain. People in therapy thus need to learn that fear is not weak, that pain will not kill, and that anger is not necessarily bad. They need to learn that rather than being signs of weakness, of losing control, or of being unable to cope, these emotions can facilitate problem resolution. Therapy seen in terms of this framework involves a certain amount of affective reeducation.

Clients often come into therapy unable to discriminate what they are feeling. Not only lacking a data base against which to check what they are feeling but also being out of touch, they are vulnerable to being led by a more knowing therapist into believing anything that might explain their problem. Incorrect labeling of emotion by the therapist then simply compounds their own confusion. The therapist must therefore be careful not to impose a label on the client's emotional experience. Instead, he or she must support emerging experience in the client until it is felt vividly as a subjective experience.

AFFECTIVE-CHANGE PROCESSES IN THERAPY

Having discussed the importance of assessment of emotional expression in therapy and the significance of awareness of primary emotion to adaptation and therapeutic change, we discuss below the different ways in which emotion plays a role in therapeutic change. A variety of orientations have addressed the importance of emotional processes in psychotherapy. However, none provides a comprehensive or systematic framework for understanding emotion. For example, acknowledgment of warded-off affect has been proposed by dynamic therapists as important in change, implosion or flooding has been proposed by behaviorists as a means of reducing anxiety, and experience of one's feelings or attention to a bodily felt sense has been seen as central to change in experiential therapy.

A variety of terms have been used to denote more specific affective-change processes in therapy. Terms such as abreaction, catharis, corrective emotional experience, releasing emotion, and experiencing emphasize some of the possible change processes involved in the expression of affect, whereas other terms, such as making the unconscious conscious, becoming aware, symbolizing, gaining insight, and focusing, emphasize the idea of creating meaning and the discovery aspects of working with affect. Yet another set of terms—defense, denial, distortion, avoidance, warding off, disavowing, incongruence, and blocking—emphasize the processes by which certain emotions are kept out of awareness.

The occurrence of affect in psychotherapy is not a singular phenomenon but rather involves a number of different processes that are best treated separately. Differentiation of different emotional-change processes will help to illuminate the function of emotion in change and will help to distinguish the different processes from the process of catharsis.

We have delineated six types of affective-change processes involved in therapy (Greenberg & Safran, 1987b). In our description of these six processes we attempt to capture the actual in-therapy processes in which the client is involved while undergoing affective change. The first five processes focus on the client alone, whereas the sixth involves emotional processes in the therapeutic relationship. The first five processes are (1) *acknowledging* primary affective responses, (2) *creation of meaning* through synthesis, (3) *arousal* of affect, (4) *taking responsibility* for affective experience, and (5) *modifying* dysfunctional affective responses. The sixth, more interpersonal process is the *expression of feelings* in the therapeutic relationship.

Although the sixth process focuses on the therapeutic relationship, the first five processes also take place within the context of a relationship with another human being. In the therapeutic relationship, however, the importance of the therapist's acceptance of the client's developing affective experience during all these processes must not be overlooked as an important factor in change. Acknowledging or arousing affect in a hostile or unsupportive environment is not the same event as the experience of affect in an appropriate therapeutic environment, in which primary emotions are validated and supported. In addition to the general importance of a good working alliance (Bordin, 1979) and a close bond, there are some specific therapeutic events in which *expressing and responding to primary emotions in the relationship* constitute an identifiably independent process of great significance.

It should be noted that the above six processes are not necessarily mutually exclusive. In practice there is definitely some degree of overlap between them. We have categorized them as distinctive processes in order to draw attention to different aspects of the change process that we believe are sufficiently important to warrant further exploration.

ACKNOWLEDGING

Acknowledging emotional experience is probably one of the most discussed processes of therapeutic change. The bringing into awareness of affectively laden information that was previously not in awareness has been discussed in a variety of ways by all dynamically and experientially oriented theorists. It is generally recognized that it can be therapeutically useful for people to "get in touch" with affective responses that are not normally attended to (Davison, 1980; Wexler, 1974) and to own disclaimed-action tendencies (Eagle, 1984; Schafer, 1983). The importance of the acknowledgment of affect results from the adaptive nature of primary affective responses and from the importance of accessing this information to aid problem solving. Organisms that ignore their own affective feedback are not well situated to behave adaptively. Acknowledging affective responses that were previously disallowed makes certain reactions and moods more understandable, and acknowledging disclaimed tendencies provides new impetus for action and need satisfaction. Acting in the world to satisfy certain needs is a sine qua non of competence and satisfaction. Without acknowledgment of feelings and desires, people feel empty, confused, and fragmented, and they lack the impetus from the action tendencies to motivate action.

One of the thorny questions regarding the acknowledgment of emotion has been whether the emotion existed in some form out of awareness, prior to acknowledgment. In our view, acknowledgment of emotion involves the synthesis of subsidiary information that is not in awareness. This synthesis occurs in real time, in the present, and it is this current construction that produces the conscious experience of emotion. Conscious emotion exists only as a potential prior to its construction and acknowledgment. But subsidiary components, such as the expressive motor response, do actually exist outside of awareness and can be more or less accurately synthesized. Acknowledgment is a process of both discovery and creation in which certain constitutive elements, such as expressive motor responses, schematic memories, and tacit rules, are synthesized along with perception of the situation into a particular current emotional experience and self-organization. States such as feeling vulnerable or angry emerge as present constructions.

Often in therapy this synthesis involves the client forming an awareness or organization of experience previously regarded as unacceptable, and then accepting this experience. With the acceptance of the feeling comes the recognition of the action tendency associated with it. Fully accepting the feeling implies accepting the want or desire that goes with it. Wants and desires need to be symbolized in awareness and their implications explored. The acknowledgment and experience of emotion brings relief when the action organized by the emotion can be expressed in some acceptable form. Acknowledgment is facilitated by a variety of awareness-generating methods of intervention, the major ones being reflections of feeling, interpretation, and feedback. The key process in all of these methods appears to be a focusing of attention on experiences that are currently not being fully processed.

CREATION OF MEANING

The second important process involving affect in therapy is a process in which strongly felt new meanings emerge. This process is similar in some ways to acknowledging affect but is sufficiently distinct to be characterized as a separate process. In the creation of new meaning, the process is less one of experiencing and expressing unacknowledged emotion than it is of searching for and generating new symbols to adequately describe one's current experiencing and to thereby carry forward this experience. Rather than leading to statements of feeling sad or angry, in this process a complex symbol such as feeling ''hypocritical'' or feeling ''over the hill'' is generated. The important issue is that this is a *creation that is occurring at the moment* by an interaction between prereflective experience and symbolic processes. It is not a process of moving from concept to concept by reasoning or inference, but rather a process of moving between concept and experience in a circular and ongoing process of explication and creation of meaning. A new perspective or new meaning often grows out of what Gendlin (1981) refers to as a bodily felt sense of meaning. When there is a shift in the bodily felt sense in some domain, this change is usually difficult to symbolize at first because a whole new constellation of meaning is being formed and has to be explicated and constructed into a new conceptual framework. This is the process of creating new meanings. The previous ways of viewing one's concern no longer fit; new concepts and new ways of symbolizing in words what is occurring are needed to capture the new meanings.

Explicit new concepts thus emerge from the felt sense as a way of describing a complex whole that is not yet known (Gendlin, 1981). These new meanings, such as ''I felt like a hypocrite,'' ''I feel empty,'' ''I feel like I'm over the hill,'' or ''It's like nobody cares about what happens to me,'' were not there preformed *in* the felt sense. Rather, a new deeply felt meaning emerges from the felt sense. There is no split between cognition and affect in this process of creating meaning. The act of symbolizing the felt sense is the creation of a unified cognitive–affective structure, a new complex meaning, which in turn is part of a process of creating new feelings and thoughts. In the creation of meaning, intense emotional experience in the absence of further symbolizations does not carry forward experiencing, whereas abstract concepts not connected to feelings are empty and have no subjective significance. Creation of meaning is an experientially based symbolization process. Meaning creation is facilitated both by experiential responses that help synthesize the client's experience into a symbol that fits the experience and by encouraging the client to focus inwardly and to symbolize. The emphasis here, more than in acknowledging, is on creation of symbols and explication of experience rather than on sheer acceptance of experience.

AROUSING AFFECT

The arousal of certain affects and their possible intensification represents another important affective-change process. Many clients report how experiences of simply sobbing, crying out, or expressing deeply felt hurts, resentments, and so forth represent significant moments in therapy. Therapists often observe that people cry when in the process of undergoing major changes in therapy. This arousal or mobilization of affect in the process of therapeutic change comes closest to what is often called catharsis. In this process, emotion is experienced in a heightened manner and expressed vividly. The process includes both arousal of emotion and its natural expression, which leads to recovery and relief. This process of arousal, expression, and recovery is an important natural sequence in an emotional experience. Interference with the expression of emotion leads to tension because of the muscular constriction used to interfere with expressive tendency. The behavioral–expressive components, be they sobbing, yelling, kicking, or less dramatic expressions, are important in completing the action tendency associated with the emotion.

One of the other effects of this type of arousal and expression of affect is, paradoxically, to produce some form of cognitive reorganization of the person's view of the world. The fact that the end goal of expression of affect is cognitive change may at first seem contradictory because the purpose often appears to be the expression of affect. In fact, many affective therapists talk about "letting go" of the feeling or "getting into the feeling" as being inherently therapeutic because it allows the completion of the natural sequence of arousal and expression. But lasting change comes about because people give *meaning* to their experience.

Close inspection of episodes of affective arousal in therapy (Greenberg & Safran, 1987b) reveals that it is the combination of the relief after the expression of affect with the subsequent cognitive reorganization that leads to change. This process, involving the arousal of affect and cognitive reorganization, appears to be at the core of a set of interventions that we have labeled emotional restructuring. In restructuring events, affectively charged emotional schemas are aroused in order to make them amenable to change. In restructuring, the underlying response program needs to be accessed and run in order to make it amenable to modification. As Lang (1983) has pointed out, the more the stimulus configuration matches the prototype or internal structure, the more likely it is that the network will be evoked. The presence of the emotional responses themselves, such as the experience of fear, sadness, or anger, is necessary before the experience can be restructured. The therapeutic situation needs to be used as a laboratory for evoking and reprocessing reactions in order to restructure the cognitive–affective–behavioral network or schema.

Restructuring is achieved by admitting new information to the schema and thereby altering its organization. Interventions ranging from evocative responding (Rice, 1974) to use of imagery (Shorr, 1974), enactments, and gestalt two-chair-dialogues (Greenberg, 1984; Greenberg & Safran, 1987b) help access and set in motion the cognitive and behavioral response patterns that need to be modified. Once the network is accessed, different processes of change such as the challenging of beliefs, provision of new evidence, generation of schema-inconsistent information, and success experiences can all be used to produce restructuring.

Evocation of the network also makes possible the modification of mood-congruent or state-dependent cognitions (Bower, 1981) and maladaptive cognitive–affective sequences. As we have elaborated elsewhere (Greenberg & Safran, 1987b; Safran & Greenberg, 1986), it is often the accessing of the hot or emotionally laden cognition that is important in cognitive therapy. Thus, by deepening the emotional experience of particular events and intensifying relevant emotional states, the full impact of irrational or pathogenic beliefs and their effect on experience can become evident to the client. Once the experience is sufficiently evoked, the core beliefs can be accessed and understood in terms of both how they act to structure experience and how they came about.

As we stated earlier, clear assessment of when and for what purpose affect should be aroused in therapy is essential. It is not appropriate to arouse any affect at any time. At certain times primary affect needs to be aroused as a mobilizer of change to help provide direction for action. At other times affect needs to be aroused in order to evoke underlying networks for restructuring. At still other times emotion should not be aroused at all. Arousal can be distinguished from acknowledgment in that the mechanism in arousal is less one of bringing the emotion into awareness (since the emotion has already been brought to awareness) than one of amplifying and increasing the level of arousal in order to increase the salience of the experience so that it cannot be overlooked. Its salience then acts to influence the person's concepts of self and situation. Affect, when aroused in these instances, helps to mark the person's experience as noteworthy and to increase its importance in organizing his or her view of self, world, and other.

Primary emotions can be aroused to motivate new behaviors. This has been a much-neglected means of behavior modification. The arousal of particular emotions will greatly increase the probability of activating certain behaviors in a person's repertoire. Thus, the arousal of anger is useful in helping people become more assertive and self-defining, whereas the arousal of sadness or affection may incline people to be more comforting or gentle. Assessment of those emotional responses that appear to be missing from someone's repertoire allows for appropriate therapeutic work to arouse the missing emotion. Arousal then enhances the probability of the activation of certain more adaptive behavioral responses.

TAKING RESPONSIBILITY

Taking responsibility is ultimately linked with the preceding processes. However, the quality of seeing oneself as the agent of one's own experience and of *owning* this experience at the moment is sufficient to establish it as a process in its own right. Taking responsibility involves shifting the locus of control from an external source to an internal source and taking the stance "It is I who am doing or feeling this." Rather than experiencing oneself as a passive recipient of an emotion or a desire, or experiencing these as belonging to someone else, they are owned. One does not say, "You're making me angry or sad," or "*You* are angry or sad," but rather "*I* am angry or sad." Taking responsibility involves recognizing the cause of the emotional experience as internal rather than external. In this process, the person accepts responsibility for feeling sad or angry rather than explicitly or implicitly blaming some other source for the feeling. In other words, the person ceases to experience his or her feelings in terms such as "You have made me sad or angry" and instead begins to experience them in terms such as "I am the agent of being sad or angry in response to my perception of the situation." Affective change is possible only when people see their experience as theirs and as self-created; only then are they in a position to choose either to accept or to modify it.

But it is not sufficient to appreciate abstractly that one is the creator of one's own affective experience. People must actually experience the emotions or desires in question, while they are taking responsibility for the experience; only then are they able to become aware of the process—or at least part of it—through which they are constructing that experience. Because a substantial portion of this constructive process takes place outside of focal awareness, it is usually important in taking responsibility for the client to learn to attend to tacit processes.

Taking responsibility thus involves a process of transforming automated processing into controlled processing (Greenberg & Safran, 1981; Shiffrin & Schneider, 1977). Clients thereby choose to do in awareness what they were already doing outside of awareness. In this fashion, the client is able to establish a metaperspective on his or her own emotional experience. In other words, clients are able to establish a representation of their experience for themselves at a higher conceptual level. Once this becomes possible and clients experience themselves as active agents in the construction of their own emotional experience, the meaning of the experience begins to change, and thus its quality changes as well.

MODIFYING MALADAPTIVE
AFFECTIVE RESPONSES

In certain situations, a direct modification of affective responses is required. There are, as we have discussed in our assessment of emotion, instances in which emotional responses have become dysfunctional or maladaptive. Some maladaptive affective responses are highly entrenched and present major problems in therapy. For example, a type of conditioning process may have led to specific conditioned-anxiety responses to cognitively mediated stimuli, such as fear of heights. More generally, children from a young age may have received messages from parents, usually nonverbally, that they should not exist, are unworthy, and so forth. In the conditioning process it is the intuitive appraisal and associated feeling that have become conditioned (Greenberg & Safran, 1987a). In these situations, the maladaptive emotional responses cannot be overcome except by direct modification.

The process of modification of maladaptive affective responses other than fear has not been extensively explored, but it certainly lends itself to investigation using principles of learning theory and behavior modification. Some of the possible processes of affect modification that we have observed in therapy have involved the substitution of one affect for another, training in alternate affective responses, graduated exposure to the emotional experience, and modification of the attentional allocation processes in order to disrupt a maladaptive emotional-synthesis process. In the case of maladaptive fear, exposure is probably the most clear example of affective modification, and, as Rachman (1978) has pointed out, music, drugs, and other agents can be used to control and to modify moods. An important means of modifying secondary emotions is by assessing the underlying structures that are generating the bad feelings and modifying these.

EMOTIONAL EXPRESSION
IN THE THERAPEUTIC RELATIONSHIP

Expression of emotion in the therapeutic relationship, or what is often referred to as ''encountering'' or ''being genuine,'' has been written about as the essence of therapy in a number of approaches. Our concern here is not to evaluate whether this is indeed a key general factor of successful therapy but rather to gain an understanding of the process by which an expression of genuine feeling between therapist and client can lead to change.

One of the most significant aspects of this process appears to be the client's experience and expression of some hitherto unacceptable feeling followed by an *affirming and validating* therapist response. In this process, a form of experiential learning takes place wherein clients experience themselves as being cared for and valued. Affirmation confronts certain presuppositions clients hold about themselves, such as being unworthy. It is the experience of being responded to and cared for that is important. Actually experiencing this sense of caring in therapy is what leads to schematic and conceptual reorganization. If a client accepts the therapist as truly valuing, the information forces a schematic reorganization. People cannot continue to process at a schematic level in the way they did before because they have had to accommodate to and incorporate the information that they are lovable, acceptable, worthy human beings. They can no longer believe that nobody cares or regard the world as totally unresponsive and people as totally insensitive to them. A new possibility has been experienced.

A second aspect of this process of therapist affirmation occurs when clients express *current feelings toward their therapists* and learn that they can be themselves without some dreaded negative consequence. For example, clients may learn that when they express anger to their therapists or express their feelings of being neglected or uncared for, they do not destroy their therapists or their relationships; they are taken seriously and accepted or responded to rather than attacked. Feelings of closeness or intimacy with the therapist can be acknowledged and not sexualized, which also allays certain fears. Being able to encounter the therapist with whatever is occurring at the moment and finding that the therapist responds in a therapeutic fashion provide an experience that confirms clients' sense of validity and allows them to feel entitled to their experience and view of the world.

Therapy, therefore, actually provides a relationship in which new ways of being are experienced with the therapist; this process acts as a first step toward trying out new ways of being outside of therapy. Given that an important part of any interpersonal relationship is the feelings one has about oneself and the other in the relationship, the opportunity for clients to have an open and honest relationship in which they can truly deal with these feelings, many of which have been problematic to them, is a potentially invaluable experience. It is possible to have a corrective emotional experience by developing a positive human relationship in the course of therapy; one learns that one is worthy, that one's responses are understandable and acceptable, and that it is possible to form a trusting relationship. Clearly the expression of emotion in real-life relationships, such as between friends, group members, and couples (Greenberg & Johnson,

1985, 1986, 1988), in and out of therapy can also be of great significance. Our focus here, however, is on individual therapy, in which the only people involved are the therapist and the client.

AFFECTIVE-CHANGE EVENTS

As we have stressed throughout this chapter, affect does not play a simple uniform role in change. Not only are there different affective-change processes but these different processes play different roles in different episodes of change. In order to understand the role of affect in change, in addition to specifying a number of change processes there are also a number of therapeutic events in which these processes occur in a variety of combinations. A therapeutic event begins with a client experiential state that marks a particular type of processing difficulty, is followed by an intervention designed to facilitate resolution of the processing difficulty, and ends with an identifiable resolution state. The identification of client markers is therefore a method of making process diagnoses of processing problems amenable to intervention. When a particular client marker is followed by an intervention designed to change the processing problem, the characteristics of client performance that lead to resolution of the problem can be specified. This combination of marker, intervention, and resolution performance constitutes a change event (Rice & Greenberg, 1984).

We briefly describe below, by way of example, three of the seven affective change events that we have identified (Greenberg & Safran, 1987b). These events recur in therapy across situations and across clients. They involve complex therapeutic performances in which all of the six change processes described earlier—acknowledging, arousing, creating meaning, taking responsibility, modifying, and expressing—appear to operate to differing degrees. Notwithstanding some overlap or similarity of the processes involved from event to event, all three are discriminable performance events that lead to change in therapy; and each differs in its structure, the performance demands on the client and therapist, and the sequence of processes observed. The three events described below, at a clinical level, are (1) allowing and accepting painful emotion, (2) completing interrupted expression, and (3) accessing core beliefs.

ALLOWING AND ACCEPTING PAINFUL EMOTION

Allowing previously unacceptable aspects of experience into awareness and accepting them as one's own involve a process of overcoming the avoidance that has kept the experience out of awareness. This type of event is frequently a turning point in therapy. When clients experience emotional difficulties because they fear and avoid certain emotional memories, feelings, and impulses, those unacceptable feelings and perceptions are generally avoided so automatically that they do not become adequately symbolized in awareness. This unprocessed information then operates outside of awareness and not only results in inexplicable bad feelings but also is unable to play its proper role in the client's solution to life problems. Valuable emotional information has been too anxiety arousing to be processed.

The best *marker* of clients' avoidance of internal experience is their expression in therapy either of a vague general sense of threat or vulnerability, such as "I feel shaky" or "I don't know why but I just feel like crying," or of a tendency to be hypersensitive to comments from others about their experience, such as "I can't stand it when he says that to me." It is important for the therapist to take notice of this state in order to help clients allow the unacceptable experience to emerge into consciousness. Such clients may appear overly careful about admitting to an experience that is contrary to some standard they hold for themselves. They may express fear of being overwhelmed by their own feelings or may negatively evaluate aspects of their experience. These are clear signs of disallowing, as are "shoulds" and "oughts," which abound in such clients' language in their attempts to control the unwanted aspects of their experience.

In addition, many nonverbal signs of avoidance, such as tensing of the jaw, clenching of the fist, averting of the eyes, and deadness of expression, are apparent. Paradoxically, allowing painful emotions to emerge into consciousness and accepting the previously warded-off emotion seem to provide the client with relief. Although the avoidance process is an activity utilizing internal resources that usually takes place outside of awareness, it is nevertheless an activity. Thus, at the point of allowing, there is an experience akin to that of relaxing at the end of a struggle. Ceasing to control the warded-off experience allows for the availability of new information concerning the state of the organism, and this facilitates a change in perspective. The resolution performance in an allowing event, then, is a process of *overcoming the avoidance* of the experience, *approaching* the previously avoided experience, and *giving in* to this experience—accepting it, expressing it, and allowing it to run its course. The process of accepting the experience is crucial since something regarded as dangerous is transformed into a potential resource. This performance primarily involves changes in processes of acknowledging and taking responsibility.

For example, a woman who came to therapy to deal with her inability to cope initially held a strong negative view of her "vulnerability." She said, "I'm too vulnerable, I cry too easily, and it gets me into trouble. I don't allow myself to cry. I need to be strong and independent. I shouldn't cry. It's silly." In the session, the therapist helped her acknowledge her pain and distress by responding to nonverbal signs of her suppression of emotion, asking her to become aware of the tightening in her throat and to intensify the biting of her lip. An empathic response, recognizing how important it was for her not to cry but how painful and lonely it was to hold in her tears in order to appear strong, led to a release of the tensing of her muscles and an expression of emotion. At this point the client burst into tears, allowing the experience, and said, "Yes, I had to hide my feelings in my family because no one else could bear their own pain."

This event, in which the client allowed and began to accept her "pain and vulnerability," was a significant therapeutic turning point. She took responsibility for this aspect of her experience, moving from statements such as "It's so silly to cry" and "I have to be strong but I'm too messed up to do it" to saying, "I feel a lot of pain about the death of my parents" and "I felt very alone without them." This then put her in a position of being able to work through her feelings of loss. Through the process of therapy, her fear of abandonment emerged more fully, and she came to accept her need for support and comfort as a part of her that she needed to pay attention to and cherish, rather than controlling this need and then feeling depressed, vulnerable, and inadequate. Although cognitive change was involved in changing her belief about her "weakness," this woman did not suffer from cognitive distortions alone but also from an impaired ability to allow feelings of loss and sadness, and from an inability to accept these feelings and to act adaptively in response to them when she did feel them. She consistently and actively avoided feelings of fear, sadness, and anger and did not recognize any needs she had for comfort and real interpersonal contact. The more she avoided and controlled these feelings and needs, the more unhappy and desperate she became, and the less able to cope with life. Only after she acknowledged and felt these needs could she go about trying to satisfy them and to integrate them into her life.

COMPLETING INTERRUPTED EXPRESSION

An event that occurs repeatedly in therapy is one in which some previously interrupted emotional expression is completed by fully expressing and processing the emotions in the therapy situation. This process—expressing previously interrupted or unexpressed emotions in order to experience them and incorporate them into one's view of the situation—is similar to the process required in grieving, but it is applicable to more than the grieving process alone. The important change process involved in completing unfinished business (Perls, Hefferline, & Goodman, 1951) is the arousal and expression of emotions to their natural completion. This is accompanied by the reprocessing of the experience in order to bring about a cognitive reorganization or reevaluation of the experience.

A number of unfinished situations appear to require the kind of arousal and expression of emotion that helps to process unresolved grief. Expressions of unexpressed anger, resentment, rage, hatred, pain, sadness, and fear of abandonment appear to relieve the person of an internal burden in the same way that grief work does. When these feelings are not adequately symbolized and expressed in the original situation, the memories and fantasies associated with them linger. They affect present functioning and seem to nag at individuals, demanding attention and influencing their current behavior. People benefit by reprocessing in an emotionally vivid manner the situation in which they restricted their experience. In this type of therapeutic event, clients need to symbolize new meanings. Anger is often the most damaging, incompletely processed emotion (Daldrup, Beutler, Engle, & Greenberg, 1989). When people do not adequately deal with their anger, they become resentful and stuck. They cannot let go of the old hurt, nor can they be open to new experience until the resentments have been expressed and fully processed. Expression of the anger previously denied or suppressed allows the completion of a natural process that was interrupted and allows an opportunity for further differentiation of all the feelings involved in the situation.

Feelings such as resentment, anger, fear, or grief are carried, in part, as bodily states of tension, of which the person may be unaware. These tension states can be relieved through arousal and expression. Once this tension has been relieved, new meanings generally emerge. Often new meanings arise, accompanied almost reflexively by images of by phrases. At other times, one needs to work on differentiating the feelings and symbolizing new meanings. The release of tension seems to free people to continue a process of differentiation of meanings. This is a process that appears to have been impeded by the tension and discomfort of unexpressed feelings in that area.

Often clients inhibit emotion because it is experienced as too dangerous to express in a specific relationship. There is, however, a hanging-on reaction and a holding-on of old resentments, frustrations, hurts, guilt, grief, or even unexpressed feelings of love and appreciation. This quite often can result in a self-pitying attitude, or even a blaming or complaining attitude toward the person who is not present, or a feeling of hurtful resignation and hopelessness. These are all markers of the need to complete unfinished business. Such markers are characterized by four features: (1) a lingering unresolved feeling toward (2) a significant others, (3) which is currently felt (4) but is being visibly interrupted. Whether an unfinished situation is from the distant past or is contemporary, it will clamor for attention until the expression is completed, the experience reprocessed, and the closure attained. Closure is brought about by reorganizing perceptions so that one no longer perceives the situation as thwarting one's attempts to achieve satisfaction. Once a therapeutic relationship has been established, the expression of the full range of inhibited feelings can be greatly facilitated by a reenactment procedure. A reenactment is a dramatization of the unfinished situation in which the expression of feelings is encouraged in order to facilitate a letting-go of the situation (Perls et al., 1951).

Often, a person can be stimulated to an expression of feeling by having him or her repeat a particular relevant sentence until an apparent well of unexpressed feeling is tapped. Motoric and nonverbal activities that involve the body's sensory system create heightened contact with bodily reactions and promote arousal of emotion. Acting out certain expressions bodily, as well as paying attention to and exaggerating expressions such as facial reactions, clenching fists, pointing fingers, and the like, provide an opportunity for heightened expression. Enacting an unfinished situation seems to generate a powerful type of emotional change. When a person who felt rejected by a parent repeats a sentence such as "I want to be loved," or when someone who felt abandoned says to himself or herself, "I'll look after you" or "poor child," a deep experience of the feelings of pain associated with these sentences can be realized. Experiencing the pain that has been avoided, by actually saying how one has suffered or what one has missed, can be tremendously relieving. Dramatizing one's earliest scenes of distress can be a particularly potent experience. Repeated reworking of a scene until it is fully explored in its many different facets, and repeated reenactment of the scene with profuse emotional expression (e.g., weeping or screaming), seem to be helpful in reprocessing the situation.

It is not, however, the emotional discharge alone that leads to change but what occurs cognitively as well. In these reenactments, people seem to be simultaneously experiencing themselves as both participant and observer. Once they have expressed the feelings involved, they are able to discriminate different aspects of the experience to achieve a more differentiated perspective on the situation. In reliving the situation, part of the person's attention is in the past, absorbed in reliving a distressing experience that has been restimulated by the present context; but another part of the person's attention is in the present, realizing that there is no real threat. It is the realization that one is actually safe in the present that allows the person to relive the situation, feel the emotions associated with it, and express those emotions. The ability to maintain a balanced distance between being fully engaged and observing leads to a reprocessing of the situation and the opportunity to become more differentiating about what occurred and to symbolize it in a new way.

For example, a client who had been feeling depressed for some time started a session by complaining about how her mother should not have treated her so rejectingly as a child. During a dialogue with her mother in an empty chair, she expressed her anger and then her deep hurt and fear at being pushed away and left alone. The client relived an incident in which as a small child she had been left alone in the house at night, and as she reentered the scene she could remember hearing the thunder outside and the storm noises in the house. In the dialogue she expressed how she needed her mother's support as a child. She told her mother in a childs voice, "I needed you, I needed to feel loved and wanted," and then differentiated these feelings into the statement "It wasn't my fault that you didn't want a child.'' She then recalled some of the occasions when her mother had been supportive of her, such as when she had lost her dog and her mother had helped find him and when she was sick and her mother looked after her. She then experienced and expressed some understanding of the way in which her mother had been prevented from fulfilling her career aspirations by having to stay home as a mother. Through this dialogue the client came to feel more empowered. She affirmed that her needs for support and encouragement were important and valid and was able to let go of her complaint, while still holding her mother accountable for her actions. She was able to separate her mother's actions toward her from her own self-esteem and finally arrive at a sense of both forgiveness and self-affirmation.

Resolution performances in this type of event entail the arousal and expression of interrupted feelings toward the imagined other. The aroused state stimulates emotional memory and allows the differentiation of anger from hurt and a complete expression of previously interrupted feelings. It appears that the emergence of the harsh, punitive, internalized other followed by a more compassionate, loving representation of the internalized other are essential components of resolution. When these performances are attained and are followed by the client's ability to see the world from the view of the other and to understand this view, resolution of the unfinished business can be achieved.

ACCESSING CORE BELIEFS

Core organizing beliefs about the self govern much of peoples' experience of themselves. Modification of these beliefs has been shown to be important in therapeutic change (Beck, 1976; Ellis, 1962; Meichenbaum, 1977). Accessing core beliefs and the automatic thoughts and feelings associated with them is not always straightforward, however. As Bower (1981) has shown, the likelihood of certain cognitions becoming conscious can be highly dependent either on the presence of the state in which these cognitions were acquired or on a mood congruent with the cognitive state. Many maladaptive cognitions are constructed in states of high affective arousal, such as when a person is feeling deeply sad or very angry. Access to these key cognitions may be dependent on being in these aroused states. Once the affective state has been evoked in therapy, the core cognitions or the sequence of different feelings and/or thoughts associated with the state can be assessed. Often it is only when clients begin to feel lonely and sad that they are able to access thoughts such as ''I can't rely on anyone'' or ''No one cares for me'' and ''I feel worthless.'' Accurate assessment of maladaptive cognitions thus often requires arousal of affect. In addition, assessment of sequences, rather than of beliefs in isolation from their context, is important. For example, a client may in the face of the repeated self-criticism collapse into tears, give up, feel tremendously hopeless and defeated, and think, ''what's the use, its no good even trying.'' The accurate assessment of this cognitive–affective sequence leading to resignation provides valuable information to guide the nature of the therapist's intervention.

A clear marker for evoking core beliefs occurs when a client seems to experience certain bad feelings repeatedly or draws certain general conclusions that indicate the obvious involvement of some inner belief. The therapist's task is to access the core belief and the associated cognitive–affective sequences. A core belief is best accessed by arousing the emotional state associated with it and then helping the client to explicate the belief. During this process the clinician probes deeply for what the client is thinking and feeling. The interventions used range from speaking in vivid, metaphorical language, to reflecting the client's feelings, to heightening awareness of nonverbal expression. The fact that sensory experience and muscular and perceptual motor behaviors play a central role in the emotion process (Izard, 1977; Leventhal, 1979; Zajonc, 1980) suggests that interventions that manipulate or draw attention to physical changes can be useful in helping people bring emotional states alive.

In accessing core beliefs the process moves from present experience to beliefs, memories, and images that operate in generating current experience but that come from the past. The beliefs governing experience are then clarified and transformed by incorporating new information. Beliefs such as ''I'm not wanted'' or ''If I say what I need you will suffer'' are transformed into new, more life-enhancing beliefs about one's self-worth or rights. These new beliefs in turn generate new feelings and new behaviors. This transformation is a complex change process in its own right, but it is dependent on accessing the core organizing beliefs. It is our contention that emotion is the best route to core organizing beliefs.

The process of accessing core beliefs involves evoking the cognitive–affective network and symbolizing in words the core principle that organizes the network. When the experience is lively and engaging and the person is feeling what is being talked about, the core organizing belief becomes readily available and apparent from the experience itself. Thus evocation of the experience and symbolization of the organizing belief generating this experience are the key components of successful performances. Processes of arousal and creation of meaning, followed possibly by some form of modification, are often operative in this type of event.

ANXIETY AND DEPRESSION

To this point the primary focus has been on the examination of affective processes that can lead to change in psychotherapy. This focus departs from the more common practice of viewing emotions as targets for therapeutic intervention rather than as active components of the change process.

In the more common approach, anxiety and depression are often identified as negative affective states that are in need of modification. We do not, however, regard anxiety and depression as simple emotions but rather as complex organismic response constellations, which involve various types of dysfunctional emotional processing (Safran & Greenberg, 1988; Greenberg, Elliot, & Foerster, 1989). In this section we will explore some aspects of the dysfunctional emotional processing involved in anxiety and depression and look briefly at their therapeutic implications.

Anxiety is a complex response constellation that can consist of a variety of behavioral and subjective components, including "freezing," withdrawal, hypervigilance, and acute emotional distress. When viewed from an evolutionary perspective, the function of anxiety in promoting survival is not too difficult to see. Anxiety functions like a red light. It immediately alerts the organism to impending danger and results in either a cessation of activity or withdrawal from any object or event that may be the source of this danger. Humans are genetically biased to respond to the properties of noise, strangeness, sudden approach, and darkness by taking avoiding action or running away—they behave in fact as though danger were actually present.

One of the more clinically significant types of anxiety in the human being is fear of the impending loss of contact with the attachment figure (Bowlby, 1980). The function of this type of anxiety can be understood in terms of its survival value in the human environment of evolutionary adaptedness. The infant is completely dependent upon parental figures for his or her physical safety and well-being. In more primitive times the human being, even on reaching maturity, was dependent on other human beings on a daily basis for his or her survival. The fear of interpersonal isolation can thus be understood as a biologically wired-in fear with survival value.

Because human beings are genetically programmed to respond to the threat of interpersonal isolation or abandonment with anxiety, either disapproval or withdrawal of emotional availability by parental figures automatically evokes an anxiety response. A child thus has a tendency to associate anxiety with specific behaviors and expressions of his or her subjective experience that have resulted in the withdrawal of attachment figures in the past. For example, the child whose parents become distressed or disapproving when he or she becomes needy or dependent may associate anxiety with feelings of vulnerability or need. The child whose parents have difficulty accepting his or her expression of anger may associate incipient feelings of anger with the experience of anxiety. This experience of anxiety will result in an automatic avoidance of any behavior or incipient feeling that becomes associated with it. In information-processing terms, what happens is that expressive motor behaviors consistent with specific feelings that have led to a disruption in interpersonal contact do not become fully synthesized.

In this situation, the anxiety is not simply an undesirable response to be extinguished. It can provide the therapist with important clues about the nature of potentially adaptive primary emotions and action dispositions that are not being fully synthesized.

In therapy at least two different types of anxiety can be discriminated, each requiring a different form of intervention. One form of anxiety, related to the disruption of interpersonal relationships or attachment difficulties, is experienced as a basic ontological insecurity. This is a more global form of anxiety in which the person's sense of coherence and intactness as a functioning self is threatened. In this experience of anxiety there is an experience of threat and vulnerability to basic self-organization. When this threat to basic self-organization occurs, the ongoing supportive quality of the therapeutic bond is crucial in helping the person to affirm a sense of self and internalize the therapist's support. This bond ultimately leads to the development of an internal capacity to calm the self and the ability to provide support for action from within.

A second type of anxiety occurs when the individual anticipates *future* negative events or catastrophic consequences of imagined action but reacts to these in the present as though they were actually occurring *now*. In this situation, fear is evoked in response to the catastrophic expectation and the appraised threat. Because the person realistically appraises the current situation as safe, however, the fear response is appraised as inappropriate, the action tendency associated with the response (e.g., running away) is prevented, and the person experiences anxiety. The person is mobilized for action but interrupts its expression, often by interfering with breathing, constricting muscles, and not moving. This high arousal accompanied by constriction produces the experience of anxiety. Bringing the catastrophic expectations into awareness and highlighting the individual's role in their production makes the anxiety process more manageable, brings it more under the person's control, and thereby renders it more amenable to change.

While anxiety can be thought of as an organismic response to appraised threat, depression can be thought of as an organismic response to perceived futility of effort. Anhedonia in depression can be viewed as a biologically wired-in response constellation that can lead to a conservation of energy in situations in which further expenditure of energy will be useless. Thus, although anhedonia is typically a pathological state, it has survival value in the environment of evolutionary adaptedness.

It is important to distinguish between depression and sadness. Sadness is a normal and healthy response to misfortune and loss. A sad person knows whom or what he or she has lost, yearns for the return of what is lost, and will mobilize efforts to regain what is lost. The sad person will turn to others for help and comfort, hopeful that the loss can be recovered or repaired.

In contrast, the cardinal feature of depression is hopelessness. The depressed person has given up. While depression is sometimes thought of as a state of heightened emotionality, it is in fact often accompanied by either blunted or restricted emotional expression. We hypothesize that this type of blunting of affective experience often results from what Bowlby (1980) has referred to as a deactivation of a behavioral system. When a person is hopeless about the possibility of establishing a satisfactory effect through his or her own efforts, or believes that the activation of potentially adaptive behavioral systems associated with feelings such as sadness, yearning, or anger will meet with rejection or failure, these behavioral systems can become deactivated by blocking the processing of the associated emotions. Our clinical experience has been that in situations of this type, accessing primary emotions that are currently not being synthesized can be an important therapeutic intervention.

Clinically, at least, two different types of depression, one associated with interpersonal loss and emotional isolation, the other with low self-esteem and self-criticism, can be differentiated and need to be treated differently. The abandonment depression requires dealing with the interrupted emotions of grief and anger and working them through to completion. This type of completion of unfinished business leads to a cognitive restructuring in the form of assimilating and/or relinquishing of the lost object and a remobilization of the self. The self-critical depression, on the other hand, requires a mobilization of the person to overcome the negative self-critical thoughts that dampen affective responses to situations. This can be done in a variety of different ways, all of which provide the person with new experiential evidence that acts to disconfirm the negative depressogenic schema. Accessing adaptive primary emotions can be helpful in challenging negative self-critical thinking (Greenberg & Safran, 1987b). If certain emotions such as anger or joy, or experientially based needs such as the need for contact and comfort or the need for mastery, can be mobilized, these can be used to challenge the thoughts that produce hopelessness and despair. Promoting an actual dialogue in a therapy session between the mobilized experience of self and the negative cognition can be very helpful as a method of combating depressive cognition with adaptive emotion (Greenberg & Safran, 1987a).

CONCLUSION

Emotion plays a significant role in the therapeutic process. The importance of clear conceptualization of emotional processes in healthy functioning and psychopathology cannot be overstressed. Theoretical clarity will promote much needed research on emotional-change processes in therapy. Research on emotion in therapy has begun (cf. Greenberg & Safran, 1987b, 1989) but is still in its infancy. Concentrated efforts are needed to generate integrated theory and research in order to demystify the role of emotional processes in therapy and to allow these irrepressible therapeutic processes to be fully recognized as valid and effective means of therapeutic change.

REFERENCES

Arnold, M. B. (1960). *Emotion and personality* (Vols. 1–2). New York: Columbia University.
Arnold, M. B. (1970). *Feelings and emotions*. New York: Academic Press.
Beck, A. T. (1976). *Cognitive therapy and the emotional disorders*. New York: International Universities Press.
Bordin, E. (1979). The generalizability of the ppsychoanalytic concept of the working alliance. *Psychotherapy: Theory, Research and Practice,* **16,** 252–260.
Bower, G. H. (1981). Mood and memory. *American Psychologist,* **31,** 129–248.
Bowlby, J. (1969). *Attachment and loss: Vol. 1. Attachment*. New York: Basic Books.
Bowlby, J. (1980). *Attachment and loss: Vol. 3. Loss: Sadness and depression*. London: Hogarth Press.
Buck, R. (1985). Prime theory: An integrated view of motivation and emotion. *Psychological Review,* **92,** 389–413.
Daldrup, R., Beutler, L., Engle, D., & Greenberg, L. (1988). *Focused expressive therapy*. New York: Guilford Press.
Davison, G. (1980). Psychotherapy process. Special issue. *Cognitive Therapy and Research,* **6,** 269–306.
Eagle, M. (1984). *Recent developments in psychoanalysis*. New York: McGraw-Hill.
Ekman, P. (Ed.). (1973). *Darwin and facial expression: A century of research in review*. New York: Academic Press.
Ellis A. (1962). *Reason and emotion in psychotherapy*. New York: Lyle Stewart.
Gendlin, E. T. (1981). *Focusing*. New York: Bantam.
Greenberg, L. S. (1984). A task analysis of intrapersonal conflict resolution. In L. N. Rice & L. S. Greenberg (Eds.), *Patterns of change: Intensive analysis of psychotherapy process*. New York: Guilford Press.
Greenberg, L. S., Elliot, R., & Foerster, F. (1989). Experiential processes in the psychotherapeutic treatment of depression. In D. McCann & N. Endler (Eds.), *Depression: Developments in theory research and practice*. Toronto: Thompson.
Greenberg, L. S., & Johnson, S. (1985). Emotionally focused couples therapy: An affective systemic approach. In N. Jacobson & A. Gurman (Eds.), *Handbook of clinical and marital therapy*. New York: Guilford Press.
Greenberg, L. S., & Johnson, S. (1986). Affect in marital therapy. *Journal of Marital and Family Therapy,* **12,** 1–10.
Greenberg, L. S., & Johnson, S. (1988). *Emotionally focused therapy for couples*. New York: Guilford Press.
Greenberg, L. S., & Safran, J. D. (1981). Encoding and cognitive therapy: changing what clients attend to. *Psychotherapy Theory, Research and Practice,* **18,** 163–169.
Greenberg, L. S., & Safran, J. D. (1984). Integrating affect and cognition: A perspective on the process of therapeutic change. *Cognitive Therapy and Research,* **8,** 559–578.
Greenberg, L. S., & Safran, J. D. (1987a). Emotion, cognition and action. In H. Eysenck & I. Martin (Eds.), *Foundations of behavior therapy*. New York: Plenum.
Greenberg, L. S., & Safran, J. D. (1987b). *Emotion in psychotherapy: Affect and cognition in the process of change*. New York: Guilford Press.

Greenberg, L., & Safran, J. (1989). Emotion in psychotherapy. *American Psychologist,* **44,** 19–29.

Harlow, H. (1958). The nature of love. *American Psychologist,* **13,** 673–685.

Izard, C. E. (Ed.). (1977). *Human emotions.* New York: Plenum.

Izard, C. E. (Ed.). (1979). *Emotion in personality and psychopathology.* New York: Plenum.

Lang, P. J. (1983). Cognition in emotion: Concept and action. In C. Izard, J. Kagan, & R. Zajonc (Eds.), *Emotion, cognition and behaviour.* New York: Cambridge University Press.

Lang, P. J. (1984). The cognitive psychophysiology of emotion: Fear and anxiety. In A. H. Tuma & J. D. Maser (Eds.), *Anxiety and the anxiety disorders.* Hillsdale, NJ: Erlbaum.

Leventhal, H. (1979). A perceptual-motor processing model of emotion. In P. Pliner, K. Blankstein, & I. M. Spigel (Eds.), *Perception of emotion in self and others* (Vol. 5). New York: Plenum.

Leventhal, H. (1980). Toward a comprehensive theory of emotions. In L. Berkowitz (Ed.), *Advances in experimental social psychology* (Vol. 13). New York: Academic Press.

Leventhal, H. (1982). The integration of emotion and cognition: A view from the perceptual-motor theory of emotion. In M. S. Clarke & S. T. Fiske (Eds.), *Affect and cognition: The 17th annual Carnegie symposium on cognition.* Hillsdale, NJ: Erlbaum.

Leventhal, H. (1984). A perceptual-motor theory of emotion. In L. Berkowitz (Ed.), *Advances in experimental social psychology* (Vol. 17). Orlando, FL: Academic Press.

Leventhal, H., & Tomarken, A. (1986). Emotion: Today's problems. *Annual Review of Psychology,* **37,** 565–610.

Meichenbaum, D. (1977). *Cognitive behavior modification: An integrative approach.* New York: Plenum.

Perls, F., Hefferline, R., & Goodman, P. (1951). *Gestalt therapy.* New York: Dell.

Plutchik, R. (1980). *Emotion: A psychoevolutionary synthesis.* New York: Harper & Row.

Rachman, S. (1978). *Fear and courage.* San Francisco, CA: Freeman.

Rice, L. (1974). The evocative function of the therapist. In D. Wexler & L. Rice (Eds.), *Innovations in client-centered therapy.* New York: Wiley (Interscience).

Rice, L., & Greenberg, L. (1984). *Patterns of change: Intensive analysis of psychotherapeutic process.* New York: Guilford.

Safran, J. D., & Greenberg, L. S. (1986). Hot cognition and psychotherapy process: An information processing/ecological approach. In P. Kendall (Ed.), *Advances in cognitive-behavioral research and therapy* (Vol. 5). Orlando, FL: Academic Press.

Safran, J. D., & Greenberg, L. S. (1988). The treatment of anxiety and depression: The process of affective change. In P. Kendall & D. Watson (Eds.), *Anxiety and depression: Distinctive and overlapping features.* Orlando: Academic Press.

Schafer, R. (1983). *The analytic attitude.* New York: Basic Books.

Shorr, J. E. (1974). *Psychotherapy through imagery.* New York: Intercontinental Medical Corp.

Shiffrin, R., & Schneider, W. (1977). Controlled and automatic human information processing. II. Perceptual learning, automatic attending and a general theory. *Psychological Review,* **84,** 127–190.

Wexler, D. A. (1974). A cognitive theory of experiencing self actualization and therapeutic process. In D. A. Wexler & L. N. Rice (Eds.), *Innovations in client-centered therapy.* New York: Wiley.

Zajonc, R. B. (1980). Feeling and thinking: Preferences need no inferences. *American Psychologist,* **33,** 151–175.

Part II

PSYCHOANALYTIC FOCUS

Chapter 4

EMOTION AND THE ORGANIZATION
OF PRIMARY PROCESS

HENRY KELLERMAN

ABSTRACT

In conventional psychoanalytic usage, primary process is a metapsychological formulation defined for the most part as that kind of mental process considered to be abnormal or psychopathological. Thus, for example, primary process material includes the expression of irrational impulses, the appearance of bizarre behavior, verbal contents that ignore categories of time and space, autistic logic, and dreams.

In the general psychoanalytic and psychiatric literature, primary process has not been systematically connected to other domains of personality such as emotion or diagnostic disposition. In this chapter, a series of specific links of primary process to various components of personality are proposed. These links within the personality network form into particular alignments referred to as emotion-diagnostic chains. The use of a theory of emotion reveals a basic family of such chains. Each emotion-diagnostic chain reflects a distinctive personality organization composed of the specific elements of that chain: emotion, trait, cognitive orientation, defensive structure, diagnostic disposition, dream and nightmare, intrapsychic property, and primary process manifestation. The array of primary process manifestations are organized with reference to the basic chains of the personality that are revealed by the structure of the theory of emotion.

EMOTION
Theory, Research, and Experience
Volume 5

INTRODUCTION

From the psychoanalytic point of view, the metapsychological formulation of primary process is defined as a mental process that generates abnormal or psychopathological responses. In clinical terms, primary process material is expressed through emotions, impulses, cognitive elements, fantasy, dream material, and behavior.

Primary process behavior is at worst considered to be bizarre, incoherent, primitive, and hallucinatory, and at best, severely idiosyncratic. Primary process presumably contains impulses usually associated with the intrapsychic concept of the id. The psychoanalytic conception of id includes references to illogical and irrational psychic productions. These id productions are characterized by the Freudian principle of immediate responses to pleasure needs within the personality, rather than on responses that would be based on the demands of reality and normal social functioning. Magical thinking, hallucinations, delusions, cannibalistic fantasy, neologisms, and syncretistic thinking all qualify as primary process products. Contributors to art, literature, and music are also credited with access to primary process, but such access is attributed to the analytic concept of "regression in the service of the ego," which refers to the capacity of the individual to utilize primary process primitive material but not to become inextricably bound up with it. Thus, for all intents and purposes, primary process, in clinical terms, is considered characteristic of severe psychopathology.

Although he originally credited Breuer with the concept, Freud first presented the idea of primary process in 1895 in his *Project for a Scientific Psychology* (Freud, 1877–1902/1954), and the concept appeared in 1900 in his classic text *The Interpretation of Dreams* (Freud, 1900/1953). Freud called primary process a kind of thinking—the kind of mental activity in which images become fused and can quite easily symbolize and substitute for one another. Thus, primary process productions were proposed to be those that ignore categories of time and space; such thinking was then described by Freud as governed both by the pleasure principle and by repressed wishes.

In the topographical psychoanalytic model—a model of the interaction of id, ego, and superego—primary process is a mode of thinking typical of id productions and is also experienced in dreaming. If dream material were to become manifest in the awake state then this expression would be considered a psychotic product and would be called maladaptive. In this respect, Holt (1956) describes primary process as including nonsensical associative links, apparently implying the presence of random associations. In more sophisticated psychoanalytic understanding, even a so-called raging superego could be characterized as containing primary process urges.

Primary process as the essence and extreme of psychopathology may also include verbal productions that can be correlated to a number of thinking mechanisms. For example, primary process has been linked to the kind of thinking that equates correlational data with direct cause and effect processes—also referred to clinically as paralogical thinking. Further, primary process has been defined by a number of theoreticians and clinicians to reflect extensive condensation of ideas, to include displacement of emotion onto irrelevant or inappropriate substitute targets, to operate by using opposites in verbal expression, and to reflect an extensive reference to symbols (Arieti, 1966; Freud, 1900/1953; Fromm, 1978–1979; Palombo, 1985). Examples of these properties of primary process include Freud's formulation of dream work mechanisms that ostensibly translate the unacceptable latent dream—the dream from below—into the manifest or descriptive dream—the dream from above. Through references to opposites (up means down), symbolism (as in the presence of emblematic references or even symptoms), and displacement (the transfer of emotion onto indirect figures), just about all the pathological phenomena in schizophrenia have been related to the emergence and dominance of primary process.

Further, Arieti (1966) discusses specific components of primary process, such as in the psychotic person's use of words as phonetic entities independent of meaning. Arieti points out that primary process constitutes a stage of regression in which the person confuses identifications. By this, Arieti is referring to the person's apparent confusion between objects; that is, similarities of objects or part objects are instantly equated with one another.

Arieti (1966) cites the example of a schizophrenic woman who suffered from a finger infection. She looked at the reddened infected spot on her finger and proclaimed, while pointing to it, "This is my red and rotten head" (p. 726). In this example, Arieti interprets the meaning of this ostensible primary process response as one in which finger and head—a part object response combined with a property of identification, that is, finger with rotten head, respectively—have been made congruent or identical.

Fromm (1978–1979) suggests that the multiple productions of primary process reflect mental functioning that resembles productions of early childhood before the development of language and before the development of reality orientation. The aspect of early childhood typically congruent with the expression of primary process production is the inability to delay gratification. Further, Palombo (1985) refers to primary process as primordial, primitive, and preemptive. By this, Palombo indicates that primary process tends toward immediate discharge.

With respect to cognition and defense, Fast (1983) presents the conception of primary process as a thought process that encompasses defenses, wishes, and experience:

> The primary processes represent a different mode of thought from that of the everyday waking life of adults, analogous to an alternative language in which ideas may be presented. In this thought form an idea occurs not as a thought but as an experience. . . . Belief is (uncritically) attached to it. It occurs in the present, without placement in such reality

frames as time (an event remembered), judgment (I think . . .), or denial (It is not . . .).
It is egocentric, organized around the fulfillment of the subject's aims or wishes. (p. 200)

In an earlier refinement, Rapaport (1957) makes the distinction between primary process itself and primary process thinking by indicating that primary process can operate both in thinking as well as in action. Here Rapaport implies the ubiquitous nature of primary process as a psychopathological product. This view is also echoed by Urist (1980): "It is probably impossible to overstate the centrality of the idea of the primary and secondary process to Freud's theory of mental functioning. . . . [It] continues to play a fundamental almost unquestioned part in day to day clinical practice" (p. 137).

Finally, Meloy (1986) summarizes the agreement among clinicians that the essence of primary process concerns the mechanisms of displacement and condensation in the sense that these mechanisms permit bizarre expressions of primary process as they surface, for example, in dreams, albeit in disguised form. In this disguised form, the subject is not awakened in a frightened state by the fundamental primary process dream content. Nightmares only occur, presumably, when individual defense mechanisms fail to operate successfully, a point developed by Kellerman (1987). Meloy suggests that in the process of condensation, correlational events are considered causative while, through the mechanism of displacement, connotational meaning is equivalent to denotation—a concretization.

PRIMARY AND SECONDARY PROCESS

To appreciate primary process as psychopathology, it can be contrasted with secondary process in which conscious thinking and logic govern the person's responses. In secondary thinking, the person obeys the laws of grammar and logic, and behavior is governed by what Freud called the reality principle. In terms of secondary process, the reality principle reduces discomfort through the implementation of adaptive behavior. Secondary process ostensibly develops concomitantly with the ego and according to Freud is inextricably associated with verbal thinking. The correspondence of ego functioning, secondary process, and verbal thinking leads to the capacity for adaptation and learning. Freud warns, however, that "good" secondary process is only possible if repression operates to block any possible channel through which the primary process can have access to consciousness. Thus, secondary process is identified solely with thinking and reality testing, processes that are coherent and focused and that correspond to adaptational considerations. In contrast, primary process is identified with idiosyncratic, intuitive, and impulsive responses that are based on the internal signal rather than on conditions of reality or convention.

In the following section a theory of primary process activity and its relation to emotion will be proposed. A relationship between primary process and emotion is implied by Freud's proposition that primary process responses are modes of activity that have been freed from inhibition and from repression and that they are basically intuitive and experiential. Although Freud refers to such modes in a general sense, these modes also may be correlated to specific, basic emotion patterns or prototypes. In this chapter, the prototypes or patterns of emotion explicated by Plutchik (1962, 1980a, 1980b) shall be proposed as the basis for a theory of basic modes of primary process.

PRIMARY PROCESS AND EMOTION

As noted above, in addition to conceiving of primary process as a product of emotional thinking, or even as the source of irrational thinking, Freud also proposed that primary processes are modes of activity that have been freed from inhibition. For example, in a dream, activity that has been freed from inhibition is not considered to be pathological. Yet, in the awake state, the presence of such primary process activity is pathological. For example, people can dream of supernatural activities such as flying by virtue of willpower. In the awake state, however, an actual attempt to fly by jumping from a high place, such as a building or mountain precipice, would certainly indicate pathological judgment and behavior.

Further, regarding the expression of emotion and its relation to primary process, Rapaport, Gill, and Schafer (1970) understand primary process to be forms of concept formation represented by the prelogical unconscious interplay between ideas, intuition, and emotion. This primary process experience presumably comprises an amalgamation of the structure of perceptions and memory infused into the person's particular emotional organization. Kellerman (1979) has also proposed that in intuition lies the kernel of the secondary idea in its primary uncrystallized form—a mass of sense impressions exemplified by the person's particular emotional configuration or particular emotional profile.

Thus, primary process may not be merely a random expression of primitive unconscious material. Rather, primary process manifestations may reflect the person's particular emotional configuration. Such primary process material is primitive and presumably results from an internal amorphous bombardment of stimuli to which the subject responds with confusion, disturbance, bizarreness, inappropriateness, neologisms, and any number of maladaptive equivalents. It is likely, however, that primary process material of the paranoid person would be different, for example, from that of the hysteric. This difference in primary process experience could be expressed in a number of ways: in feeling tone; in associative productions; almost certainly in terms of expression of emotion; in basic personality style; in general proclivities of the personality such as expansiveness or constriction; and finally, even with reference to specific character structure that gives to personality its particular cast.

In the following section an attempt is made to relate primary process to basic characterological states and their proposed respective core emotions.

THE PERSONALITY NETWORK

In a series of publications, Kellerman (1979, 1983, 1987) has suggested basic cognitive, defense, and intrapsychic categories that are hypothesized to be derived from the basic emotion system developed by Plutchik (1962, 1980a, 1980b, 1984). Kellerman points out that the disparate levels of personality can also be understood within this emotion system. The emotion system is an epigenetic phenomenon, a given biological set of dispositions that are affected by experience. Within this system, cognitive concepts are related to emotion dimensions, defenses, and diagnostic dispositions. Hypotheses are then formulated to suggest how the cognitive and defense levels of this proposed epigenetic emotion system can reveal the connection between primary process material and the emotions. This specific linkage between primary process and emotion has not been explicitly proposed before, although there are some references in the psychoanalytic and psychological literature that implies an intertwining of emotion and primary process. Yet, fundamentally, the issue of primary process thinking has been treated clinically and scientifically as a different domain from that of the emotions.

It is proposed here that the emotion–personality system is very much implicated in the appearance of primary process material and, more specifically, that there may be different kinds of primary process material just as there are different basic emotions. Further, it is proposed that this primary process thinking can be a component of the morphology of each basic emotion of the system and can be identified, and in fact understood, within the context of this epigenetic emotion–personality network.

THE EMOTION SYSTEM

The system of emotion and its vicissitudes, especially with respect to personality structure, are largely set forth by Plutchik and by Kellerman in this series: Volume 1, *Theories of Emotion* (see Kellerman, 1980; see Plutchik, 1980);

Volume 2, *Emotions in Early Development* (see Kellerman, 1983; see Plutchik, 1983); Volume 4, *The Measurement of Emotion* (see Kellerman, 1989; Plutchik, 1989); this volume; and other publications (Kellerman, 1979, 1987; Plutchik, 1962, 1984). The correlations and proposed theoretical connections of the emotion–personality system to abnormal psychology, psychoanalytic formulations, psychopathology, and personality structure are presented in these publications. For example, Plutchik's formulations concerning the crystallization of personality traits from the action of the emotions are further applied to suggest additional correlations with other levels of personality.

Kellerman (1979, 1987) has proposed that particular links within personality exist, permitting distinctions to be proposed between personality types. Thus, the paranoid personality, for example, can be distinguished from the hysteric along a number of personality dimensions. These dimensions include basic emotions linked to particular clusters of personality traits, specific defense patterns, identifiable dream and nightmare themes, palpable intrapsychic (id–superego) influences, cognitive orientations, diagnostic dispositions, and even primary and secondary processes. These linkages are conceived as emotion–personality chains, and eight basic chains are proposed within the basic theoretical system. As an illustration of the relation between personality and emotion, the following exposition of the paranoid pattern or chain is presented.

THE PARANOID CHAIN

The paranoid character is considered a basic type derived from the prototypic behavioral mode of rejection. In this mode of rejection, the subject resists the assimilation of new objects or rejects anything that has been inadvertently taken in. The emotion that reflects this rejection impulse is disgust or revulsion. The emotion of disgust enables the person to identify aversive stimuli either that have been already taken in or that are perceived at least as potentially noxious. In terms of personality traits, a cluster of rejection traits becomes dominant in such paranoid types. These traits include needs to criticize others, to repudiate, to become suspicious of others, to distrust others, and to quarrel.

In an interpersonal sense, the criticalness trait represents the subject's need to reject all new ideas or attempts by others to create personal associations or to ask for commitments. On the diagnostic level, this rejection–criticalness tendency of the subject becomes a central manifestation of paranoid character. A central need of a paranoid character is to always demonstrate derivative behavior that, in an overall sense, attempts to fortify and underscore the continuous distinction made by the subject between self and other. In this overall sense, the rejection mode or prototype pattern is represented by the emotion of disgust or revulsion and by the traits of criticalness, repudiation, and suspiciousness. This mode then coalesces in a diagnostic paranoid syndrome. In a more specific sense, the distinction made between self and other consists of a need in the subject to maintain a negative focus on the object or other. It is in this way that the basic emotion system reveals emotion-diagnostic chains of the personality.

There are additional aspects of personality that constitute other links on each basic emotion-diagnostic chain. For example, this disgust–rejection–paranoid chain is linked to the defense structure of personality through the mechanism of projection. The use of projection as a typical paranoid mechanism enables an individual to externalize all negative feelings, thereby directing hostility, suspiciousness, and critical feelings toward others. Such outward direction of criticalness is presumably projected in order for the subject to avoid the experience of the perception of one's own personal imperfection—the underlying dynamic in paranoid functioning. This underlying dynamic of the paranoid constellation regarding an unconscious belief in one's own inferiority creates the need for strong projective defenses so that all imperfection is attributed to others. The subject, therefore, avoids noticing any personal imperfections whatsoever.

With respect to dreaming, when projective defenses are operating efficiently, such persons are able to dream and not become disturbed by their dreams. In these cases, hostility and criticalness find interpersonal targets in the dream. When projective defenses are not effective, however, dreams become transformed into nightmares, and such paranoid types then awaken with distress. The nightmare content reflects the central dynamic of the paranoid type in which hostility and criticalness, in the absence of projection, are now directed against the self. Thus, nightmares include themes of body parts missing, self-mutilation, and other such self-punishment dream contents reflecting the extreme of self-doubt and feelings of inferiority. The emotion-diagnostic chain of the personality can now also be seen to include particular dreams and nightmares that are intrinsically connected to specific defense mechanisms.

Through the self-punishment themes emerging in paranoid dreams and nightmares, the basic intrapsychic nature of paranoid character is revealed. The typical self-punishment themes of this type suggest the punitive nature inherent in this personality structure. In psychoanalytic terms, such punitive structure is defined as representing superego manifestations, that is, the kind of nature seeking to punish, scold, criticize, blame, or, in any number of ways, reflect the subject's attempt to expiate guilt, ostensible wrongdoing, or feelings of dread. Thus, it is proposed that at the core of the disgust–emotion chain there exists a paranoid–superego nature.

A final example of the connection of various aspects of the personality to particular emotion–personality structural chains concerns the consideration of basic cognitive orientations to any given chain. The connection of personality and emotion to possible cognitive categories that can be conceived as derivatives of the basic emotion system has been previously proposed by Kellerman (1983, 1987). With respect to the paranoid disposition, the basic cognitive orientation of this emotion-diagnostic chain concerns the search for certainty. The paranoid person seeks to avoid ambiguity or uncertainty. Indeed, such a person is in a continual state of affirming and reaffirming a sense of certainty, a belief in personal perfection, and the attribution of imperfection to others. The objective in this constant search for certainty is to create and sustain a self–object difference. This difference between self and object then results in the continuous separation of self and object by an inexorable critical and negative focus on the object—the paranoid stance. The task of maintaining a negative focus on the object is defined as a secondary process aim. It is this secondary process aim and cognitive connection to the emotion–personality system, along with the thematic material of the dreams and nightmares of each basic diagnostic type, that constitute a bridge to the understanding and the inherent organization of primary process. That is, failure of the secondary process aims, the loosening of cognitive orientation as well as the surfacing of nightmare dream contents, can reveal the nature of particular primary process material corresponding to each of the structural chains of the entire emotion–personality system.

In the example of the paranoid type, when the subject is unable to maintain a negative focus on the object and cannot sustain the condition of certainty, then the distinction between self and object can become obscured. When the distinction between self and other is obscured, the paranoid's projected target for criticism is no longer clear. Tension is then released and associated with the condition of uncertainty that the subject experiences toward the object. Along with this tension of uncertainty and in the absence of an effective projective defense, dream material of the nightmare typical of this type will include themes of self-criticism and self-punishment, appearing in the form of missing body parts as well as of mutilation or part mutilation of the subject. In addition, references to feelings of revulsion and decaying matter are seen in response to projective testing material. The florid behavioral samples of such primary process breakthrough, reflecting this paranoid pattern, can include punitive or superego references of the persecutory delusional kind as well as corresponding hallucinatory experiences. Table 4.1 presents the rejection–paranoid, emotion–personality chain in which the various aspects or levels of personality are linked.

In light of the illustration and definition of the paranoid chain offered above, in the remainder of this chapter the connection of primary process to the categories of the emotion–personality system shall be proposed. The nature of the subject–object relationship as a basis for the development of object-relations theory provides the interpersonal context for the dynamic operation of the entire emotion–personality system.

TABLE 4.1
EMOTION–PERSONALITY STRUCTURE OF THE DISGUST–PARANOID CHAIN

Prototype pattern or mode: Rejection
Behavioral act: Riddance reaction
Basic or core emotion: Disgust, revulsion
Personality traits: Criticalness, suspiciousness, distrustfulness
Diagnostic disposition: Paranoid
Defense mechanism: Projection
Dream and nightmare: Self-punishment, self-depreciation, mutilation, fragmentation of body parts
Intrapsychic property: Superego
Cognitive orientation: To establish certainty in order to preserve separation between self and object
Secondary process aim: To maintain a negative focus on the object
Primary process manifestation: Dream material of mutilation, references to decay and revulsion on
  projective material, hallucinatory experiences, and punitive delusional themes

---

EMOTION, PRIMARY PROCESS,
AND THE SUBJECT–OBJECT TIE

In relating emotion, primary process, and the subject–object tie, two basic conceptions can be aligned. First is the idea that the dynamic operation of the emotion–personality system crystallizes within an interpersonal framework. Second, the relationship of emotion to the subject–object tie can be understood as the basis of overall object-relations development.

The fundamental conception of object-relations development concerns the fact that one person can become attached, invested in, or, in psychoanalytic terms, cathected to another person, that is, the emotional attachment of self to other or, in object-relations terminology, subject to object. The nature of this subject–object tie consists of the emotional connection, the emotional investment, or the emotion involved in the cathexis to the other person. In clinical usage, this emotional connection of subject to object is frequently referred to as the psychological premise that *emotions take objects*. This premise means that the mortar responsible for the attachment of self to other is composed of investment of emotion in the other that is cemented by a corresponding response from the object. Thus, the nature of the subject's investment in the object refers specifically to the subject's emotional response to the object, or even to the pattern of emotion that characterizes the typical responses between subject and object.

It is this habituation in emotional communication between subject and object (self and other) that constitutes the basis of object-relations development. Further, in a developmental sense, when such emotional communication facilitates adaptive responses between subject and object, then the clinical adage that emotions take objects also becomes the main mechanism in the development of secondary process. When the demands of the subject and the responses of the object are not emotionally resonant, however, but instead produce typically maladaptive interactions, then the probability of the eventual appearance of primary process material is likely to increase. Interestingly, Rapaport (1957) refers to the free transfer of cathexis as the basic idea of primary process so that, according to Rapaport, on the level of primary process, emotion does not become firmly bound to any permanent object. In contrast, in the development and crystallization of secondary process, emotion presumably does become bound to a permanent object.

In the illustration of the disgust–paranoid chain, primary process material of mutilation, self-punishment, and fragmentation reflected the undefended, depersonalized, and, most importantly, emotionally decathected aspect of this diagnostic chain; a condition where the subject–object cathexis was not sufficiently entrenched. In the following sections the remaining primary process modes, as they correspond to the basic emotion-diagnostic entities, are described.

THE HYSTERIC CHAIN

The emotion-diagnostic structure of the hysteric personality is portrayed in Table 4.2. In contrast to the paranoid type, whose interpersonal aim is to create a separation between subject and object and to maintain a negative focus on the object, the aim of the hysteric is to gain the attention of the object in order to incorporate or blend with the object. Cognitively, the hysteric accepts and needs to attend to the object and to avoid any deflections from this task. This cognitive

TABLE 4.2
EMOTION–PERSONALITY STRUCTURE OF THE ACCEPTANCE–HYSTERIC CHAIN

Prototype pattern or mode: Incorporation
Behavioral act: Assimilation behavior
Basic or core emotion: Acceptance
Personality traits: Trustfulness, suggestibility, gullibility
Diagnostic disposition: Hysteric
Defense mechanism: Denial
Dream and nightmare: Sarcasm, alienation themes
Intrapsychic property: Id
Cognitive orientation: To attend to object or to assimilate positive information of the object in order to preserve the subject–object relationship
Secondary process aim: To maintain a positive focus on the object
Primary process manifestation: Sarcasm, incorporative needs now serve the purpose of destroying object, negative impulses toward the object expressed through fantasies of devouring object

orientation of attending to the object and the aim of maintaining a positive focus on the object, along with the screening out of all negative information, form the essence of the secondary process. The secondary process functions help to sustain interpersonal stability for persons with this hysteric-diagnostic configuration through such attachments with the object.

The emotion of acceptance constitutes the core of this emotion-diagnostic chain and reflects an incorporative behavioral mode. On the defense level, the subject utilizes denial mechanisms as a way of screening out negative information or distractions that could in any way interfere with the subject's positive or attentive focus on the object. Correspondingly, traits of trustfulness, suggestibility, and even gullibility represent the typical interpersonal orientation of this hysteric type. When denial mechanisms become ineffective, then the subject experiences a dreaded separation from the object and an associated weakening of the secondary process. Primary process responses can then begin to appear. These responses are characterized by sarcasm and by fantasies of devouring the object, that is, destruction through incorporation. In addition, on the level of primary process, the hysteric experiences profound and continuous negative and hostile impulses toward the object. This expostulation of negative impulses can occur because secondary process is no longer the dominant mode of the personality. Therefore, denial defenses—typically utilized in the successful functioning of the secondary process—can no longer help the hysteric to screen in only positive information about the object and, correspondingly, to screen out all negative information.

On the level of primary process the basic nature of each emotion-diagnostic chain is revealed to be one of either id or superego. Kellerman (1979, 1983, 1987) has proposed that the id or superego nature of each emotion-diagnostic chain is a given aspect of each basic emotion dimension and is not developed within the emotion program as a result of adaptational influences. That is, those emotion dimensions correlated with primary process material and characterized by the release of impulse generally, and aggression and sexuality specifically, are considered to reflect id imperatives that are inherent in the particular morphology of that dimension of emotion. Similarly, primary process material composed of depersonalization anxiety, grief that results in suicidal acting-out, and overall suffering reflects superego imperatives inherent in the morphology of those particular emotion dimensions associated with such primary process. Only ego and the degree to which ego is developed are considered a function of adaptational influences. On the level of primary process, then, a basic id nature is reflected in the hysteric-diagnostic chain in the sense of the chaotic release of hostile impulses.

In the paranoid structure, the subject is impaired because the absence of the object and the ineffectiveness of the projective mechanism of defense now direct the usual criticalness toward the self instead of toward the object. Thus, because of the punitive quality implicit in the paranoid's self-loathing, the true nature of this type is revealed to be one of superego. In the hysteric, merger with the object leads to denial of negative impulses toward the object and ensures that only positive information about the object is admissible. When a separation between subject and object occurs, then negative impulses toward the object can flood the personality because of a weakening of secondary process and a corresponding ascendancy of the primary process.

THE PASSIVE CHAIN

It is proposed that the cognitive orientation and defensive aim of the passive personality are designed to assist in the repression of the memory of the early subject–object relationship. To recall and remember the nature of this original subject–object tie is to jog into memory early feelings of apprehension concerning the object's demand for the subject to maintain a comprehensive attachment and continual focus on the object. It is a demand by the object for adherence, compliance, and obedience. To comply with such demands implies that the subject becomes extremely dependent. Yet, in terms of conventional individuation–separation theory, the subject also needs to maintain some semblance of autonomy in order to meet the demands made by the world with respect to adaptation and development. This psychodynamic conflict between dependence, on the one hand, and autonomy, on the other, presumably contributes to the emergence of a passive stance. In this passive stance, the subject rejects any assertive and obvious behavior in favor of a more anonymous transference position in the world—that is, the position of passivity.

In the passive stance the individual can deny the presence of any pressing personal needs. With the aid of the repressive defense, the person remains out of view of the punitive and demanding eye of the object or parental figure. In this way the passive stance can become the person's method of retaining a sense of autonomy. In psychoanalytic understanding, such a passive stance is considered an effect of derivative castration anxiety, that is, inordinate fear of the authority figure. The traits that coalesce with respect to the diagnostic disposition of passivity are mostly determined by a cluster of emotions related to apprehension and fear. The presence of such emotions presumably reflect the so-called castration fear as well as support the development of related traits of compliance and timidity. Such passive persons are described as being unable to be assertive. The difficulty in becoming assertive is also considered in psychoanalytic understanding to be the central derivative problem reflecting the phallic psychosexual level. It is out of the phallic period that the psychoanalytic concept of castration fear is derived. Thus, the passive stance is considered a phallic-period derivative pattern influenced by the metapsychological concept of castration anxiety—a reference to the child's fear of punishment from the parent or parental transference figures.

In the absence of the main defense of repression, the object, or parental transference object, as a punitive figure and profound source of dependence can be remembered. Since the aim of secondary process in this cognitive and defensive orientation is to forget, avoid, or escape this punitive transference person, then recalling and remembering in the absence of repressive defense can create a sense of foreboding. In addition, fear of a loss of self is also a likely effect of the failure of secondary process. On the level of primary process, therefore, the passive dispositional type reflects oppressive superego imperatives supported by early experiences of a punitive subject–object tie.

Table 4.3 displays the emotion–personality structure of this fear–passive chain. When defenses are incapacitated or otherwise neutralized and under the pressure of excessive stress, any primary process material that surfaces can contain themes of alarm. An alarm or fear reaction can represent typical fears of the subject regarding subjugation and even supplication demands by the object, along with the subject's corresponding fear of losing a sense of personal autonomy and freedom. The appearance of a dream in which an attacker tries to kill the dreamer–subject, and the subject awakens in terror, is an example of the kind of primary process material that emerges in this passive-dispositional type. Thus, the appearance of an attacker in a dream is considered a reflection of a conflict regarding passivity. Nightmares of terror that result from such a dream content also suggest that the defense of repression has been threatened. The effect of passivity in the personality can apply to any dispositional type whenever the element of passivity, in the personality becomes prominent. Of course, the nightmare in which the dreamer awakens in terror in response to an attacker is theoretically more likely to appear in the passive dispositional type or whenever passive periods gain prominence.

TABLE 4.3
EMOTION–PERSONALITY STRUCTURE OF THE FEAR–PASSIVE CHAIN

Prototype pattern or mode: Protection
Behavioral act: Caution, escape
Basic or core emotion: Fear, apprehension
Personality traits: Timidity, obedience, compliance
Diagnostic disposition: Passive
Defense mechanism: Repression
Dream and nightmare: Life-threatening attacker appears
Intrapsychic property: Superego
Cognitive orientation: To forget object in order to preserve autonomy
Secondary process aim: To support separation of subject from object
Primary process manifestation: Conscious expectation and terror of threat
    from others in face of loss of autonomy, person in state of alarm

THE AGGRESSIVE CHAIN

The secondary process task and defensive aim of the aggressive personality are to attenuate the expression of dissatisfaction, annoyance, and anger toward the object. On the level of secondary process the operation of the displacement defense is utilized to minimize or control any undue aggression toward the object. Thus, because of the displacement of anger only a moderately negative focus on the object occurs. This moderately negative focus substitutes for a more direct expression and fully reconstituted measure of anger toward the object were the defense of displacement not to be effective. With the operation of displacement, the subject's cognitive orientation is to reinforce all attenuation of anger. This process of managing anger is here labeled condensing operations. These condensing operations prevent the possibility of more fully reconstituted anger expressed toward the object; that is, when no longer in condensed form through the operation of displacement mechanisms, the anger becomes fully reformed with respect to its original target—it is reconstituted.

On the primary process level, when displacement mechanisms become inoperative, anger and aggression are then reconstituted and the subject expresses rageful, uncontrolled impulses. In the primary process state, the expression of emotion serves the purpose of directing fully destructive impulses and intentions outward. Primary process responses of this aggressive chain are essentially id expressions; that is, the expression of anger to its fullest measure concerns the subject's desire to attack the object without the usual social concerns and restraint. On the level of secondary process, the trait profile that develops for this type includes quarrelsomeness, protest behavior, and a host of somewhat controlled, yet hostile, aggressive responses. In contrast, primary process themes, which are also reflected in the dreams and nightmares of this aggressive dispositional type, include general dyscontrolled aggression and fully developed rage reactions toward the object. Table 4.4 describes the emotion–personality structure of this anger–aggressive chain.

The passive and aggressive lines of development reflect opposite dispositions. In the passive personality the secondary process aim is to forget or repress memories of the object, or parental figure, thereby neutralizing the subject's fear of the power and potentially destructive threat of the object. The secondary process aim of the aggressive person is to neutralize potentially destructive behavior toward the object, that is, to be less angry. For the passive dispositional type, power resides in and is attributed to the object or authority figure. For the aggressive type, power resides in the subject or self, while the object is targeted for attack.

The primary process expressions of the passive type include inordinate startle responses and a variety of seclusive, cautious, and highly idiosyncratic fear and even terror responses. The primary process reactions of the aggressive type

TABLE 4.4

EMOTION–PERSONALITY STRUCTURE OF THE ANGER–AGGRESSIVE CHAIN

Prototype pattern or mode: Destruction

Behavioral act: Hostility and aggression expressed toward object

Basic or core emotion: Anger, rage

Personality traits: Aggression, protest, quarrelsomeness

Diagnostic disposition: Aggressive

Defense mechanism: Displacement

Dream and nightmare: Subject attacks the object

Intrapsychic property: Id

Cognitive orientation: To displace anger through condensing operations

Secondary process aim: To attenuate intensely destructive feelings toward object largely through displacement mechanisms

Primary process manifestation: Obliteration of object through direct rageful responses

---

include a variety of rage and emotionally dyscontrolled, expansive, or explosive impulses.

THE OBSESSIVE CHAIN

The cognitive orientation and defensive aim of the obsessive personality are to utilize a cluster of defenses in the service of control of the object. When the subject is successful in controlling the object, then, assuming the availability of the object, the subject and object can remain in a regulated relationship. If the object can sustain a relationship, then such a regulated relationship would largely be determined by the extent to which the subject is able to tolerate intimacy. The cluster of defenses utilized in this obsessional chain centers around the defense of intellectualization. This defense of intellectualization enables the subject to analyze, examine, categorize, and further discover the object, all in the service of control of the object. In the ordering of the subject–object relationship through such control needs and controlling behavior, the subject is able to avoid any scatteredness, chaos, or appearance of impulse in the subject–object relationship. In the attempt to control the object, the subject is involved in a series of scanning behaviors so that the anticipation of events and circumstances of the subject–object relationship becomes more possible. The emotion of expectation or anticipation reflects this particular obsessive–diagnostic chain.

Secondary process mechanisms of the obsessive chain are designed to further aid in the mapping of the environment in order to contribute to the regulation and control of the subject–object relationship. The breakthrough or appearance of primary process material, then, naturally creates a loss of control of the object. The subject presumably will experience a scattered state during the surfacing of primary process material, in which, in the absence of typical and successful control operations, the self seems vulnerable and disoriented. Further, in the absence of control over the object, former impulse-ridden experiences consisting of feelings of trepidation and anticipation quickly lead to sensations of dyscontrol as subject becomes disoriented.

During experiences of pathological stress, should the usual cluster of controlling obsessional defense mechanisms of intellectualization, sublimation, rationalization, and undoing become impaired, then the content of a typical dream of this dispositional type can become transformed into a nightmare. In such nightmares, the subject loses control and is overwhelmed by sensations of dyscontrol. Dream and nightmare themes of this obsessional type include falling from high places—mountain peaks, roofs of buildings—or even the letting-go that permits the act of bed-wetting. Kellerman (1979, 1987) has pointed out that such impulse-dominated dyscontrol reactions reveal this obsessional type actually to be defending against a basic dyscontrolled or id nature. This configuration of an underlying dyscontrol nature of the obsessive can be a basis for understanding the inordinate cluster of defenses that have developed to manage the obsessional pattern.

It is proposed that the personality traits that develop for this obsessional type are designed to order and create controls in the presence of the underlying id nature, a nature that seeks to express dyscontrol. These traits include orderliness, parsimony, neatness, hoarding, stinginess, and a host of tendencies that contribute to the secondary process motive of control. Of course, on the primary process level, opposite proclivities and tendencies are seen such as outbursts. Table 4.5

TABLE 4.5
EMOTION–PERSONALITY STRUCTURE OF THE
EXPECTATION–OBSESSIVE CHAIN

Prototype pattern or mode: Exploration
Behavioral act: Mapping
Basic or core emotion: Expectation
Personality traits: Control, orderliness, parsimony
Diagnostic disposition: Obsessive
Defense mechanism: Intellectualization, sublimation, rationalization, undoing
Dream and nightmare: Loss of control
Intrapsychic property: Id
Cognitive orientation: To continue to analyze, map, and monitor subject–object relationship
Secondary process aim: To assure subject–object connection through subject's control of relationship
Primary process manifestation: Loss of control over object resulting in disorientation and dyscontrol behavior in subject

---

presents the emotion–personality structure of this obsessive chain in which the various levels of the personality are displayed and includes the secondary process aim as well as the primary process manifestation of this type.

THE PSYCHOPATHIC CHAIN

In a general sense, and specifically with respect to the psychopathic type, dyscontrol as a characterological feature suggests the presence of pervasive impulsivity. This general impulsivity is typically expressed as an impatience with the object or with others.

In terms of subject–object interaction, the cognitive orientation and defensive aim of the psychopathic type with respect to impatience with the object are to prevent the object from controlling the subject. This secondary process attempt by the psychopathic subject to undermine any potential control that the object may attempt to exert stands in sharp contrast to the secondary process aim of the obsessive type who merely tries to control the object. The psychopathic type seeks to function with fewest possible restrictions. To this end, the defense of regression is relied upon by dyscontrolled psychopathic types to assure a motoric condition in which dyscontrol, in the form of moving, talking, or otherwise being involved in a continuous series of acts, is designed to create endless, externally stimulating conditions. The need for externally stimulating conditions refers to the psychopath's proclivity and attraction to events that require some motoric act. Such persons are frequently labeled immature, delinquent, and even hyperactive. The profusion of stimulation, along with the presence of typical regressive defense patterns, then tends to undermine any potential control the object may want to exert on the subject—that is, it is not easy to control such motoric types. The subject thus continues to surprise or disorient the object with unexpected behavior, thereby neutralizing most attempts by the object to control the basic subject–object relationship.

Secondary process mechanisms of this psychopathic type can be said to be operating effectively when a dyscontrol of impulse is assured, that is, when the subject feels an absence of any inner restraint. Impulsive dyscontrol as a major feature of the psychopathic personality constitutes the basic psychological equilibrium for this type; that is, it is the normal condition for the psychopathic type to function with free expression of impulse and without restraint. A major defensive function of the ego, therefore, is to permit the condition of dyscontrol to operate effectively in the personality.

Primary process material begins to appear when the regressive defense is rendered ineffective so that motoric and dyscontrol imperatives are neutralized. The appearance of primary process and the ineffectiveness of the regressive defense are also correlated with the overall ineffectiveness of the secondary process aim that ensures the characteristic equilibrium of the psychopathic type. This characteristic equilibrium refers to the free expression of impulse and the usual motoric condition of this type. The primary process material then surfaces in the form of a sensation of being stopped. This primary process condition of neutralized dyscontrol is experienced by the subject as an overall psychological paralysis. In the state of unexpected inertia or paralysis, this type feels vulnerable to control by the object and can no longer utilize typical or characteristic traits of manipulation, expansiveness, or impulsivity. It is this dreaded control by the object over the subject that generates the basic fear of annihilation of the self. Thus, on the secondary process level, the emotions and personality traits of impatience and impulsivity ensure typical characterological functioning while, on the primary process level, the experience of paralysis and vulnerability can create catatonic-like responses of inertia and paralysis.

On the level of primary process, the inertia, vulnerability, or psychological paralysis of this psychopathic type is also apparent in dreams and nightmares. Examples of contents that transform the dream to a nightmare for this psychopathic type include themes of the subject drowning and being unable to breathe, being buried alive and not having room to move or escape, or being pursued by an attacker but not being able to flee. In such nightmares the subject awakens in a state of terror and disorientation. The dreamer experiences a collapse of protective defenses and is then flooded by feelings of the annihilation of self. In this sense of the threat to the ego in the form of annihilation fears, the intrapsychic nature of the psychopathic type is revealed to be punitive and is assumed to reflect superego imperatives; that is, the psychopathic type is fundamentally afraid of inevitable disaster, suggesting superego fears.

Table 4.6 presents the emotion–personality structure of this psychopathic chain in which the various levels of the personality can be seen.

TABLE 4.6

EMOTION–PERSONALITY STRUCTURE OF THE
SURPRISE–PSYCHOPATHIC CHAIN

Prototype pattern or mode: Orientation
Behavioral act: To undermine object
Basic or core emotion: Surprise
Personality traits: Dyscontrol, impulsivity, impatience
Diagnostic disposition: Psychopathic
Defense mechanism: Regression
Dream and nightmare: Paralysis
Intrapsychic property: Superego
Cognitive orientation: Impatience toward object
Secondary process aim: To prevent object from controlling subject
Primary process manifestation: Feeling emotional paralysis, dread, and
    terror because of inability to control object

The obsessive and psychopathic lines of development reveal opposite dispositions. In the obsessive personality the secondary process aim is to control the object and therefore to be able to regulate the degree of intimacy of the relationship. In contrast, the secondary process aim of the psychopathic personality is to prevent the object from controlling the subject. In both the obsessive and psychopathic types, control of the relationship is the central motive. On the primary process level, however, the typical trait clusters of each type shift. The controlled obsessive reveals a plethora of impulse-laden behavior, while the dyscontrolled psychopathic type shows hypercontrolled behavior indicative of a behavioral and psychological paralysis and dysfunction of regressive motoric mechanisms, as in the dream—nightmare contents of overall paralysis. Thus, the psychopathic type is dyscontrolled with respect to secondary process but hypercontrolled on the primary process level. In contrast, the obsessive type is quite controlled with respect to secondary process but dyscontrolled on the level of primary process.

THE MANIC CHAIN

In the manic state, industriousness and gregariousness are personality traits that translate into the person's need to be involved in multitudes of projects. The manic person's behavior seems infused with purpose and energy so that the subject seems to want to accomplish enormous work aims. It is proposed that such a person's cognitive orientation can be understood as one of purposiveness, a goal-oriented attitude.

The assumption made with respect to the manic person is that this work energy is originally experienced as sexual energy. Because of the undesirability of flagrant sexuality, defenses are brought to bear on the overall sexual id nature of this manic type. Through the defense of reaction formation, the person responds aversively to sexual experiences. In addition, through the defense of compensation and especially sublimation, the sexual energy then becomes transformed into work energy. Thus, inherent to this purposive cognitive orientation, and in the secondary process of this manic type, is the drive involved in motivation and work.

In terms of the relation of emotions to the manic disposition, Kellerman (1979, 1987) and Kellerman and Plutchik (1977) have presented possible theoretical connections between the emotions of pleasure and joy and the manic disposition. Together, the emotions of pleasure and joy; the defenses of reaction formation, compensation, and sublimation; and the cognitive element of purposiveness reflect the sublimated nonsexual object-focus that becomes sustained through secondary process efforts. Through goal-oriented aims, the subject envelops or possesses the object within the context of the typical manic work frenzy. Possessing the object serves and accomplishes such secondary process aims so that the nonsexual envelopment of the object qualifies as a form of accomplishment for the subject. In this sense, possession of and nonsexual focus on the object constitute the aim of secondary process in the manic disposition.

Secondary process aims of maintaining a nonsexual focus on the object, the cognitive orientation of purposiveness, and the defenses of reaction-formation, compensation, and sublimation no longer influence the manic person's behavior with respect to primary process behavior. Thus, on the level of primary process, the nature of the subject–object relationship changes. On the primary process level, no longer does the possession of the object (other person) reflect nonsexual achievement of goals. Rather, under psychological conditions of primary process, the subject can develop a state of loss of control in which formerly sublimated work energy becomes reconstituted into more primary sexual needs, and the subject may then reveal a variety of sexually dyscontrolled behaviors and a correspondingly basic id nature. This id response on the level of primary process is also evident in the dream content of the manic person during a nightmare. The nightmare is usually precipitated because in the absence of typical defenses, the subject has an orgastic dream and awakens sexually aroused to any number of sexual dream contents. The sexual nature of the dream becomes so powerful that a condition of dyscontrol obtains and reveals the release of intense sexual impulses—considered here to reflect the underlying id imperative.

Table 4.7 presents the emotion–personality structure of this manic chain in which the various levels of the personality are revealed, including secondary process goals as well as primary process manifestations.

TABLE 4.7

EMOTION–PERSONALITY STRUCTURE OF THE JOY–MANIC CHAIN

Prototype pattern or mode: Sexuality

Behavioral act: Possession of object

Basic or core emotion: Pleasure or joy

Personality traits: Gregariousness, industriousness, exuberance

Diagnostic disposition: Manic

Defense mechanism: Reaction formation, compensation, sublimation

Dream and nightmare: Sexually dyscontrolled dream

Intrapsychic property: Id

Cognitive orientation: To accomplish work aims, purposiveness

Secondary process aim: To possess and maintain a nonsexual focus on the object primarily through reaction-formation, compensation, and especially sublimation defenses

Primary process manifestation: Separation of subject and object because of impairment of defenses designed to nullify sexuality; this inability to control sexuality results in sexually dyscontrolled behavior

THE DEPRESSIVE CHAIN

In the depressive disposition, the object is usually experienced as lost or as having abandoned the self. Despite the fact that grief, anger, or despair result from loss of the object, secondary processes and cognitive aims nevertheless are brought to bear on the issue of the lost object in an attempt to reintegrate this lost object. This attempt to reintegrate the object consists largely of fantasy preoccupation with the object. For the most part, preoccupation in fantasy with the lost object is equivalent to continuous rumination about the object.

Together, the emotions of sorrow or grief and the cognitive element of rumination reflect this continuous focus on the lost object. The entire secondary process enterprise is an attempt not to accept the loss of the object but rather to seek, regain, and reintegrate the object. Therefore, rumination represents the chief cognitive orientation of this depressive type and such rumination generates a continuous focus on the object. During the time when the object is absent, then, the continuous rumination on the object also now represents a compensatory attempt to regain the strength of the intact subject–object relationship. The rumination and its compensatory mechanism express the wish for the object.

This entire sequence associated with focusing on the object represents the depressive person's psychological attempt to reestablish or reintegrate the object into the original subject–object relationship. Such reintegrating attempts are governed by the secondary process. The compensation defense mechanism of the depressive person is utilized by secondary process to prevent any permanent demoralization of the subject with respect to acknowledgment of loss of the object. Rather, the implementation of secondary process aims, the use of compensatory processes, and the rumination about the object prevent the final relinquishment of hope for the reintegration of the object.

In the absence of compensatory defense, a relinquishing of the object does occur and expressions of primary process then include profound signs of depression and loss. In the absence of compensatory defense and in the actual relinquishing of the object, the subject is finally and totally bereft. The emotional state of the subject during such primary process manifestations can reveal intense despair, resignation, suicidal ruminations, as well as suicidal acting-out. During such depressive and despairing times, the magnitude of such pain can be considered psychically equivalent to experiences of punishment. The sense of punishment is evident in familiar phrases repeated by individuals in such painful circumstances: "Why is this happening to me?"; "What did I ever do to deserve this?"; or "Why is God punishing me?" This depressive dispositional state is here considered to contain a superego nature or to suggest superego imperatives. Even in the dreams of such persons, when the dream content contains the death of a loved one, feelings of grief are so vivid and penetrating that the dreamer awakens crying or sobbing. Despite the realization that it was a nightmare, the subject's feelings of despair and grief are so poignant that such feelings remain etched in the person's psyche. Years later, such nightmares are still soberly remembered and constitute one example of the kind of psychological product generated by primary process experiences that characterize the depressive disposition.

Table 4.8 represents the emotion–personality structure of this depressive chain in which the various levels of the personality are listed, including secondary process aims as well as primary process manifestations.

On the level of secondary process, the manic and depressive lines of development reflect opposite dispositions. In the manic personality the secondary process aim is to accomplish enormous work aims and, through this output of energy, to possess the object. The secondary process aim of the depressed personality is to attempt to reintegrate the object in order to regain the equilibrium of the subject–object relationship. In both cases, the manic and the depressed, an intense focus on the object reveals the importance of the object to the subject and the overall deep emotional investment in the object.

On the primary process level however, the manic person reveals dyscontrolled behavior in the form of flagrant sexuality. It is assumed that this sexual dyscontrol is, with respect to its psychic nature, attributable to an id quality. In contrast, the depressed personality, under the pressure of primary process superego urges and in the absence of compensatory mechanisms, finally relinquishes the continuous focus on the object. The subject then shows bizarre and strongly directed self-destructive impulses usually expressed in suicidal gestures.

TABLE 4.8
EMOTION–PERSONALITY STRUCTURE OF THE
SORROW–DEPRESSIVE CHAIN

Prototype pattern or mode: Reintegration
Behavioral act: Reaction to loss
Basic or core emotion: Sorrow, grief
Personality traits: Despondent, gloomy
Diagnostic disposition: Depressed
Defense mechanism: Compensation
Dream and nightmare: Crying grief
Intrapsychic property: Superego
Cognitive orientation: Rumination, continuous focus on object
Secondary process aim: Attempt to reintegrate object with subject
Primary process manifestation: Relinquishment of object and experiences of loss and abandonment, suicidal rumination as well as suicidal acting out

CONCLUSION

This overview of the emotion–personality system, as well as the proposed connection of the system to secondary process aims and the organization of primary process, suggests that psychopathological behaviors associated with primary process are not random or in any way less consistent within the infrastructure of personality than any other aspect of personality. Rather, the myriad pathological products and varieties of psychopathology identified as primary process are proposed here to be determined by the nature of particular emotion-diagnostic dispositions, to which they correspond as well as by the breakdown of secondary process associated with each emotion-diagnostic chain.

The primary process has been conventionally considered the purest example of severe psychopathology, and, further, it has been understood solely as a phenomenon of scattered, random, and bizarre productions that are untraceable and not connected in any systematic way to the secondary process. Yet, the formulations presented in this chapter offer one way to understand the relation of psychopathology and personality within the infrastructure of a basic system of emotion-diagnostic chains that include direct references to the domain of primary process.

REFERENCES

Arieti, S. (1966). Creativity and its cultivation: Relation to psychopathology. In S. Arieti (Ed.), *American handbook of psychiatry* (Vol. 3). New York: Basic Books.

Fast, I. (1983). Primary process cognition: A reformulation. In *The annual of psychoanalysis* (Vol. 2). Chicago, IL: Chicago Institute for Psychoanalysis.

Freud, S. (1954). The origins of psychoanalysis: Letters to Wilhelm Fliess, drafts and notes. *Project for a scientific psychology,* New York: Basic Books. (Original work published 1887–1902)

Freud, S. (1953). The interpretation of dreams. In J. Strachey (Ed. and Trans.). *The standard edition of the complete psychological works of Sigmund Freud* (Vols. 4 and 5). London: Hogarth Press. (Original work published 1900)

Fromm, E. (1978–1979). Primary and secondary process in waking and in altered states of consciousness. *Journal of Altered States of Consciousness,* **4**(2), 115–128.

Holt, R. (1956). Gauging primary and secondary process in Rorschach responses. *Journal of Projective Techniques,* **20**, 14–25.

Kellerman, H. (1979). *Group psychotherapy and personality: Intersecting structures.* New York: Grune & Stratton.

Kellerman, H. (1980). A structural model of emotion and personality: Psychoanalytic and sociobiological implications. In R. Plutchik & H. Kellerman (Eds.), *Emotion: Theory, research and experience: Vol. 1. Theories of emotion.* New York: Academic Press.

Kellerman, H. (1983). An epigenetic theory of emotions in early development. In R. Plutchik & H. Kellerman (Eds.), *Emotion: Theory, research and experience: Vol. 2. Emotions in early development.* New York: Academic Press.

Kellerman, H. (1987). Nightmares and the structure of personality. In H. Kellerman (Ed.), *The nightmare: Psychological and biological foundations* (pp. 271–356). New York: Columbia University Press.

Kellerman, H. (1989). Projective measures of emotion. In R. Plutchik & H. Kellerman (Eds.), *Emotion: Theory, research and experience: Vol. 4. The measurement of emotion.* San Diego, CA: Academic Press.

Kellerman, H., & Plutchik, R. (1977). The meaning of tension in group therapy. In L. Wolberg & M. Aronson (Eds.), *Group therapy 1977.* New York: Stratton Intercontinental Medical Book Corp.

Meloy, J. R. (1986). On the relationship between primary process and thought disorder. *British Journal of Medical Psychology,* **14**(1), 47–56.

Palombo, S. R. (1985). The primary process: A reconceptualization. *Psychoanalytic Inquiry,* **5**(3), 405–435.

Plutchik, R. (1962). *The emotions: Facts, theories and a new model.* New York: Random House.

Plutchik, R. (1980a). *Emotion: A psychoevolutionary synthesis.* New York: Harper & Row.

Plutchik, R. (1980b). A psychoevolutionary theory of emotion. In R. Plutchik & H. Kellerman (Eds.), *Emotion: Theory, research and experience: Vol. 1. Theories of emotion.* New York: Academic Press.

Plutchik, R. (1984). Emotions: A general psychoevolutionary theory. In K. R. Scherer & P. Ekman (Eds.), *Approaches to emotion.* Hillsdale, NJ: Erlbaum.

Plutchik, R. (1989). The measurement of emotions and their derivatives. In R. Plutchik & H. Kellerman (Eds.), *Emotion: Theory, research and experience: Vol. 4. The measurement of emotion.* San Diego, CA: Academic Press.

Rapaport, D. (1957). *Seminars on advanced metapsychology* (Vols. 1 & 2). Stockbridge, MA: Austin Riggs Center (mimeo).

Rapaport, D., Gill, M. M., & Schafer, R. (1970). *Diagnostic psychological testing.* London: University of London Press.

Urist, J. (1980). The continuum between primary and secondary process thinking: Toward a concept of borderline thought. In J. Kawar *et al.* (Eds.), *Borderline phenomena and the Rorschach Test* (pp. 133–154). Madison, CT: International Universities Press.

Chapter 5

NEW PERSPECTIVES
IN PSYCHOANALYTIC AFFECT THEORY

OTTO F. KERNBERG

ABSTRACT

*A theory of affects is proposed, based upon the exploration of affects in the psycho-
analytic situation. The correspondence between structural characteristics of affects as
revealed in the psychoanalytic situation and recent neuropsychological and developmental studies of affects is noted. Affects are seen as the "building blocks" of drives. The
latter are conceived as hierarchically supraordinate motivational systems that organize
their component affects along a "libidinal" and "aggressive" line and are clinically
reflected in signal affect states.*

*Early object relations are seen as determining the cognitive aspects of affects. Early
representations of self and others, framed in the context of an affect state, are fixed in the
form of an affective memory. It is further proposed that internalization of early object
relations determines the organization of the tripartite structure. These findings are correlated with Mahler's developmental schemas. Thus the psychoanalytic theory of drives and
an object-relations theory are linked by the structural and developmental character of
early affects.*

Marjorie Brierley (1937) was the first to point to a strange paradox regarding
the role of affects in psychoanalytic theory and practice. Affects, she said, play a
central role in the clinical situation but a peripheral and ambiguous one in
psychoanalytic theory. Brierley thought that if the part played by affects could be
clarified, it might correspondingly lead to clarifying issues in drive theory that

were still unresolved. I believe the paradox Brierley drew attention to half a century ago still existed until recently. Brierley opposed the tendency of analysts to explore drive theory without regard to the role of affects. Only in the last 10 years has this situation begun to change. In the following, a reexamination of the relation between affects and drives in psychoanalytic theory is presented. I shall examine Freud's changing theories of drives and affects and recent psychoanalytic contributions—including my own—to these issues, and I shall propose an integrated psychoanalytic theory of affects and drives. I shall then examine both the nature of affects as they emerge in the psychoanalytic situation and their distortions under the impact of defensive processes and conclude with a developmental model based upon my conceptual frame.

DRIVES AND INSTINCTS

Although Freud recognized the ultimate biological sources of the drives as psychic motivational systems, he repeatedly stressed the lack of information available regarding the processes that would transform these biological predispositions into purely psychic motivation. His concept of libido or the sexual drive was that of a hierarchically supraordinate integration or organization of developmentally earlier, partial sexual drives. This idea of the organization of early partial sexual drives is in accordance with his concept of drives as psychic in nature. According to Freud, the partial drives (oral, anal, voyeuristic, sadistic, etc.) are psychologically integrated in the course of development and are not physiologically linked. The dual drive theory of sexuality and aggression (1920/1955) represents his final classification of drives as the ultimate source of unconscious psychic conflict and psychic structure formation.

While Freud described biological sources of the sexual drives according to the excitability of the erotogenic zones, he did not describe such concrete biological sources for aggression. In contrast to the fixed sources of libido, the aims and objects of both sexual and aggressive drives were characterized as changing throughout psychic development, and the developmental continuity of sexual and aggressive motivations could be recognized in a broad variety of complex psychic developments.

I agree with Holder (1970) that Freud clearly differentiated drives from instincts. He saw the drives as supraordinate, psychological, and constant rather than intermittent sources of motivation. He saw instincts, on the other hand, as biological, inherited, and intermittent in the sense that they are activated by physiological and/or environmental stimulation. Freud conceived of drives as on the boundary between the physical and the mental; they were psychic processes rooted in biological dispositions. He proposed (1915/1957a, 1915/1957b) that the only way we can know about drives is through their psychic representatives—ideas and affects. Libido is a drive, hunger is an instinct.

Both Holder (1970) and Laplanche and Pontalis (1973, pp. 214–217) have stressed the purely psychic nature of Freud's dual drive theory and have pointed to the loss of this distinction between psychological drives and biological instincts in the *Standard Edition's* consistent translation of both *Instinkt* and *Trieb* as 'instincts'. In my view, that translation has had the unfortunate effect of linking Freud's drive concept too closely with biology and has inhibited psychoanalytic research into the nature of the mediating processes that link biological instincts to drives defined as purely psychic motivation. The very term instinct stresses the biological realm of this concept and discourages, therefore, psychoanalytic exploration of motivation. It is my view—to be elaborated upon in what follows—that the concept of drives as hierarchically supraordinate psychic motivational systems is valid and that Freud's dual drive theory is satisfactory to explain such motivation.

As Laplanche and Pontalis (1973) appropriately stress, Freud always referred to instincts as discontinuous, inherited behavior patterns that vary little from one member of the species to another. It is impressive how closely Freud's concept of instinct relates to modern instinct theory in biology as represented, for example, by Lorenz (1963), Tinbergen (1951), and Wilson (1975). These investigators consider instincts as hierarchical organizations of biologically determined perceptive, behavioral, and communicative patterns, released by environmental factors that activate inborn releasing mechanisms. Such a biological–environmental system is considered an epigenetical phenomenon. As Lorenz and Tinbergen illustrated in their animal research, the maturational and developmental linkage of discrete inborn behavior patterns, their overall organization within a particular individual, is very much determined by the nature of environmental stimulation: hierarchically organized instincts represent the integration of both inborn dispositions and environmentally determined learning. Instincts, in this view, are hierarchically organized biological motivational systems. They are usually classified along the lines of feeding behavior, fight–flight behavior, or mating and perhaps of other such dimensions.

Freud changed his definition of the concept of affects at least twice (Rapaport, 1953). He originally (Freud, 1894/1962) considered affects pretty much equivalent to drives; later (1915/1957a, 1915/1957b), he considered them discharge processes of drives (particularly their pleasurable or painful, psychomotor, and neurovegetative features); eventually (1926), he considered them inborn dispositions (thresholds and channels) of the ego. In my view, affects are instinctive structures, that is, biologically given, developmentally activated psychophysiological patterns that include psychic components, and it is this psychic aspect that becomes organized to constitute the aggressive and libidinal drives described by Freud. The partial sexual drives, in this view, are more limited, restricted integrations of corresponding affect states, while libido as a drive is the hier-archically supraordinate integration of them, that is, the integration of all erot-ically centered affect states. Therefore, in contrast to the still quite prevalent view within psychoanalysis of affects as merely discharge processes, I consider them the bridging structures between biological instincts and psychic drives. I shall present supportive arguments for this conclusion following further elabora-tion of my definitions of affects and emotions.

AFFECTS AND EMOTIONS

Following Brierley (1937) and Jacobson (1953/1971a) from the clinical psy-choanalytic field, and Arnold (1970a, 1970b), Izard (1978), Knapp (1978), and Emde (1987; Emde, Gaensbauer, & Harmon, 1978) from the field of empirical research on affective behavior in neuropsychology, I define affects as psycho-physiological behavior patterns that include a specific cognitive appraisal; a specific expressive facial pattern; a subjective experience of a pleasurable, re-warding, or painful, aversive quality; and a muscular and neurovegetative dis-charge pattern. The expressive facial pattern is part of the general communicative pattern that differentiates each particular affect.

There exists today fairly general agreement that affects from their very origin have a cognitive aspect and contain at least an appraisal of "good" or "bad" of the immediate perceptual constellation, an appraisal that, in Arnold's (1970a, 1970b) formulation, determines a felt motivation for action either toward or away from a certain stimulus or situation. In contrast to the older James–Lange theory (James, 1884; Lange, 1885, 1887/1922), which held that the subjective and cognitive aspects of affects follow or are derived from the perception of the muscular and neurovegetative discharge phenomena, and in contrast to the de-rived position of Tomkins (1970) that the cognitive and felt aspect of affects follow or are derived from the perception of their facial expression, I think—for reasons to be spelled out below—that the subjective quality of felt appraisal is the core characteristic of each affect.

Affects can be classified as primitive or derived. The former make their appearance within the first 2 to 3 years of life and have an intense, global quality, with the cognitive element diffuse and not well differentiated. Derived affects are more complex; they consist of combinations of the primitive affects cognitively elaborated; unlike primitive affects, they may not show all their original compo-nents with equal strength and their psychic aspects gradually come to dominate the psychophysiological and facial communicative ones. For these more complex phenomena I would reserve the term *emotions* or *feelings*. The distinction corre-sponds to the clinical observations regarding primitive affect states and complex emotional developments in the psychoanalytic situation.

AFFECTS AND DRIVES

Freud had proposed (at the time he formulated his second affect theory) that drives are manifest by means of psychic representations or ideas—that is, the cognitive expression of the drive—and affect. In this second theory of affect (which replaced the first one in which the concepts of affect and drive were practically interchangeable), Freud proposed that affects are discharge processes that can reach consciousness but do not undergo repression, and that only the mental representation of the drive is repressed, together with a memory of or a disposition to the activation of the corresponding affect (Freud, 1915/1957a, 1915/1957b).

In clinical psychoanalysis, the idea that affects could not be dynamically unconscious has been a conceptual problem, and one could ask to what extent Freud's exclusive stress on the discharge aspects of affects in his second theory was a consequence of the then dominant James–Lange theory of affects. In any case, we now have important neuropsychological evidence to show that affects may be stored in the limbic brain structures as affective memory (Arnold, 1984, Chaps. 11 & 12).

If affects and emotions are complex structures, including subjective experiences of pain or pleasure with particular cognitive and expressive–communicative implications, and neurovegetative discharge patterns, and if they are present—as infant research has demonstrated (Emde, 1987; Emde et al., 1978; Izard, 1978; Stern, 1985)—from the earliest weeks and months of life, are they the primary motivational forces of psychic development? If they include both cognitive and affective features, what is left in the broader concept of drive that is not contained in the concept of affect? Freud implied that the drives are present from birth on, but he also implied that they matured and developed. It can be argued, of course, that the maturation and development of affects are expressions of the underlying drives, but if all the functions and manifestations of drives can be included in the functions and manifestations of developing affects, a concept of independent drives underlying the organization of affects would be difficult to sustain. In fact, the transformation, combination, and integration of affects throughout development; the integration of drives with internalized object relations; and their overall developing dichotomy into pleasurable ones building up the libidinal series versus painful ones building up the aggressive series all point to the enormous richness and complexity of their cognitive as well as affective elements. I believe the following, mutually complementary considerations are relevant.

First, the traditional psychoanalytic concept of affects as only discharge processes, and the assumption that decrease of psychic tension leads to pleasure whereas increase of psychic tension leads to unpleasure, has unnecessarily complicated the analysis of affects in the clinical situation. Jacobson (1953/1971a), called attention to the fact that tension states (such as sexual excitement) may be pleasurable and discharge states (such as anxiety) may be unpleasurable, and she concluded, in agreement with the view already suggested by Brierley (1937), that affects are not only discharge processes but complex and sustained intrapsychic tensions.

Jacobson also described in great detail how the cognitive aspects of affects refer to their investment of self and object representations in both ego and superego. She concluded that affective investments of self and object representations constitute the clinical manifestations of drives. In other words, whenever a drive derivative in the clinical situation is diagnosed, for example, a sexual or aggressive impulse, the patient's total experience at that point always includes an image or representation of self relating to an image or representation of another person ("object") under the impact of the corresponding sexual or aggressive affect. And whenever an affect state of the patient is explored, a cognitive aspect of it is found, usually a relation of the self to an object under the impact of the affect state. The cognitive elements of drives, Jacobson went on, are represented by the cognitive relations between self- and object representations, and between self and actual objects.

In clarifying the relations between affects and moods, Jacobson (1957/1971b) defined moods as a temporary fixation and generalization of affects throughout the entire world of internalized object relations, that is, a generalization of an affect state throughout all self- and object representations of the individual for a limited time span. Moods are thus extended yet relatively subdued affect states that color, for a time being, the entire world of internalized object relations.

AFFECT AND OBJECT

I propose that early affective development is based on a direct fixation of early, affectively imbued object relations in the form of affective memory. In fact, the work of Emde, Izard, and Stern points to the central function of object relations in the activation of affects. This connection of object relations to the activation of affects supports the proposal of fixation in memory of early affect states involving such object relations.

Second, I propose that the activation of different affect states toward the same object takes place under the dominance of different developmental tasks and biologically activated, instinctive behavior patterns. This variety of affect states directed to the same object may provide an economic explanation for how affects are linked and transformed into a supraordinate motivational series that becomes the sexual or aggressive drive. For example, the pleasurable oral stimulations during nursing and the pleasurable anal stimulations during toilet training may bring about a condensation of pleasurable interactions with mother that link such oral and anal libidinal developments. In contrast, the enraged reaction to frustrations during the oral period and the corresponding power struggles during the anal period may link consonant aggressive affect states, thus integrating the aggressive drive. Further, the infant's intense positive affective investment of mother during the practicing stage of separation individuation (Mahler, Pine, & Bergman, 1975) may become linked with a sexually imbued longing for her derived from the activation of genital feelings in the oedipal stage of development.

Third, if we consider affects as the primary, psychobiological "building blocks" of drives, and as the earliest motivational systems, we still have to explain how they become organized into supraordinate hierarchical systems. Why not say that the primary affects themselves are the ultimate motivational systems? In my view, there exists a multitude of complex secondary combinations and transformations of affects, so that a theory of motivation based on affects rather than on two basic drives would be complicated and clinically unsatisfactory. I also believe that the unconscious organization and integration of affectively determined early experience requires assuming a higher level of motivational organization than that represented by affect states per se. We need to assume a motivational organization that does justice to the complex integration of all affective developments in relation to the parental objects.

By the same token, an effort to replace both drive and affect theory with an attachment theory or an object-relations theory that rejects the concepts of drives naturally leads to a restriction of the complexity of intrapsychic life by stressing only the positive or libidinal elements of attachment and by neglecting the unconscious organization of aggression. Although, in theory, this should not be necessarily so, in practice, those object-relations theoreticians who have rejected drive theory have, in my view, also seriously neglected the motivational aspects of aggression.

AFFECT AND INTRAPSYCHIC FORCES

For all these reasons, I think we should not replace a drive theory by an affect theory or by an object-relations theory of motivation. In short, it seems eminently reasonable to consider affects as the building blocks of drives. Affects are thus the link between biologically determined instinctive components, on the one hand, and intrapsychic organization of the overall drives, on the other. The correspondence of the series of rewarding and aversive affect states with the dual lines of libido and aggression makes sense from a clinical and theoretical perspective.

This concept of affects as the building blocks of drives, I believe, resolves some chronic problems in the psychoanalytic theory of drives. The concept of affects as the building blocks of drives broadens the concept of erotogenic zones as the "source" of libido into a general consideration of all physiologically activated functions and bodily zones that become involved in affectively invested interactions of the infant and child with mother. These functions include the shift from concerns with bodily functions to concerns with social functions and role enactments. My proposed concept also provides the missing links, within psychoanalytic theory, of the sources of aggressively invested infant–mother interactions, the "zonal" function of aggressive rejection of oral ingestion, anal control, direct physical power struggles linked with temper tantrums, etc. It is affectively invested object relations that energize physiological "zones."

The sequential psychophysiological activation of early distress, rage, and fear and, later on, of depression and guilt determines the corresponding series of aggressive self- and object investments. These investments are reactivated in the unconscious conflicts with respect to aggression that are expressed in the transference. The direct internalization of libidinal and aggressive affective dispositions as part of self- and object representations (in technical terms, "internalized object relations") integrated within ego and superego structures represents, within my formulation, the libidinal and aggressive investments of these structures.

The id, according to this concept of the relation between drives and affects, consists of repressed, intensely aggressive or sexualized internalized object relations. The condensation and displacement characteristic of id formations reflects the linkage of affectively related self- and object representations of the corresponding aggressive, libidinal, and, later on, combined series.

This concept also permits us to do justice to the biologically determined input of new affective experiences throughout life. These new affective experiences include the activation of intense sexual excitement during adolescence, where erotically excited affect states become integrated with the corresponding genital excitement and erotically charged emotions and fantasies derived from the oedipal stage of development. In other words, the intensification of drives (both libidinal and aggressive) at various stages of the life cycle is determined by the new incorporation of psychophysiologically activated affect states into the preexistent, hierarchically organized affect systems.

More generally speaking, in my view, once the organization of drives as the supraordinate hierarchical motivational systems has been consolidated, any particular activation of drives in the context of intrapsychic conflict is represented by the activation of a corresponding affect state. This affect state includes an internalized object relation, basically, a particular self-representation relating to a particular object representation under the impact of a particular affect. The reciprocal role relation between self and object that is framed by the corresponding affect is usually expressed as a concrete fantasy or wish. Affects, in short, become the signals or representatives of drives as well as their originating building blocks. This view of affects, while in contrast to Freud's second theory of affects, is in consonance with both his first and third theories: with the first theory, in linking affects and drives; with the third theory, in stressing the inborn disposition to affects that characterize the original ego–id intrapsychic matrix.

AFFECTS IN THE PSYCHOANALYTIC SITUATION

Having described a theory of drive development, I return to the clinical manifestations of affects to support the suggestion formulated by Brierley and Jacobson that clinically we always work with affects or emotions, and that affects are complex intrapsychic structures rather than simply discharge processes.

The psychoanalytic situation provides a unique way of exploring all kinds of affects—from primitive (such as rage or sexual excitement) to cognitively differentiated, toned-down affect states. As Brierley (1937) and Jacobson (1953/1971a) pointed out, affects include a basic subjective experience of a pleasurable or a painful quality. The subjective experiences of pleasure and pain are usually differentiated from each other but can under certain conditions be mixed or combined.

Affects differ quantitatively as well as qualitatively: the intensity of subjective experiences varies, usually observable in physiological "discharge" patterns and/or psychomotor behavior. The patient's behavior also serves to communicate to the analyst the patient's subjective experience. Thus, the communicative functions of affects are central to the transference and permit the analyst to empathize with and internally respond emotionally to the patient's experience. The ideational content of affects is important in relation to the psychoanalytic exploration of all affects, particularly primitive ones that, on initial impression, may seem to be almost devoid of cognitive content. Psychoanalytic exploration of intense affect storms in regressed patients, in my experience, consistently demonstrates that there is no such thing as a "pure" affect without cognitive content.

The affects we observe in the psychoanalytic situation not only always have cognitive content, but—and this is, I think, a crucial finding—they always have an object-relations aspect as well; that is, they express a relation between an aspect of the patient's self and an aspect of one or another of his object representations. Furthermore, the affect in the psychoanalytic situation either directly reflects or else complements a reactivated internal object relation.

In the transference, an affect state recapitulates a significant past object relation of the patient. Indeed all actualizations of an object relation in the transference contain a certain affect state as well.

DEFENSIVE DISTORTIONS

In earlier work (Kernberg, 1984, Chap. 13) I proposed that clinically the manifestations of impulse–defense configurations in the psychoanalytic situation may be conceptualized as the activation of certain object relations in conflict; one side of the configuration is defensive, the other reflects the impulse or drive-derivative side of the conflict. The masochistic suffering of an hysterical patient who experiences the analyst as frustrating and punitive may serve as a defense against the patient's underlying sexual excitement, fantasies, and implied positive oedipal strivings: the mixture of sorrow, rage, and self-pity may reflect an affect state with defensive functions directed against repressed sexual excitement. In fact, whenever, clinically speaking, we point to the defensive use of one drive against another, we are actually referring to the defensive function of one affect against another.

The defensive process itself, however, frequently disrupts the affect state. For example, the cognitive aspects of the affect may be repressed or, in other cases, the subjective experience of it; or else, all but the psychomotor aspects of the affect may undergo repression. When the affect state is disrupted then the predominant object relation in the transference is interfered with and the patient's full awareness of his own subjective experience is obscured. The analyst's capacity for empathic understanding is also thereby thwarted. Consider, for example, listening to an obsessive patient's ruminating sexual thoughts but not to their affective, sexually excited qualities, which remain in repression; or a hysterical patient's intense and dramatic affect storm, which obscures the cognitive content of the experience; or a narcissistic patient speaking in what sounds like highly emotional tones while his or her total behavior bespeaks an absence or unavailability of any emotional communication. This dissociation of various components of affects in the service of defense may give the impression that the subjective experience of affects is separate from their cognitive, behavioral, and communicative aspects, particularly in the initial stages of treatment or when resistance is high.

This defensive dissociation seems to illustrate the traditional psychological view that affect, perception, cognition, and action are separate ego functions. But when these defensive operations are worked through, and as the deeper layers of the patient's intrapsychic experience gradually emerge, the psychoanalyst encounters the integration of these various components of affects. When the nature of the unconscious conflict that develops in the transference is more primitive, then the affects appear as full-blown, complex processes centering on a subjective experience, but with a full complement of cognitive, physiological, behavioral, and communicative aspects, and expressing a specific relation between the patient's self and the corresponding object representation in the transference.

These observations confirm, I believe, recent neuropsychological research on affects, which contradicts the traditional idea that affects, cognition, communicative behavior, and object relations develop separately (Emde, 1987; Emde et al., 1978; Hoffman, 1978; Izard, 1978; Plutchik, 1980; Plutchik and Kellerman, 1983; Stern, 1985). Affects thus can be seen as complex psychic structures that are indissolubly linked to the individual's cognitive appraisals of his immediate situation, and that contain a positive or negative valence with regard to the relation of the subject to the object of the particular experience. Affects, therefore, because of this cognitive appraisal component, have a motivational aspect.

Arnold's (1970a, 1970b) definition of emotions—that they are a felt action tendency based on appraisal—is relevant here. Arnold's concept of "emotion" corresponds to what I refer to as "affect." I prefer to reserve the term emotion for affects with highly differentiated cognitive contents and relatively mild or moderate psychomotor and/or neurovegetative components. Arnold described two components of emotion: one static, the appraisal; and one dynamic, the impulse toward what is appraised as good or the impulse away from what is appraised as bad. If Arnold reflects, as I believe she does, a general trend of contemporary neuropsychological research on affects, this trend is remarkably concordant with the clinical findings on affects in the psychoanalytic situation spelled out by Brierley (1937) and Jacobson (1953/1971a).

When intense affect states are activated in the transference, a gratifying or frustrating, corresponding past object relation is recalled, together with the effort either to reactivate that object relation if it was gratifying or to escape from it if it was painful. This process of juxtaposition, in fact, defines the origin of fantasy, namely, the juxtaposition of an evoked remembered state with a future desired state in the context of a current perception that motivates the desire for change. This formation of fantasy is thus a juxtaposition that reflects the simultaneity of past, present, and future that is characteristic of the id, predating the awareness and acceptance of objective space–time constraints that characterize the differentiated ego (Jaques, 1982).

PRIMITIVE REPRESENTATIONS AND PEAK AFFECT STATES

From such a primordial integration of primitive affective memory linking "all-good" or "all-bad" peak affect states stems the development of more specific wishful fantasies linking self and object that characterizes unconscious fantasy in general. Peak affect states represent, by definition, extremely desirable (pleasurable) or undesirable (painful) experiences that motivate intense desires to reinstate or, respectively, to avoid similar affective experiences. These desires, expressed in concrete unconscious wishes, determine the motivational repertoire of the id.

Peak affect experiences may facilitate the internalization of primitive object relations organized along the axis of rewarding or "all good" versus aversive or "all bad." In other words, the experience of self and object under the impact of extreme affect activation acquires an intensity that facilitates the laying down of affective memory structures. Originally, in these internalizations, self- and object representations are not yet differentiated from each other. Fused, undifferentiated or condensed "all-good" self- and object representations are built up separately from equally fused, undifferentiated or condensed "all-bad" self- and object representations. These earliest intrapsychic structures of the symbiotic stage of development (Mahler & Furer, 1968) would correspond both to the beginning of structure formation of internalized object relations and to the beginning of overall organization of libidinal and aggressive drives. The structural characteristics associated with the id are based upon a combination of several factors: (1) the primitive, diffuse, and overwhelming nature of early affective memory derived from peak affects; (2) the undifferentiated quality of early subjectivity and early consciousness; and (3) the rudimentary nature of symbolic functions in the context of condensation of past, present, and evoked future.

Peak affect states may have very different developmental consequences from low-level, mild, or modulated affect states: these latter ones may directly contribute to ego development. Parallel mother–infant interaction and learning under conditions of mild or modulated affect states might set up memory structures reflecting more discriminatory and instrumental relations to the immediate psychosocial environment. In other words, ordinary learning may occur under conditions of low or mild affect activation, where alertness is focused on the immediate situation and tasks, with little distortion derived from affective arousal, and no particular defensive mechanism interferes with learning. These memory structures constitute the early forerunners, we might say, of more specialized adaptive ego functioning, the affective memory structures of early consciousness.

AFFECTS AND EARLY
SUBJECTIVE EXPERIENCE

What evidence do we have that the early manifestations of affects imply the infant's subjective awareness of pain or pleasure? This question implicitly argues against early subjectivity, early intrapsychic experience before the development of linguistic capacities, and early activation of intrapsychic motivational systems. In response to this question of relating the manifestations of affects to the infant's subjective awareness of pain or pleasure, the study of tension states in infants following the presentation of stimuli that activate affects in them—as for example, in the study of heart rate—indicates modification in tensions (either increase or decrease) according to the cognitive implications of such stimuli. In other words, there is beginning evidence of an increase or decrease of intrapsychic tension prior to the time when the expressive and discharge patterns of affect become apparent (Sroufe, 1979; Sroufe, Waters, & Matas, 1974).

There is also evidence that the diencephalic centers that mediate the experience of aversive or rewarding qualities of perception are fully mature at birth. The maturity of these centers supports the assumption of an early capacity for experiencing pleasure and pain. In addition, the surprisingly early infant capacities for cognitive differentiation provide indirect evidence for a potential of affective differentiations as well. It seems reasonable to assume that the 3-month-old is able to experience emotions and not only show behavioral evidence of pleasure as well as of rage or disappointment (Izard, 1978). This point is developed at great length in Plutchik and Kellerman's (1983) *Emotions in Early Development.*

DEVELOPMENT OF CONSCIOUSNESS

Regarding the nature of early subjectivity and early self-experience, it is reasonable to assume that affective subjectivity constitutes the primordial experience of an experiential self, self as subjective awareness of states of pleasure and unpleasure that simultaneously imply a certain degree of general arousal and a certain degree of neurovegetative tension as well. Affective subjectivity, the primordial experience of self, probably contributes to the integration—in the form of affective memory—of the perceptual, behavioral, interactional, and affective schemas themselves.

It would also seem reasonable to assume that such an assembly of memory structures under the impact of peak affects may spur the earliest symbolic activities in the sense that one element of a peak affect constellation stands for the entire constellation (for example, a light going on in the room represents the presence of the feeding mother even before she herself is perceived). One could argue the question that asks at what point simple association and conditioned reflexes become transformed into symbolic thinking, in the sense that one element stands for an entire constellation of evoked experience outside the rigid linkage of conditioned associations. In any case, it would be reasonable to assume that the earliest symbolic function, an active representation of an entire sequence by one element of it, placed outside the rigid associative chain would occur precisely under conditions of peak affect states.

Peak affect states, then, would signal the transformation of affective subjectivity into mental activity with symbolic functions. These symbolic functions can be clinically represented by affective-memory structures that reflect pleasurable relations of infant and mother. In these pleasurable infant–mother relations, in spite of their highly differentiated, cognitive inborn schemata, self- and object representations are as yet undifferentiated. Affective-memory structures derived from the unpleasurable or painful peak affect states in which self- and object representations are also undifferentiated are built up separately from the pleasurable ones.

Mahler's (Mahler & Furer, 1968) symbiotic stage of development would correspond to these two parallel series of early states of consciousness that do not yet include awareness of one's awareness (or self-awareness), that is, a categorical self. Perhaps of particular importance here is the gradual development of two parallel series of "all-good" and "all-bad" fantasied characteristics of this symbiotic world. The first "all-good" world is expressed through the excited pleasure connected with the evoked and realized presence of the "good" mother. The second "all-bad" symbolic world concerns the evoked and fantastically imagined "bad" mother under conditions of extreme frustration, pain, or rage. In this connection, the fact is that infant observation is carried out mostly under conditions of the infant's "alert inactivity," facilitated by pleasurable affective states in mother–infant interaction. Infant observation has not focused sufficiently on the nature of behavioral developments under conditions of serious frustration. This restricted investigative strategy creates a problem in understanding the infant's subjectively painful, frightening, and enraged experiences that are so prevalent under conditions of severe psychopathology (Kaplan, 1987). By the same token, the transformation of painful experiences into the symbolic image of an undifferentiated "bad self–bad mother" obviously contains an element of fantasy that transcends the realistic character of the "good" self–object representations. The aggressively invested line of internalized object relations may be more unrealistic, is also traumatic and more difficult to tolerate in consciousness, and is more difficult to elaborate into the realm of the ego. Early dissociative mechanisms may defend the ego against the full awareness of these traumatic experiences and foster their repression later on. Therefore, the original fantasy material of what is to later become the repressed unconscious may reflect a predominance of aggressive imagery and affects over the libidinal ones.

The next stage of development of consciousness would naturally coincide with the beginning of the stage of separation–individuation (Mahler et al., 1975), probably beginning with the 4th or 5th month of life, in which both cognitive and affective development contribute to reducing the extreme nature of unpleasurable or painful experiences, and in which the infant gradually differentiates perceptions of the self from those of the mother under both pleasurable and painful conditions. The stability of proprioceptive experiences under varying affective interactions with mother, in short, the developing body image, contributes importantly to this differentiation. The building up of self-representations now separate from but relating to object representations implies awareness both of an interaction and of the self as subject of such interaction. At this stage, the existence of self-awareness has to be definitely assumed. Now primordial experiences reflecting affective subjectivity are transformed into the self-awareness that is a correlate of differentiated self- and object representations. This self-awareness, reflecting the consolidation of self-representations, reflects the early stage of a categorical self and is in contrast to the global, diffuse nature of awareness that preceded it.

The next stage in the development of consciousness is reflected in the completion of the stage of separation–individuation toward the end of the rapprochement crisis at the completion of the 3rd year of life (Mahler, 1972). At this point, "good" and "bad" self-representations built up under opposite affective conditions are integrated into a global concept of the self, while "good" and "bad" object representations are, in turn, integrated. Now there are manifestations of the affect of guilt, a crucial landmark signaling the integration of part into total object relations. What happens is that the capacity for experiencing guilt depends on the capacity to be aware that the "bad" object hated by the self is, at the same time, also the "good" object loved by the self, and that the "good" and "bad" self are also one. The integration of contradictory, "good" and "bad," aspects of object representations is a precondition for the related capacity for experiencing other people in depth, similar to the deepening of self-awareness and self-knowledge achieved when "good" and "bad" self-representations are consolidated into an integrated conception of the self. At this point the establishment of full continuity of self-awareness is fulfilled, and, by the same token, an integrated structure of the self, the definite categorical self, emerges within the ego.

We may now add that, in terms of the development of defensive operations, the original lack of integration of contradictory ego–id states (corresponding to contradictory peak affect states) is gradually transformed into an active mechanism of ego splitting. Splitting or primitive dissociation and other related, primitive defenses culminate in the rapprochement subphase of separation–individuation, then to be replaced, at the time of the consolidation of the self, with the development of repression and other related, more advanced defensive mechanisms. This defensive process based upon repression leads to the consolidation of the dynamic unconscious, the id as an organized mental structure.

All these considerations may generate psychoanalytic hypotheses regarding certain developmental features of affects in the first 3 years of life. For example, the development of stranger aversion or anxiety around the 8th to 10th month of life (following an increased degree of stranger wariness in the 2 or 3 preceding months) may be understood in new ways. This stranger anxiety may reflect not only the maturation of an inborn affective disposition to fear responses. It may also reflect the beginning of projective mechanisms dealing with primitive, unconscious, fused "all bad" self- and object representations or "negative schemata," which represent the earliest organization of aggression as a drive. The projection of "all-bad" object relations on the feared stranger may protect the image of the "all-good" mother from "contamination" with aggression.

One of the unresolved problems of infant-affect research is the necessarily limited nature of experiments carried out under conditions of infant suffering or aversive stimulation. It is as if the aggressive side of human experience were being neglected, thus implicitly colluding with the natural tendencies of the human being, including, presumably, the infant, to mobilize all resources available to deny or escape from painful experience.

To conclude, I have suggested that the understanding of affects as complex intrapsychic structures, as important features of the manifestations of impulse–defense configurations in the transference and as developmental markers of the growing world of internalized object relations, should contribute to clarifying further the place and nature of drives in psychoanalytic theory.

REFERENCES

Arnold, M. B. (1970a). Brain function in emotion: A phenomenological analysis. In P. Black (Ed.), *Physiological correlates of emotion* (pp. 261–285). New York: Academic Press.

Arnold, M. B. (1970b). Perennial problems in the field of emtion. In M. B. Arnold (Ed.), *Feelings and emotions* (pp. 169–185). New York: Academic Press.

Arnold, M. B. (1984). *Memory and the brain* (Chaps. 11 & 12, pp. 117–152). Hillsdale, NJ: Erlbaum.

Brierley, M. (1937). Affects in theory and practice. In *Trends in psychoanalysis* (pp. 43–56). London: Hogarth Press.

Emde, R. N. (1987, July). *Development terminable and interminable.* Plenary presentation at the 35th International PsychoAnalytical Congress, Montreal, Canada. Unpublished manuscript.

Emde, R. N., Gaensbauer, T. J., & Harmon, R. J. (1978). Emotional expression in infancy. 1. Initial studies of social signaling and an emergent model. In M. Lewis & L. Rosenblum (Eds.), *The development of affect* (pp. 125–148). New York: Plenum.

Freud, S. (1955). Beyond the pleasure principle. In J. Strachey (Ed. and Trans.), *The standard edition of the complete psychological works of Sigmund Freud* (Vol. 18, pp. 3–64). London: Hogarth Press. (Original work published 1920)

Freud, S. (1957a). Repression. In J. Strachey (Ed. and Trans.), *The standard edition of the complete psychological works of Sigmund Freud* (Vol. 14, pp. 141–158). London: Hogarth Press. (Original work published 1915)

Freud, S. (1957b). The unconscious. In J. Strachey (Ed. and Trans.), *The standard edition of the complete psychological works of Sigmund Freud* (Vol. 14, pp. 159–215). London: Hogarth Press. (Original work published 1915)

Freud, S. (1959). Inhibitions, symptoms and anxiety. In J. Strachey (Ed. and Trans.), *The standard edition of the complete psychological works of Sigmund Freud.* (Vol. 20, pp. 87–156). London: Hogarth Press. (Original work published 1926)

Freud, S. (1962). The neuro-psychoses of defence. In J. Strachey (Ed. and Trans.), *The standard edition of the complete psychological works of Sigmund Freud* (Vol. 3, pp. 43–61). London: Hogarth Press. (Original work published 1894)

Hoffman, M. (1978). Toward a theory of empathic arousal and development. In M. Lewis & L. Rosenblum (Eds.), *The development of affect* (pp. 227–256). New York: Plenum.

Holder, A. (1970). Instinct and drive. In H. Nagera (Ed.), *Basic psychoanalytic concepts of the theory of instincts* (Vol. 3, pp. 19–22). New York: Basic Books.

Izard, C. (1978). On the ontogenesis of emotions and emotion-cognition relationships in infancy. In M. Lewis & L. Rosenblum (Eds.), *The development of affect* (pp. 389–413). New York: Plenum.

Jacobson, E. (1971a). On the psychoanalytic theory of affects. In *Depression* (pp. 3–47). New York: International Universities Press. (Original work published 1953)

Jacobson, E. (1971b). Normal and pathological moods: Their nature and functions. In *Depression* (pp. 66–106). New York: International Universities Press. (Original work published 1957).

James, W. (1884). What is an emotion? *Mind, 9,* 188–205.

Jaques, E. (1982). *The form of time.* New York: Crane, Russak & Co.

Kaplan, L. J. (1987). Discussion. *Contemporary Psychoanalysis, 23*(1), 27–44.

Kernberg, O. F. (1984). Character analysis. In *Severe personality disorders: Psychotherapeutic strategies* (pp. 210–226). New Haven, CT: Yale University Press.

Knapp, P. H. (1978). Core processes in the organization of emotions. In M. B. Cantor & M. L. Glucksman, (Eds.), *Affect: Psychoanalytic theory and practice* (pp. 51–70). New York: Wiley.

Lange, C. (1922). *The emotions* Baltimore, MD: Williams & Wilkins. (1885 German Trans. Dr. Kurella; 1887, Engl. Trans.)

Laplanche, J., & Pontalis, J. B. (1973). Instinct (or drive). In *The language of psycho-analysis* (pp. 214–217). New York: Norton.

Lorenz, K. (1963). *On aggression.* New York: Bantam Books.

Mahler, M. (1972). Rapprochement subphase of the separation-individuation process. *Psychoanalytic Quarterly, 41,* 487–506.

Mahler, M., & Furer, M. (1968). *On human symbiosis and the vicissitudes of individuation.* New York: International Universities Press.

Mahler, M., Pine, F., & Bergman, A. (1975). *The psychological birth of the human infant.* New York: Basic Books.

Plutchik, R. (1980). *Emotions: A psychoevolutionary synthesis.* New York: Harper & Row.

Plutchik, R., & Kellerman, H. (Eds.). (1983). *Emotions: theory, research, and experience: Vol. 2. Emotions in early development.* New York: Academic Press.

Rapaport, D. (1953). On the psychoanalytic theory of affects. In M. M. Gill (Ed.), *The collected papers of David Rapaport* (pp. 476–512). New York: Basic Books.

Sroufe, L. A. (1979). Socioemotional development. In J. Osofsky (Ed.), *Handbook of infant development.* New York: Wiley.

Sroufe, L. A., Waters, E., & Matas, L. (1974). Contextual determinants of infant affective response. In M. Lewis & L. A. Rosenblum (Eds.), *The origins of fear* (pp. 49–72). New York: Wiley.

Stern, D. N. (1985). *The interpersonal world of the infant.* New York: Basic Books.

Tinbergen, N. (1951). An attempt at synthesis. In *The study of instinct* (pp. 101–127). New York: Oxford University Press.

Tomkins, S. S. (1970). Affect as the primary motivational system. In M. B. Arnold (Ed.), *Feelings and emotions* (pp. 101–110). New York: Academic Press.

Wilson, E. O. (1975). *Sociobiology: The new synthesis.* Cambridge, MA: Harvard University Press.

Chapter 6

EMOTION, TIME, AND THE SELF

JACOB A. ARLOW

ABSTRACT

All emotion has a time dimension. Each present moment is affected by fantasy wishes from the past, pressing for satisfaction in the future. Memory and anticipation are inexorable dimensions of the present reality. Time and emotion are closely intermingled from the very inception of mental life. The elements participating in the conceptualization of time develop early in connection with a psychophysiological need, accompanied by unpleasant feelings, followed by gratification of that need, leading to a relief of tension and feelings of pleasure. It is in this context that the two fundamental components of time sense, duration and succession, develop. The child learns to anticipate relief by associating it with the appearance of the need-satisfying object. He or she comes to recognize that relief is brought about by an "other." This is the beginning of a process of differentiating between one's self and others. These experiences with time and emotion influence the development of infantile narcissism, concepts of causality, self-differentiation, and the construction of reality.

In this chapter the connection between emotion and time will be discussed, and consideration will be given to how these phenomena influence the development of psychic structure, time sense, and certain aspects of psychopathology.

EMOTION
Theory, Research, and Experience
Volume 5

AFFECT, FEELING, AND EMOTION

It may be well to begin by distinguishing among affect, feeling, and emotion. This is necessary because the three terms are often used interchangeably and hence inaccurately. According to the psychiatric glossary of the American Psychiatric Association (Werner, 1984), affect pertains to the outward manifestation of a person's feelings, tone, or mood. The subjective counterpart of affect is feeling tone, which basically may be described as being pleasant or unpleasant. According to current psychoanalytic theory (Brenner, 1974a, 1974b; Rangell, 1955, 1967; Schafer, 1964; Zetzel, 1960; Zilboorg, 1933), the many varied and complex feeling states later recognizable as discrete emotions develop out of repeated experiences suffused with pleasant or unpleasant feeling tones, to which specific, concrete, ideational content becomes attached. The primordial tendency to process experiences in terms of whether they are pleasant or unpleasant in feeling is an inherited biological predisposition, the product of the evolution of the human species. The fact that certain experiences produce pleasurable feelings and others painful ones must have had survival value in the course of human evolution. For the most part, what was noxious created unpleasant feelings and was to be avoided. Conversely, safe, nurturing experiences are ordinarily connected with pleasurable feelings worthy of repetition.

Freud's two principles of mental functioning (1911) were clearly based on such biological considerations. The earliest drives, he said (1905), were anaclitic, that is, they were connected with the nurturing, biological aspect of the pleasure-giving activity. Freud regarded the pursuit of pleasurable feelings and the avoidance of unpleasant ones as the basic principle governing mental life. Let us consider the basic connection between the pleasure principle and the developing sense of time.

THE ORIGIN OF TIME SENSE

Time is not sensed by direct awareness. There are no sensory structures for time comparable to the retina and the cochlear apparatus. "Our direct experience is always of the present and our idea of time comes from reflecting on that experience" (Whitrow, 1980, p. 61). Our sense of time is an intellectual construction, dependent on psychological processes that unite thought and action. The essence of this process depends on an awareness of change. Aristotle pointed out that, without change, time does not exist.

Most observers agree that the two fundamental concepts of the sense of time are the awareness of duration and of the succession of events. The first impression of physiological duration is experienced in connection with the intervals between the experience of need and gratification. Need gratification leads to pleasurable feelings, eventuating in states of quiescence, while frustration of physiologic needs creates unpleasant feelings, leading to signals of distress and restlessness. As a rule, the longer the interval between need and gratification, the greater is the sense of painful tension. Accordingly, unpleasant feelings of frustration impress upon the mind of the developing infant the experience of duration.

In other words, the beginning of time sense is associated with the awareness of enduring unpleasant sensations, which are part of a cycle in which need tension is followed by pleasurable relief, which comes with the appearance of the need-satisfying object. A sequence of experience is established, linking the unpleasant feelings of tension with a painful sense of duration, followed by relief and pleasure. It can be seen that the concept of succession of events, which constitutes the second basic element in the building up of the time sense, evolves out of this fundamental, biological cycle. Thus, from the very outset of mental life, the two basic components out of which the time sense is conceptualized, namely, duration and succession, and the basic affects of pleasure and unpleasure are inextricably intermingled.

The implications of this correlation of time and affects are far-reaching indeed. Out of repeated experiences of need accompanied by unpleasure, followed by gratification accompanied by pleasure, events begin to fall into a pattern of need, distress signal, and gratification. The result is an ordering of happenings into a sequence that comes to have meaning. Furthermore, as a result of the ability to interpret each element in the linear sequence as one in a series of signals leading to gratification and pleasure, a more distant signal, that is, the appearance of the mother's face, may serve as a reassuring, temporary substitute for the actual experience of gratification. The child has begun to anticipate. Under these circumstances, duration becomes tinged with pleasure, a reassuring calmness pervades the present with the promise of pleasure in the immediate future. Here is the dawning of the concept of the future. For children whose early experiences have been fraught with prolonged tension and disappointment, the future does not seem quite as promising. They do not console easily. Sometimes the effects of such very early disappointments may have far-reaching and persistent influences. Freud (1917) felt that such disappointment may predispose the individual to depressive illness later in life, after the real or fantasied loss of a love object. Abraham (1924) traced the character trait of pessimism to the same constellation of early childhood disappointments.

TIME, SELF, AND OBJECT

The ability of the child to anticipate calmly that the cycle that begins with painful need tensions will, after some duration in time, lead in the more or less immediate future to the appearance of a set of sensory perceptions accompanied by pleasurable relief is, according to Kris (1950), one of the first steps in the development of object constancy. Instead of resorting to primitive wish-fulfilling hallucination about the mother's presence, the child begins to anticipate quietly that the mother will return to relieve his discomfort. This step in mental development indicates that the mother exists as a separate entity, independent of the child's immediate feelings of distress. The development of object constancy points to the evolution of an organized concept of an "other," functioning independently in time and space. As such, it also marks the beginning delineation of the self.

The emergence of the self-concept is critical for the development of time sense. The empirical philosophers, Locke, Berkeley, and Hume, agree that the notion of time originated in awareness of succession of ideas in the mind. According to Hume (1874), without a succession of perceptions, we have no notion of time. Time "is always discovered by some perceivable succession of changeable objects" (p. 342). According to Locke (1894), the perception of change is related to the awareness of the succession of one's own thoughts. Fraser (1975) says that time can be considered a construct that refers to the perception or imputation of change against some background that is taken to be relatively permanent. For a change to be perceived or imputed, there has to be both succession and duration; that is, when two successive events are separated by an interval, the interval between them is called duration. Hence duration is defined by succession. The reverse also holds true. For two events to be successive, there must be a time gap, a duration, between them.

If time can be considered a construct that refers to the perception or imputation of change against some background that is taken to be relatively permanent, the question arises of "What is that background?" or "What is it that changes and yet endures?" That relatively permanent background clearly is the self. In our awareness, it is the self that is enduring and yet continuously changing. It is the self that has a history of a succession of events that has been endured (Arlow, 1986b; see also Jacobson, 1964; Mahler, Pine, & Bergmann, 1975).

PREDICTABILITY AND SELF-ASSURANCE

The self, the construction of reality, and primitive conceptualizations of causality evolve out of affectively tinged maneuvers and manipulations correlated with changes in time and with the ability to anticipate in a reliable fashion a predictable sequence of events. Contiguity of elements in time, in this context, becomes the basic underpinning of primitive concepts of causality. This may be one of the reasons why in later life it is so hard to shed the notion of *post hoc, ergo propter hoc,* that is, the notion that an immediately contiguous event is necessarily a direct result of the preceding event. Piaget (1937, 1955) has observed that when children realize that their activities, for example, crying when hungry, are effective in getting them what they want, a feeling of efficacy is created, generating a sense that activity is the causative link between desires and their fulfillment. More recently, I. Harrison (personal communication, 1986) has suggested that the realization by the children of their power to bring about such changes through their effects on the object world may contribute to the sense of grandiosity so typical of infantile narcissism. In any event, every efficacious linkage of meaning derived from a sequence of events in time strengthens the sense of mastery and autonomy and becomes a source of pleasurable self-esteem.

Through activity, the child begins to be able to interpret a sequence of events in time that will ultimately lead to the ability to distinguish between what is internal and what is external, between image and percept, and between real and unreal. If the image appears only when the eyes are shut, it is internal. If the image appears only when the eyes are open, it is external. If the image shifts or changes relative to the child's motion, it is external. The sensations experienced when two parts of the body come in contact are distinguished from the sensations experienced when only one part of the body comes in contact with an object. In each instance, the change in sensation is related to an anticipation of the immediate future. To be convincing, the reappearance of an image in consciousness with a change of muscular activity has to be immediate. The reappearance of an image removed some distance in time presents a different problem. A considerable degree of development has to take place before the image is understood as an external object, one that is capable of being ''refound'' in repeated experience (Freud, 1925).

The ability to anticipate correctly the immediate future seems to have a reassuring quality for infants. This is a tendency that persists, in one way or another, in the human individual throughout life. For the child, when a sequence of events does not conform to established, that is, familiar, patterns of experience, this inability to predict the immediate future may be experienced as unsettling, perplexing, and even frightening. The image of a stable, predictable world and of the self in relation to it are challenged.

THE UNFAMILIAR

Children differ in their capacity to become acclimated to things that are new, unfamiliar, and alien. The classic ''stranger anxiety'' described by Spitz (1957, 1972) may be the most familiar and striking example of this reaction. During the ''rapprochement'' phase described by Mahler (1968), the child experiments in various ways with how to test and become acclimated to the unfamiliar, situations in which the immediate future is not readily predictable. To some extent, unease in the face of the unknown may enter into the psychology of all individuals. For example, Ostow (1982) has suggested that this inherent tendency towards xenophobia may be one of the root causes of the persistence of anti-Semitism.

There exists a wide range of emotions of unpleasant feeling tone connected with confrontation with what is strange and unpredictable. The reactions to confrontation with unaccustomed places and societies may vary all the way from "culture shock" to feelings of strangeness and unreality. When the immediate perceptions appear strange and unfamiliar and the sequence of events fails to conform to what is known and immediately predictable, a sense of unease develops. The ideational content of the emotional state is dominated by a threatening sense of strangeness. The feeling is characterized as "eerie." When there is a sense that the events are occurring outside of the natural order of experience, the feeling generated is described as "uncanny" (Freud, 1919). Whatever fails to conform to the ordered sequence of events that man expects to take place in the external world is described as unnatural or supernatural. Thus, in literary or scriptural descriptions of miracles, the participants are said to have responded with feelings of awe and dread. In such cases, the ideational content connected with the feeling is one of foreboding and impending disaster. Some individuals may respond to threatening, unfamiliar situations with a disturbance in the coherence of the self. They may experience feelings of depersonalization (Arlow, 1966), a defensive form of denial that attempts to convey the reassuring message "I am not the one involved in this dangerous situation."

The ability to prepare one's self mentally plays an important role in the response to what is unfamiliar, strange, and threatening. Even though there are such things as pleasant surprises, for the most part people do not respond favorably to the unexpected. Preparation for a new and strange experience, however, makes possible anticipatory assimilation of new impressions against a background of what is known, what is familiar, and what has been mastered in the past (Fenichel, 1945). We can anticipate the future much better when we have a good idea of how things will turn out. Thus, the child may tolerate and even enjoy frightening stories when, as a result of repeated retelling of the story, he or she may safely anticipate the successful resolution of even the most unpleasant of situations.

A similar mechanism seems to operate in the typical examination anxiety dreams described by Freud (1900) and in that distortion of the time experience known as the déjà vu phenomenon (Arlow, 1959). In these situations, individuals strive to achieve reassurance against current feelings of danger by reminding themselves of earlier threatening situations successfully mastered in the past. There is here a resemblance to the ability of children to enjoy magic tricks.

Only after children have established a relatively firm hold on the concepts of cause and effect in reality are they able to be amused by such tricks, secure in the knowledge that what they are observing is an illusion. Adults, for example, may interpret a motion picture run in reverse as unreal and find the experience amusing, but only in the short run. On the other hand, to a child at a certain stage of development, such a reverse showing may seem confusing and frequently frightening. The total disregard of the accustomed order of events in time is one element that brings about the feeling of unreality or absurdity that we attach to dreams. Time should behave itself and make sense.

THE SENSE OF THE PAST

It is a useful assumption, sustained by many observations, that the mind appears to process the data of perception according to the criteria of familiar or unfamiliar and pleasurable or unpleasurable (Arlow, 1980; Freud, 1925). As new perceptions are compared and contrasted with the memory traces of what has been experienced and registered previously, the organization of memory and the concept of the past begin to form. A more objective view of the past is attained as the child begins to distinguish between fantasy and perception. In order to categorize definitively the particular memory or experience as belonging to the past, it is necessary to perceive the fact that the recalled experience can no longer be altered, either by the subject's own action or by some intervention from the outside (Hartocollis, 1983). This perception not only is an important step in the development of the sense of reality but, as we shall see, also bears directly on other aspects of mental life.

The memory of the past conditions how the present is perceived and felt. At its earliest, most primitive level of functioning, the mind, as Freud (1900) postulated, responds to physiological need in a specific way. In the presence of need tension, there is a tendency, he said, to achieve relief and gratification by reexperiencing a set of pleasurable perceptions remembered from the past. If such gratification actually did not come about, there is a tendency to hallucinate appropriate, wish-fulfilling perceptions. The mind, Freud said, strives to achieve a complete perceptual identity with the memory of previous gratification. This mode of mental functioning he called the "primary process." No experience, of course, can ever achieve a complete perceptual identity with a memory of previous gratification. At best, it may be assumed that the actual perceptual experiences of gratification are only approximations rather than identical reproductions of the original experience.

Memory is only approximately recaptured. Accordingly, various memory systems may be established in which experiences are associatively linked according to the criterion of similarity, and, in the process of recollection, an approximate, rather than a precise, replication of an event may appear in consciousness. This process paves the way for the emergence of such mental mechanisms as substitution, displacement, illusion, and symbolism. It also sheds light on the human tendency to create metaphor and suggests that the successful utilization of metaphor, most of all, may reflect the exquisite functioning of emotion as it is joined with cognition. The meaningful connections among elements in a patient's free associations during therapy furnish convincing evidence of how memories and concepts are related according to the principle of similarity, that is, in a metaphoric way (Arlow, 1979).

The realization that the past is something about which nothing can be done, except in fantasy, serves as a serious blow to infantile narcissism. It undermines the sense of omnipotence and must lead at times to some feelings of lowered self-esteem. Not only is it impossible to recreate the pleasures and triumphs of the past, it is also impossible to undo the hurts and humiliations that have been experienced. Such considerations seem to be central to the psychology of depressed patients. They dwell on a past that they can neither alter nor forget, and they cannot free themselves of that dilemma (Arlow, 1986a). It is out of such considerations that modern psychoanalytic theorists (Brenner, 1974a, 1974b; Zetzel, 1960) have conceptualized the major affective components of psychopathology in terms of their time dimension. Depressive affect is related to the past, to the conflicts growing out of the catastrophes of childhood, and linked to the awareness that something bad has happened that cannot be undone. It is this ideational content, when added to the experience of unpleasurable feeling, that we recognize as depression. In the same light, anxiety has a dimension that pertains to the future. In anxiety, the ideational content of the emotion is that some catastrophe or danger impends. It involves an estimate on the part of the individual of his capacity to master the impending danger. Depending upon the intensity of the unpleasure generated, the individual may feel worried, anxious, or panic-stricken.

In the light of the foregoing, one can appreciate how the time dimension is a major component of two of the most important emotions involved in psychopathology, depression and anxiety. Emotions are not simply experiences of affective tone felt by the individual. The ideational content is of utmost significance, and a major component of the ideational content is associated with the relationship to time. Emotions can be regarded as complex mental phenomena, comprising sensations of pleasure, unpleasure, or a mixture of both, and characterized by a specific ideational content. What one experiences as an emotion is actually a combination of feeling tone and ideational content (Brenner, 1974b). The latter can be conscious or unconscious, often reflecting the effects of persistent unconscious fantasy. The influence of unconscious fantasy is particularly striking in certain cases of persistent moods, which reflect a pervasive feeling tone yet seem to be quite unconnected to any ideational content. In the analytic situation, it is possible to demonstrate how such moods, consciously experienced, nonetheless reflect an ideational content related to an unconscious fantasy (Arlow, 1969). This is another example of the importance of the time dimension in emotion. An element of the past, that is, a persistent unconscious fantasy, remains active in the present and influences anticipations for the future. The all-pervasive influence of fantasies, conscious and unconscious, on mental life demonstrates the inexorable time dimension that is part of all emotion. In a certain sense, this is the very essence of drive theory in psychoanalysis.

THE SELF IN TIME

As mentioned earlier, time is a feeling before it is an abstraction. Out of the affectively tinged experiences of duration and succession of events, a more objective time concept emerges in the course of development. "Time is a construct that refers to the perception or imputation of change against some background that is taken to be relatively permanent" (Fraser, 1975). The relatively permanent background against which change is perceived is the self. It is the self of which we are conscious. Consciousness implies the capacity to differentiate between perceptions that pertain to the external world and those that pertain to the self. The self is a time-bound concept. It is the self that is enduring and yet continuously changing. Events in the external world are ordered in terms of sequence and continuity relative to the constancy of the self. The self has a history and it is the self that has a past, present, and future. Time is what we live in. It is the container of our existence.

The sense of continuity and permanence of the self-concept is stoutly maintained by the individual. For example, when someone recovers from a lapse of consciousness, he or she is likely to experience anxiety or confusion. The discontinuity of self-awareness is experienced as a threat to the integrity and continuity of the self. Such a person will usually attempt to reorient the self in time and space while reflecting upon the experience of having lost the sense of self in time. There is an inwardly acknowledged conviction of self-identity and of continuity that parallels but remains forever stronger than the sense of continuity and permanence that pertains to objects. Identity implies that a self or an object is the same entity at different points in *time*, no matter what changes or transformations may have taken place in the intervening years. Clinical experience demonstrates how earlier representations of the self may be repudiated or disavowed, but the sense of connection to the self is hardly ever sundered in an absolute way, except possibly in severe psychotic states.

Since the appreciation of time would be impossible without the consciousness of self, it is not surprising that disturbances of the sense of self invariably are connected with distortions of the sense of time and, as a rule, are accompanied by feelings of unpleasant emotion (Schilder, 1936). Certain euphoric states of mind, induced by drugs, do bring about a concomitant distortion of the sense of self and of the sense of time. Such states would seem to be an exception to this general rule. Clinical reports, however, usually contain some reference to states of discomfort, unease, or fear connected with an awareness of alteration of the sense of self. In this connection, some mention should be made of the alterations of the sense of self that are supposed to accompany the so-called oceanic feeling and the experience of timelessness. According to Freud (1930), the sense of oneness with the universe, and the feelings of timelessness connected with the oceanic feeling, may represent a regressive reactivation of the blissful state of satiated fusion with the mother during the earliest months of life. My own clinical observations do not support the thesis linking the feelings of timelessness with the loss of the sense of self. During the analysis of two patients who experienced feelings of timelessness, it seemed possible to explain that unusual emotional state as a derivative of unconscious fantasies of a wish to extend time indefinitely. In one case, this was in pursuit of a wish to ward off death (castration anxiety); in the other, in the interest of prolonging indefinitely the life of a beloved father (Arlow, 1984).

TIME AND FRUSTRATION

In fantasy, it is possible to reorder time relationships and bring events into a sequence that is nearer to the heart's desire. In reality, this is not possible. The past cannot be undone any more than the future can be controlled. The inexorable advance of time is the great frustrater of infantile omnipotence and wishful thinking. While it leads to a consolidation of the role of the reality principle in mental functioning, it also leaves a residue of resentment and frustration, one that resonates earlier experiences of wishes inhibited or denied by the parents. Thus, time and reality may become identified with the frustrations imposed by authority figures and caretakers. Time becomes one of the chief instrumentalities imposed by the external world upon the child to limit the pursuit of self-indulgent pleasure. Through schedules, appointments, and other regulations, time comes to speak as the voice of parental authority and, to a certain degree, is for that reason forever after resented. Clinical experience is rich with examples of individuals who defy appointments and disregard schedules. Some people make a point of not wearing watches and of remaining generally oblivious of the time of day. If they cannot master time, they can at least disregard it.

Through a process of anthropomorphization and concretization, time may be treated in unconscious fantasy as a thing or a person. As a result, time may be the object of conflictual conscious and unconscious wishes. Yates (1935) described a patient whose behavior toward time was the expression of a fantasy of throwing hours and days at her mother, the hours and days representing the food and milk that had been denied her. In a previous communication (Arlow, 1984), I described a patient whose relationship to time was influenced by a fantasy growing out of the oedipal struggle for possession of the omnipotent paternal phallus. He imagined that, on New Year's Eve at the stroke of midnight, the incoming year destroys the old Father Time and takes possession of an automatically operating time machine that endlessly produces time as a stream of fluid. The concretization of time as a fluid, as well as the metaphor of time as a flowing river, make possible fantasies of manipulating time by reversing the direction of its flow or controlling the rate of its passage (Arlow, 1986a).

The gravest insult that time imposes upon the self and the individual's narcissism is, of course, the inevitable confrontation with death. In the inconography of Western civilization, time is often represented in the guise of the omnipotent father, the ultimate frustrater identified with death. When young children first learn of death, it is difficult for them to think of it as a natural process, the consequence of biological degeneration. Often clinical investigation demonstrates that death is equated with murder. Mythology concretizes this notion through the image of the angel of death and the concept of an inescapable appointment with the angel of death at a specific time and place in the future. The body of literature, legends, and stories dealing with the theme of avoiding or mastering the inevitable appointment with death is vast indeed. The same theme reverberates in Freud's analysis (1900) of the typical dream of missing the train. This dream portrayed as already fulfilled the wish to avoid the long, last journey.

Time becomes the frustrating agent that makes impossible the fulfillment of oedipal wishes. Thus, time and the oedipal father come to stand for the same common enemy. When the little boy is told by his mother that he cannot marry her because he is too young and too small, he hopes that she will wait for him so he can do so when he is grown-up. He learns, however, that time makes this impossible. As he matures, she ages. Time puts her forever out of his reach. Time imposes a barrier that cannot be overcome. The saddening realization of this fact becomes one of the sources of romantic love, the quest for the beloved who is forever unattainable and out of reach (Arlow, 1984). It also serves as the impetus for fantasies of eliminating, controlling, and suspending time indefinitely. Out of such fantasies has grown a rich literature of time warp. In these works, time experience is altered so as to make possible the loving union of two people from different generations, temporarily becoming roughly the same age in a world of suspended time. In the fairy tale, Sleeping Beauty is awakened from her suspended animation to find love and happiness with a prince of a later generation. The novel *Lost Horizons* is set in never-never land, where the intrusions of time have been suspended indefinitely, and in the Broadway musical *Brigadoon* our hero finds the woman he loves in an unchanging world that is independent of the rule of time.

Most striking, of course, are those literary creations in which the hero goes back in time and falls in love with one of his female ancestors (e.g., *Berkeley Square*) or, as in the case of a recent motion picture, with his own mother (*Back to the Future*). Time, unyielding and all-powerful, is unconsciously identified with the interposing power of the oedipal father, and the prohibitions emanating from the incest taboo reappear in terms of the realistic strictures imposed by the discrepancy in time relationships. To the dismay of our young oedipal heroes, however, in all of these fantasies as in life, the spell is broken. The magic world vanishes and the world of time and reality is reestablished.

TIME AND THE DEFENSIVE PROCESS

Finally, it should be observed that time may be experienced in a distorted way as a consequence of the ego's need to ward off the unpleasant affects of anxiety, depression, or guilt. Stein (1953) demonstrated how a feeling of premonition, a foreknowledge of a dreaded event, served to protect a patient against guilt feelings. Instead of recognizing that he entertained hostile wishes toward someone, the patient experienced instead a protective dreaded anticipation that something evil might happen to that person. Similarly, Arlow (1959) reported how a disturbance of the sense of time helped reassure a patient against fears connected with what he felt to be a dangerous confrontation with authority. Before the frightening encounter, the patient had the sense of déjà vu. Actually, in his mind, he was associating to the experience similar encounters from the past that he had "already seen" and had mastered successfully.

Many patients report that, in situations of danger, they have a sense of depersonalization, a feeling that they are not the actual participants going through a harrowing experience but rather detached observers who cannot be affected by what is about to happen. Together with this alteration of the sense of self, there is a feeling of time standing still, a feeling that nothing is going to happen, nothing will change, everything will remain as is indefinitely (Arlow, 1966). There must be many other situations in which the sense of time is altered in keeping with a need to fend off unpleasant emotions.

REFERENCES

Abraham, K. (1924). A short study of the development of the libido. In *Selected papers on psychoanalysis* (pp. 418–501). London: Hogarth Press.

Arlow, J. A. (1959). The structure of the déjà vu experience. *Journal of the American Psychoanalytic Association*, **7**, 611–631.

Arlow, J. A. (1966). Depersonalization and derealization. In R. M. Loewenstein et al. (Eds.), *Psychoanalysis: A general psychology. Essays in honor of Heinz Hartmann* (pp. 456–478). New York: International Universities Press.

Arlow, J. A. (1969). Unconscious fantasy and disturbances of conscious experience. *Psychoanalytic Quarterly*, **38**, 1–27.

Arlow, J. A. (1979). Metaphor and the psychoanalytic situation. *Psychoanalytic Quarterly*, **48**, 363–385.

Arlow, J. A. (1980). Object concept and object choice. *Psychoanalytic Quarterly*, **49**, 109–133.

Arlow, J. A. (1984). Disturbances of the sense of time. With special reference to the experience of timelessness. *Psychoanalytic Quarterly*, **53**, 13–37.

Arlow, J. A. (1986a). Psychoanalysis and time. *Journal of the American Psychoanalytic Association*, **34**, 507–528.

Arlow, J. A. (1986b). *Time and mind.* Unpublished Freud lecture, Yale University, New Haven, CT.

Brenner, C. (1974a). Depression, anxiety and affect theory. *International Journal of Psycho-Analysis*, **55**, 25–32.

Brenner, C. (1974b). On the nature and development of affects: A unified theory *Psychoanalytic Quarterly*, **43**, 532–556.

Fenichel, O. (1945). *The psychoanalytic theory of neuroses.* New York: Norton.

Fraisse, P. (1963). *The psychology of time.* (J. Leith, Trans.) New York, Evanston, and London: Harper and Row.

Fraser, J. T. (1975). *Of time, passion and knowledge. Reflections on the strategy of existence.* New York: George Braziller.

Freud, S. (1953). The interpretation of dreams. *The standard edition of the complete psychological works of Sigmund Freud* (Vols. 4 and 5). (Original work published 1900)

Freud, S. (1953). Three essays on the theory of sexuality. *The standard edition of the complete psychological works of Sigmund Freud* (Vol. 7, pp. 125–245). (Original work published 1905)

Freud, S. (1958). Formulations of the two principles of mental functioning. *The standard edition of the complete psychological works of Sigmund Freud* (Vol. 12, pp. 218–226). (Original work published 1911)

Freud, S. (1957). Mourning and melancholia. *The standard edition of the complete psychological works of Sigmund Freud* (Vol. 14, pp. 237–260). (Original work published 1917)

Freud, S. (1955). The uncanny. *The standard edition of the complete psychological works of Sigmund Freud* (Vol. 17, p. 219). (Original work published 1919)

Freud, S. (1961). On negation. *The standard edition of the complete psychological works of Sigmund Freud* (Vol. 19, pp. 235–239). (Original work published 1925)

Freud, S. (1961). Civilization and its discontents. *The standard edition of the complete psychological works of Sigmund Freud* (Vol. 21, pp. 64–65). (Original work published 1930)

Hartocollis, P. (1983). *Time and timelessness.* New York: International Universities Press.

Hume, D. (1874). *A treatise on human nature.* Vols. 1 and 2. T. H. Green and T. H. Grose (Eds.). London: Longmans, Green.

Jacobson, E. (1964). *The self and the object world.* New York: International Universities Press.

Kris, E. (1950). Notes on the development and on some current problems of psychoanalytic child psychology. *Psychoanalytic Study of the Child*, **5**, 24–46.

Locke, J. (1894). *Essay concerning human understanding.* (A. Campbell Fraser (Ed.). London & New York: Oxford University Press (Clarendon).

Mahler, M. S. (1968). *On human symbiosis and the vicissitudes of individuation: Vol. 1. Infantile psychosis.* New York: International Universities Press.

Mahler, M. S., Pine, F. & Bergmann, A. (1975). *Psychological birth of the human infant.* New York: Basic Books.

Ostow, M. (Ed.). (1982). *Psychoanalysis and Judaism*. New York: KTAV Publishing House.

Piaget, J. (1955). *The child's construction of reality*, (Ch. 4), (M. Cook, Trans.). New York: Basic Books.

Rangell, L. (1955). On the psychoanalytic theory of anxiety. A statement of the unitary theory. *Journal of the American Psychoanalytic Association, 3*, 369–414.

Rangell, L. (1967). Psychoanalysis, affects, and the 'human core': On the relationship of psychoanalysis to the behavioral sciences. *Psychoanalytic Quarterly, 36*, 172–202.

Schafer, R. (1964). The clinical analysis of affects. *Journal of the American Psychoanalytic Association, 12*, 275–299.

Schilder, P. (1936). Psychology of time. *Journal of Nervous and Mental Disease, 83*, 530–546.

Spitz, R. A. (1957). *No and yes and the genesis of human communication*. New York: International Universities Press.

Spitz, R. A. (1972). Bridges. On anticipation, duration and meaning. *Journal of the American Psychoanalytic Association, 20*, 721–735.

Stein, M. H. (1953). Premonition as a defense. *Psychoanalytic Quarterly, 22*, 69–74.

Werner, A. (Ed.), (1984). *Psychiatric glossary*. Washington, DC: American Psychiatric Press.

Whitrow, G. J. (1980). *The natural philosophy of time*. London & New York: Oxford University Press.

Yates, S. (1935). Some aspects of time difficulties and their relation to music. *International Journal of Psycho-Analysis, 16*, 341–354.

Zetzel, E. R. (1960). Symposium on depressive illness. I. Introductions. *International Journal of Psycho-Analysis, 41*, 476–480.

Zilboorg, G. (1933). Anxiety without affect. *Psychoanalytic Quarterly, 2*, 48–67.

Chapter 7

THE CHANGING ROLE OF EMOTION
IN GROUP PSYCHOTHERAPY

K. ROY MacKENZIE

ABSTRACT

This chapter explores the role of emotion in group psychotherapy. A review of the history of group theory reveals that affect was originally considered a potentially ungovernable force to be kept under control. This position has been modified over time to focus instead on the emotional meaning of interpersonal patterns as these emerge in the group process. The concepts of cohesion as a "condition for change" and of various "therapeutic factors" are considered from the standpoint of emotional dimensions. Theories of group developmental stages and social roles are presented as important organizing schemas for understanding the group as a social system. Both stage tasks and role functions are described in terms of basic emotional axes. Each stage may be considered to have a unique interactional climate that has particular relevance to members in accordance with their interpersonal style. The predominant group emotional tension drives the group to resolve related stage tasks. Through this process, the individual member must also confront parallel issues as they are revealed both internally and through group interpersonal events. The succession of stages permits the group member to experience all major emotional dimensions.

This chapter on the role of emotion in group psychotherapy will focus primarily on group-level phenomena. It is important that the group therapist and the group researcher understand the unique set of issues that are best understood from the standpoint of the group as an interactive system. Group therapy embod-

EMOTION
Theory, Research, and Experience
Volume 5

ies components that are not found in individual therapy, or, if present, are in an attentuated form. Categories of therapeutic factors include some that occur only in groups, such as altruism and vicarious learning from the interactions of others. Other therapeutic factors, while found in individual therapy, have a different quality in groups. For example, self-disclosure in a group has broader implications than in individual therapy where there can be greater confidence that the information will be treated with professional courtesy and clinical perspective.

The chapter will begin with an overview of the history of the development of group theory. From there the discussion will move to a consideration of current group issues that are particularly concerned with interpersonal mechanisms and the application of systems theory. The use of the term ''emotion'' will conform to the expanded definition provided by Plutchik (1980a):

> [Emotion is] an inferred complex sequence of reactions to a stimulus, and includes cognitive evaluations, subjective changes, autonomic and neural arousal, impulses to action, and behavior designed to have an effect upon the stimulus that initiated the complex sequence. . . . The patterns of expression associated with each chain of emotional reactions serve to signal motivation or intent from one member of a social group to another. (p. 361)

The group context is a particularly powerful environment in which to study such interactional phenomena. By its very nature, there is in the group a broader and more diverse range of interpersonal stimuli available to which the individual may respond. There is also much greater variability along the control or power dimension. In dyadic therapy there exists explicit role dichotomy between therapist–patient, healer–supplicant, and giver–receiver. In a group, the power of the leader is diluted as leadership functions are to some extent dispersed among the members.

These two features of multiple relationships and greater equality of role status encourage a broad range of emotional responses from each member. Contemporary dynamic psychotherapy places major emphasis on tracking core, dynamic interactional themes in the therapeutic situation and on relating these to similar patterns in outside relationships both present and past (Horowitz, 1979; Luborsky, 1984; Strupp & Binder, 1984). The therapy group provides a multifaceted interactional field for the application of these techniques. This process demonstrates the application of Plutchik's concept of emotion as a response to environmental stimuli.

THE ROLE OF EMOTION IN THEORIES
OF GROUP

EARLY WORK

The history of the development of group theory can to some extent be understood as the evolution of ideas regarding the understanding and management of emotional issues in the group. LeBon (1920) described the large group as a social setting in which the individual member becomes excessively suggestible and therefore susceptible to a process of contagion promoted by the influence of a charismatic leader. The civilized controls of the individual may be overcome by the "group mind," resulting in a climate of intolerance, prejudice, and uninhibited behavior. McDougall (1920) shared many of these opinions but felt that the release of such "mob" processes could be controlled through group organization and task orientation. Even under these conditions, an intensification of emotional response would occur that had to be channeled into positive accomplishment. For both of these early theoreticians, emotion was viewed as a potentially ungovernable force to be kept under control.

FREUD

Freud (1921) considered the power of the group to stem from a common attachment to the leader. This diminished individuality since "a primary group of this kind is a number of individuals who have put one and the same object in the place of the ego ideal and have consequently identified themselves with one another in their ego" (p. 116). Freud supported this theory by reference to his earlier hypothesis in *Totem and Taboo* (Freud, 1913), wherein he postulated a common genetic inheritance of the memory of the destruction of the primal father–chief, exclusive possessor of the tribe's females, by the younger men who then became a unified community of brothers. He viewed the tendency for members to become united in positive feelings toward the group leader as an illusion representing a wish-fulfilling reaction to the opposite state of affairs that had prevailed in the primal horde. This theoretical material is unsupported by evidence but does focus on the tension between group control and individual autonomy.

These earlier ideas, in themselves seldom utilized in contemporary group psychotherapy, laid the base for the first major theoretical approach to the understanding of groups.

BION

The British psychiatrist W. R. Bion, in a series of articles between 1943 and 1952, like McDougall, contrasted the orderly productive work group with "basic assumption" states in which primitive drives and reactions emerge (Bion, 1961). Once again emotion was seen as a potentially destructive and disorganizing force to be kept under organizational or cognitive control. Bion described three "basic assumption" states that might block the group from maintaining its task orientation: dependence as if a superior and wise person must be found, fight–flight as if the group must cluster together as though threatened, and pairing as if two of the members have a solution for all.

These group-as-a-whole concepts are appealing because Bion described situations that are familiar to any group therapist. At the same time they provide an inadequate general theory of group functioning. Identification of "basic assumption" states may be used as a signal that a group is moving away from a productive working position. However, both the description and the theory fail to indicate the purpose for which they might be employed except as a defense against psychological work. Moreover, the assumption that all members of the group are preoccupied with the same defensive posture seems unrealistic. An important implication of Bion's work, though, is the focus upon specific emotional dimensions. His descriptions draw attention to the power of the group to influence the emotional responses of the members, particularly under adverse circumstances. This idea of the group as an amplifier of emotion is a core conceptualization.

The most important liability of Bion's approach is the way in which it dissociates emotion from interpersonal meaning. The "basic assumption" states are seen as interfering with productive work and as indicating that individual members have been swept out of control by group forces. While this may certainly happen, Bion does not consider the constructive use of emotion as a mechanism for uncovering interpersonal meaning. Bion moved the understanding of group events from largely unidimensional concepts of contagion to a much more detailed consideration of emotional dimensions.

SLAVSON

Great impetus was given to group psychotherapy in America through the theoretical writings and organizational efforts of S. R. Slavson (1979). He applied ideas from individual analytic work in a fashion quite different from Bion. The basis of his approach is the analysis of transference through genetic interpretations linking current neurotic behavior to its early childhood origins. Slavson emphasized the importance of transference and modeling in relationship to the therapist and to other group members. This work constitutes an important progression in the development of group theory. Ideas from individual psychoanalytic work are adapted in a creative fashion to the group context. In contrast to Bion, Slavson emphasized the importance of understanding emotional dimensions in the relationships of the member to the therapist and to other group members. Recognition is made of the opportunity in groups for the emergence of several types of specific relationships that may become the material for analysis. Priority is placed on genetic psychodynamic understanding as the principal, final common pathway for therapeutic change. Group interactional events are seen as providing the experiential material from which such insight may be derived.

WHITAKER AND LIEBERMAN

A number of authors have conceptualized group phenomena as reflecting common psychodynamic themes among the members (Ezriel, 1950; Foulkes, 1964; Whitaker & Lieberman, 1964). Whitaker (1985) describes the emergence of such themes as a defence against anxiety about taking risks regarding group participation or about addressing sensitive personal issues. Such fears are contained by the development of a common belief system among the group members. These themes are then understood in terms of (1) a disturbing motive for the theme, an impulse–wish–need–intention that is striving for expression, and (2) a reactive motive, anxiety or guilt over the emergence of the desires inherent to the disturbing motive. From this tension, two possible solutions can result. A constructive "enabling solution" alleviates fear while allowing at least partial expression of the disturbing motive. A "restrictive solution" addresses only the fear and leaves the wish unacknowledged and unsatisfied.

This theory takes the focal conflict idea developed by French (1954) for individual therapy and applies it more or less intact to a group context. As this tradition has developed over time, it has become less dogmatic in regard to the expectation that all members must participate in a given theme. Whittaker in her later work (1985) clearly implies that a particular theme may be relevant only to a subset of group members. The idea of a given psychodynamic conflict being held in common by group members represents a greater degree of sophistication in analyzing group process. It expands Slavson's interest in individual relationships to group-level emotional states and the interpersonal meanings upon which they are based. The theory clearly shows its roots in earlier analytic concepts of instinctual expression. While of value to therapists in understanding some aspects of group process, it does not provide an adequate theory of group functioning.

This brief review of the evolution of group theory indicates how emotional dimensions have moved from being regarded as dangerous and antitherapeutic to being considered critical components in the context of interpersonal meaning. This brings us to current conceptualizations about group therapy that fall into two general areas: (1) The interpersonal approach focuses on the interactions among group members in terms of the therapeutic factors that are operating. This is a person-oriented tradition with roots in humanistic psychology (Rogers, 1951) and interpersonal theory (Sullivan, 1953). The group is seen as a social microcosm with important therapeutic properties. Genetic insight is downplayed as a mechanism of change. (2) Systems theory views the group as an organizational structure with interactive features based on information theory and boundary functioning (Durkin, 1981). The individual is seen in terms of his role in this system. The two approaches are in many ways complementary. The interpersonal theory focuses on the minute-to-minute transactions among the members.

Systems theory steps further back and tries to understand the group from an organizational viewpoint. Both offer their own particular understanding of therapy. The remainder of this chapter is structured around the major concepts of these two traditions and the connections they have with emotion.

COHESION

While cohesion is widely discussed as a basic therapeutic factor similar in importance to empathy in individual therapy, the term itself has suffered in both the clinical and research literature from lack of a clear definition. Yalom (1985) accepts the meaning of cohesion as "the resultant of all the forces acting on all the members to remain in the group" or "the attractiveness of a group for its members" (p. 49). However, his chapter on cohesiveness then goes on to mix these group-level definitions with the idea of the individual member's recognition of being accepted by other members. Bloch and Crouch (1985) have proposed sound reasons for considering the group definition of cohesion as a general "condition for change," and the individual definition as the therapeutic factor of "acceptance."

COHESION AS A CONDITION FOR CHANGE

Group-level cohesion can be considered one of the important conditions for change. Therapeutic factors will have greater impact in a group with strong cohesion. Cohesion refers to a sense of group esprit de corps. This includes a strong alliance with the group's goals or potential for positive therapeutic outcome. These effects may be maximized through pretherapy role-induction preparation. Cohesion can be based on attraction to a charismatic or prestigious leader. The group may appear desirable because of strong external social pressure or the need to defend against an outside threat. The individual may see the group as providing recognition or security through shared power. A member may have strong allegiance to a group despite not caring for many of the members or even experiencing a sense of being accepted (Scott, 1965). However, the usual situation is that of a circular process wherein group cohesiveness enhances participation, positive feelings about the group and its members, and a desire to know others more intimately. These effects in turn contribute to increased levels of cohesiveness.

Kellerman (1981), writing from an analytic perspective, defines cohesion according to ideas of group normative structure as "the existence of an assumed group attitude with respect to its own reason for being that is accepted by the group membership as a context and framework of affiliation" (p. 5). He suggests that these assumptions of commonality are based primarily upon a perceived similarity of the deep structure of members' punitive or superego predispositions. These can be seen as ways of managing tensions and as answers to the question "How is blame being managed?" Three basic punitive structures are described: projective mechanisms by which blame is externalized onto scapegoats, expiating mechanisms concerned with personal sin and a higher force that can offer atonement, and confronting mechanisms whereby tensions are dealt with directly. These three avenues of managing tension would seem to have considerable similarity to Bion's fight–flight, dependency, and working group conditions, respectively. Kellerman's ideas draw attention to the "assumptive reality" of group norms (MacKenzie, 1979) and how this can reflect individual internal issues not immediately tested in actual interpersonal exchanges.

AFFILIATION TO THE SYSTEM

The concept of cohesion is closely related to the idea of affiliation to a system. This is somewhat different from the emotional dimension of bonding or attachment to another individual. Membership in a social system or group can evoke high levels of commitment, but most systems of personality classification have not focused on this dimension. Three contemporary researchers have dealt in varying ways with this issue.

Schutz' (1966) tri-axial interactional system includes the dimension of "inclusion" in the form of a wish "to include others" or a wish "to be included." His self-report questionnaire, FIRO-B, has been used to measure this but with less than uniform results.

Bales, like Schutz, also uses a three-dimensional model of interpersonal functioning (Bales & Cohen, 1979). His Forward–Backward axis focuses mainly on task orientation versus emotional tension release that interrupts the task. However, lurking in his descriptions of the Forward direction are references to value judgments and social norms. "Backward behavior is justified by values of freedom from certain other value controls, while Forward behavior is justified by a positive evaluation of the value controls on impulse" (Bales & Cohen, 1979, p. 179). This axis, therefore, is in some ways related to issues fundamental to cohesion.

Plutchik (1980b) describes one of the four major adaptational problems to be overcome by all creatures as that of identity. "This refers to the basic question of who we are; alternatively, it refers to what group we belong to. This is a fundamental problem for all organisms because isolated individuals in society do not usually survive and certainly they do not propagate. Group membership, therefore, is a fundamental basis for survival" (p. 28). He characterizes the issue of identity as polarized between the interpersonal functions of acceptance and rejection. This corresponds in his circumplex model of personality dimensions to the emotional terms of trust–affiliating and distrust–repulsing.

While the above authors have provided some useful concepts, there is need for further fundamental theory and research on the issue of the connection between the individual and the group. As we have seen, many of the group ideas of cohesion come from a social psychology tradition with quite different concepts from those of traditional personality research and clinical therapy. One important issue is concerned with how the individual sees and understands the group itself as opposed to the individuals constituting it. Kellerman's notion of the link being related to internalized group expectations in the form of superego mandates is one intriguing avenue for investigation. It appropriately maintains a group level of understanding. Freud's original concept of the group being united in their identification with the leader addresses at least a component of the phenomenon of cohesion. MacKenzie (1983) has attempted to assess group-level perceptions through the use of a group-climate questionnaire, but the positive working factor in his instrument does not adequately deal with the concept of group cohesion. The question of common goals and normative expectations among the members is also important. Any discussion of cohesion contains within it the issue of the balance between individual autonomy and group influence. This matter will be discussed later under the topic of developmental phenomena.

THERAPEUTIC FACTORS

The interpersonal approach to group psychotherapy became the central force in the field with the publication of the first edition of Yalom's textbook in 1970. In many ways, this was a revolutionary book for it focused on the importance of group events, in and of themselves, as the principal vehicle of therapeutic

TABLE 7.1
THERAPEUTIC FACTORS[a]

1. Instillation of hope[b]
2. Universality[b]
3. Acceptance[b]
4. Altruism[b]
5. Catharsis
6. Self-disclosure[b]
7. Guidance
8. Vicarious learning[b]
9. Interpersonal action
10. Insight

[a]Based on Bloch & Crouch (1985).
[b]Unique presentation in group.

change. Within this populist approach, the centrality of the role of the leader was diminished and the importance of member-to-member events emphasized. Yalom developed his material around the concept of therapeutic factors, which are described in basic interactional terminology with avoidance of the metapsychological concepts commonly found in the psychoanalytic–psychotherapeutic literature. Emotions, in the broader sense of interactional dimensions with specific interpersonal meaning, form an important part of this literature.

Recently Bloch and Crouch (1985) have contributed a critical review of this literature and the following list of 10 categories is modeled on their approach. Many of these therapeutic factors can occur in dyadic therapy as well. However, some are either available only in a group context or else the nature of the experience is quite altered in groups.

Morale Factors

1. Instillation of hope: The patient sees that other group members have improved or are improving and that the group can be helpful to its members in accomplishing their goals; he or she is thus optimistic about the group's potential helpfulness.
2. Universality: The patient realizes that other group members have similar problems and feelings, that one is not alone with reactions and problems, and that one's situation is not unique.
3. Acceptance: The patient experiences a sense of belonging, acceptance by the group, closeness, warmth, reassurance, and support.
4. Altruism: The patient experiences a change in attitude toward the self through a process of helping others by offering support reassurance, or help; the desire to help another is recognized.

This first group of four therapeutic factors share a number of common features. All are related to a general process of opening the self to interaction with others. They do not include specific interactions with specific individuals so much as a global response to positive personal relatedness. In a recent publication, these four have been linked together as a "morale" group (MacKenzie, 1987). They are closely related to the work of Jerome Frank (1973) and Carl Rogers (1951) regarding common helpful factors. Lacoursiere (1980) has linked development of group stages to variations in morale levels. From an information-processing viewpoint, these categories focus on various ways of identifying and experiencing similarity with others, or on membership in a common state. Universalization is a crucial early group phenomena for it allows the process of identification to develop. It makes other members in the group understandable so that work with them seems possible. It also helps to forge a sense of a common task to deal with common problems. In terms of emotional dimensions, these therapeutic factors lie in a positive affiliative direction. They are accompanied by increased levels of sociability, trust, and dependence.

Even though general in nature, these therapeutic factors are responsible for powerful effects in a group. They are indispensable in creating a positive and cohesive group in the early sessions and remain important as sustainers of morale throughout the group's life. The interpersonal opening process involves the need to listen and understand others and to give and take in exchange. This counterbalances the tendency of morbid self-preoccupation commonly found in psychotherapy patients. Also, the process allows an increased objectivity in viewing the self. A common theme running through these factors is the linkage between positive contact with others and improved self-perception. In effect, "if I can be acceptable to others, perhaps I can be acceptable to myself." By building a social network, these factors increase the sense of security and acceptability of the group to the individual and therefore its power to influence members.

Finally, it should be borne in mind that interactional events can work in reverse. A group in which these four therapeutic factors are found in a negative direction is usually in significant trouble. It is that kind of atmosphere that is associated with negative effects and outright casualties (Dies & Teleska, 1985).

Self-Revelation Factors

5. Catharsis: The patient experiences ventilation of feelings, positive or negative, about self or life events. The principal effect must be one of release that brings relief. Often this is described as an "uncorking" of material previously unexpressed or else expressed with great difficulty.
6. Self-disclosure: The patient reveals personal information that is usually kept secret. This may deal with real or fantasied material about past life or current events outside the group.

These two categories comprise a self-revelation process. The first four morale factors are of a general nature. The self-revelation factors deal with specific emotional events that provide highly personal information to the group. These two may be part of a universalization process but this latter process can occur through more superficial self-revelation than covered in the present two categories. For example, a group of somatizing patients may compare symptoms and experience considerable universality without disclosing personally powerful information or emotion. These two factors represent a deepening of the interpersonal work from the standpoint of the individual's revelation of self.

Catharsis is the only therapeutic factor that is specifically affective in nature, the others include a cognitive or interpersonal dimension. Catharsis or ventilation is based on the pure release of emotion. Research suggests that this can be of value in such situations as an acute grief reaction or acute stress situation, but that it is of limited value in more complex interpersonal circumstances. The emotional expression may pave the way for further learning, but this added cognitive dimension appears to be important for maintaining the beneficial effects. One component of the encounter-group movement and related evocative therapies was based on the assumption that the release of emotion is of paramount importance; "let it all hang out." However, the Stanford Encounter Group study concluded that expression of affect without concomitant cognitive integration of the material was not associated with positive change (Lieberman, Yalom, & Miles, 1973).

Self-revelation has been linked to the development of a cohesive group. This is a mutually reinforcing process whereby "self-disclosure is both facilitated by, and contributes to, members' attraction to their group" (Bloch & Crouch, 1985, p. 135). A number of studies have suggested a similar reciprocal effect between self-revelation and attraction and acceptance between members.

Information Factors

7. Guidance: The patient receives useful information, advice, or suggestions, for example, facts about mental illness, theories of etiology, or specific instructions about how to approach a problem.
8. Vicarious learning: The patient learns something of value to the self by observing others interacting within the therapy setting. This includes modeling on other members or therapist, identifying with other members, imitating others, and seeing a personally relevant pattern enacted by others and learning from this.

These two categories of guidance and vicarious learning are appropriately considered together as mechanisms in which outside information is used to modify behavior and perceptions of self and others. They are both relatively simple processes, although the effects may be profound. In themselves they do not employ specific emotional components, although the results may affect self-esteem and confidence through the mastery of situations, as well as through the stimulation of an introspective process.

Psychological Work Factors

9. Interpersonal action: The patient learns from actual interactional behavior with others in the group. This includes trying to have more open relationships with members or the therapist, trying out new ways of relating, learning from feedback about one's behavior, seeing distortions in one's construal of relationships, and trying out alternative methods on the basis of new understanding.

10. Insight: The patient learns something important about the self, personal conduct, self-presentation to others, and the nature of one's problem. Past experiences that led to the present patterns may also be identified.

These categories refer to the entire range of applied interpersonal behavior that may occur in a group. They are at the core of Yalom's "self-reflective loop": The here-and-now interactional experience in the group is subjected to here-and-now self-examination driven by the intense emotional arousal accompanying the process. The emotional process must be subjected to efforts to understand it, to relate it to other situations and interpersonal meanings, and to derive new patterns of interaction.

In many ways the last two categories are the least satisfactory. We have seen progression through mechanisms of increasing complexity. The morale factors are quite basic relationship issues. The self-revelation and information (cognitive-input) factors represent reasonably discrete output and input components, respectively. These three clusters of therapeutic factors have referred to emotion in a rather simplified form of arousal, reactivity, or discharging. In the psychological work categories we see the application of the more complex, "interpersonal meaning" concept of emotion described by Plutchik (1980a). The concepts underlying the importance of interpersonal action in promoting insight include, but go beyond, the idea of transference distortions. A positive learning orientation is taken rather than a negative defense–resistance position. The therapeutic factor approach has led us to this most interesting part of things but then left us without guidelines. The two psychological work categories, while intensely emotional in execution, cover such a wide spectrum of potential issues that at best they are useful nonspecific markers of a "work" environment. They cannot address the question of how best to dissect the complex processes by which interpersonal meaning is derived and acted upon.

GROUP AS A SYSTEM

Now a different perspective will be introduced for understanding groups. This is centered on concepts of the group as an organizational system that develops in functional complexity over time. The individual members can be seen as occupying social roles that have functional importance for the system. Informational boundaries provide the structure upon which the system rests.

An extensive research literature suggests that groups can be seen to progress through different stages of development. Tuckman (1965) popularized this material in his comprehensive review with the terms "forming," "storming," "norming," and "performing." Beck (1974) updated this review and found that while authors identified phenomena in different terms, there was considerable

TABLE 7.2
GROUP DEVELOPMENTAL STAGES WITH PROTOTYPIC THEMES

Stage	Theme
1. Engagement	"We're all the same."
2. Differentiation	"I'm somewhat different."
3. Individuation	"I'm a complex but whole person."
4. Intimacy	"I can be important to someone else."
5. Mutuality	"What I do has implications for someone else."
6. Termination	"I can exist even though alone."

agreement in the descriptions and sequencing of stages. MacKenzie and Livesley (1983) augmented this descriptive literature with a detailed consideration of the functional importance of each stage for both the group and the individual member. Table 7.2 presents a standard formulation of group developmental stages and themes.

The concept of developmental stages is complemented by that of social roles: clusters of behaviors which have functional significance for the group system (Livesley & MacKenzie, 1983). Since the behaviors constituting a role arise under the combined influence of social context and individual personality dynamics the concept of social role provides a theoretical construct for integrating individual characteristics with the functional requisites of the group. Most research concerning social role behavior is reported in the social psychology literature concerning the study of task-oriented groups. Table 7.3 presents a standard formulation of group social roles and attitudes.

The system of the group and the subsystems of the members may be considered to be identified by boundaries. Psychological boundaries exist when there is an awareness that two entities are different; this information about differences constitutes the boundary. Within a therapy group, important boundaries include the external group boundary; the personal boundary of each member; the various interpersonal boundaries, including that between the leader and the group; and

TABLE 7.3
SOCIAL ROLES WITH PROTOTYPIC ATTITUDES

Role	Attitude
1. Sociable	"Let's get along together."
2. Structural	"Let's get the job done."
3. Cautionary	"I'm not sure I belong in this group."
4. Divergent	"I don't agree with the way you people see things."

the internal boundaries within each member, for example between what is recognized and what is hidden from awareness. Many therapeutic processes can be usefully conceptualized as dealing with issues across particular boundaries. The clarification of transboundary differences and mediation between the divergent points of view are important therapist tasks. Figure 7.1 illustrates these various group boundaries.

Brief descriptions of group developmental stages and social roles will be presented. Further details can be found in chapters by MacKenzie and Livesley (1983). After this brief overview, these intersecting theoretical positions of the group task, together with the function of the individual member in accomplishing it, will be discussed from the standpoint of emotional relevance. The descriptions provided below should be seen as prototypical clusters that actual group and individual behaviors will approximate to varying degrees.

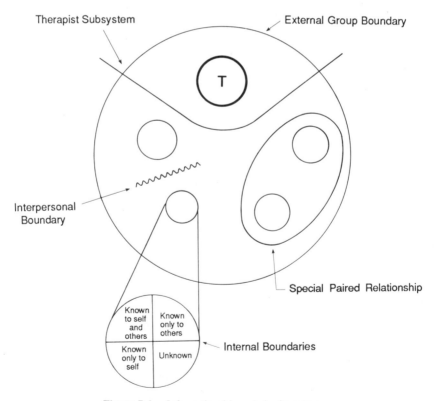

Figure 7.1. Informational boundaries in groups.

GROUP DEVELOPMENTAL STAGES

Stage 1. Engagement: The fundamental task in the first stage is to resolve the issue of engagement of members in the common task of therapy. This is necessary if the group is to emerge as a social system with its own identity. The parallel task for the individual member is to allow participation in an affiliative process and overcome tendencies of isolation and withdrawal. The group climate during this stage is characterized by increasing levels of openness and positive attitudes toward the group and its members. The various aspects of universalization form the central interactional mechanism.

Stage 2. Differentiation: In the second stage, the task is to recognize that differences exist between the members. This moves the group forward from the uncritical sense of cohesion that may come to characterize the engagement stage. The individual member must deal with the management of hostility and the need to incorporate social expectations. This stage involves the polarization of opinion and challenge to the leader. Conflict and confrontation force the examination of differences and lead to the development of conflict resolution mechanisms.

Stage 3. Individuation: The group must now promote an exploratory process to allow a deeper appreciation of the complexity of each member. This is achieved through active interpersonal challenge in a supportive atmosphere. The individual must become open to psychological exploration and become more clearly aware of ambivalences, contradictions, and split-off parts of self. Working dimensions of self-disclosure, challenge, and cognitive mastery are evident. The cohesion of the engagement stage and the conflict resolution style of the differentiation stage are now put to productive work.

Stage 4. Intimacy: The task of this stage is to experience and explore the implications of close relationships. This work is built upon the extensive personal information revealed in the individuation stage. The focus shifts from the individual member to the relationships within the group. The individual members must deal not just with themselves but also with the idea of having relevance to someone else. The interaction climate is characterized by high engagement, at times almost euphoria. In some respects this stage reworks many of the issues and challenges of the engagement stage at a more complex and personalized level.

Stage 5. Mutuality: In this stage, the meaning of closeness is explored, and an appreciation gained of the fundamental uniqueness of each member. This involves questions of personal autonomy and interpersonal responsibility. The individual must address the threat of being used or abandoned in the context of close and meaningful relationships. This involves addressing the meaning of deep levels of trust. The interactional atmosphere is one of interpersonal openness but with greater confrontation and conflict than before as members react to the system's demands for deeper commitments.

Stage 6. Termination: The group task is to promote disengagement from this "artificial" social system and at the same time to encourage incorporation of the experience and the learning that it has allowed. If termination is viewed in a negative fashion, earlier progress may be undone. The individual member must deal with loss and separation and the necessity to assume personal responsibility without the forum of the group for support.

SOCIAL ROLES

1. Sociable Role: Members enacting the sociable role are gregarious and trusting. They try to ensure that all members have a positive experience by providing support, by encouraging participation, and by minimizing differences or negative reactions. In return, these members are rapidly incorporated into the group and are regarded as popular members. These same qualities may imply naivete and the potential for exploitation. Sociable members may also become overly dependent on the group.
2. Structural Role: These members are concerned that the group attends to its task and are therefore involved in organizing group activity and establishing goals. They may have difficulty recognizing and dealing with affect and compensate for this with an advice-giving and concrete problem-solving style. The need for cognitive mastery and sense of purpose are stabilizing features, but these same features may lead to a formalistic, compulsive style that makes interpersonal exchanges difficult.
3. Cautionary Role: Members taking on this role behave in a circumspect and defensive fashion. They are hesitant to reveal important aspects of themselves and demonstrate reluctance to commit themselves to the group. Their resistance may have an angry, distrustful quality. They emphasize the importance of autonomy and self-responsibility. These qualities interfere with the effective use of the group and may lead to rejection by other members.
4. Divergent Role: These members' behavior is characterized by a challenging and questioning interpersonal stance. Members who show such behavior emphasize differences between viewpoints and often do so in an impulsively blunt fashion. There is often an angry and aggressive component to their interpersonal style. They are highly involved in the work of the group and serve to force the examination of contentious but important issues. These same qualities may become disruptive to the group and lead to the scapegoating of these members.

SYSTEM ISSUES

It is clear from these descriptions that stages and social roles are characterized along basic emotional dimensions. As the group approaches its developmental task in each stage, there is a polarization along a particular emotional axis. This creates a state of dialectical tension around issues related to that dimension, and members representing particular role positions will align themselves accordingly. Thus each stage will have unique importance to each member. Some will lead the group in addressing the stage task, others will struggle to come to grips with the relevant issues. The developing group therefore presents a series of interactional environments that in total represent a reasonable sampling of major emotional dimensions.

Affect plays a central role at several different levels in the system. At the level of the group, affect forces resolution of the polarization inherent to the group task. For example, during the differentiation stage the high level of conflict in the group pushes members to justify their positions and thereby establish their individual identity within the group more clearly. Thus the group becomes a more confrontational environment in which effective work can take place. At the same time, the process of successfully presenting and defending one's viewpoint results in an enhancement of self-esteem for the individual. In this interactive process the individual may also become aware of aspects of the self that had previously been hidden from oneself, though not necessarily from others. The work of confrontation therefore applies internally as well as externally, indicating an isomorphism between group-level mechanisms and individual ones. System theory goes one step further to suggest that change in one level of the system will induce change at other levels. Thus it is not critical if an intervention is made to the group or to the individual, since the effects will move throughout the system.

The group leader has the important task of managing the affective climate of the group. Through a knowledge of the developmental sequence that will best facilitate the emergence of constructive working group climate, the therapist is equipped with broad guidelines in regard to stage-appropriate material. The expected issues will undoubtedly appear within the group interaction. The therapist may then selectively reinforce or dampen particular interactional dimensions through a process of knowledgeable operant conditioning. For example, in the engagement process it is important that a sense of positive cohesion develop before the group attempts to come to grips with more conflictual issues. The therapist therefore will soften and deflect confrontational patterns. Initially, this may be done by selective ignoring or redirection. If that is not sufficient, then specific interventions may be made suggesting that "it is important to explore differences but that members need to get to know each other better first." This employs positive connotation of the behavior followed by explicit reasons for the deferral.

Generally, the therapist is able to draw on role behaviors present among the members to promote stage tasks. It is important in this process that members do not become labeled for particular qualities even if these are useful for the group. These same qualities may also reflect areas of conflict for them, and excessive attention by the therapist or group members may make it difficult to address the less functional side of the role behavior. At times the therapist may need to promote stage-appropriate themes by modeling them for the group. The important general point is that the therapist has a responsibility to see that the group deals with the stage-relevant emotional issues. Particularly in the early stages, formation of a working group must take priority over issues of individual members.

There is substantial evidence to suggest that therapist behaviors drawn from the sociable and structural role repertoires are most conductive to effective group therapy. In the Lieberman-Yalom-Miles study (1973), these were labeled caring and meaning-attribution. Leaders who promote heightened emotional states and who pull members into the group interaction through their charismatic exhortations may have some positive results but also an increase in negative effects (Dies & Teleska, 1985). These are behaviors drawn especially from the divergent role spectrum. Therapists who act mainly with cautionary role behaviors have lower success rates. This would include a "classical" analytic nonresponsive withholding style. Group-as-a-whole interpretations are of limited value and when used exclusively tend to promote an antitherapeutic environment. It appears important that therapists deal directly with in-group interpersonal events, particularly to increase understanding of distortions in interpersonal perceptions and reactions.

Groups will move through the developmental stages at varying rates related to composition, member characteristics, therapist strategies, and the context in which the group is taking place. For example, outpatient groups for long-term schizophrenic patients may progress over a time scale of years, while the development of experiential training groups for professionals may be measured in hours. There are groups, such as some for addictive behaviors, that may purposefully stay in engagement stage patterns forever. Constancy of group membership and frequency of sessions will hasten group development. Changes in therapist or in members will necessitate the reworking of early group development issues. It is important that the therapist encourage and lead the group toward its developmental tasks but, at the same time, not get too far ahead. The therapist needs to take cues from emerging group interaction and reinforce stage-appropriate components. As the ancient saying puts it, "It's easier to ride a horse when its going in the right direction."

In the following discussion, the language to be used in identifying emotional dimensions is based on that used by Plutchik (1980a) in his circumplex model of emotions. These basic interactional dimensions are considered to form the building blocks of more complex patterns. A major advantage of this tradition lies in its origins in an extensive ethological literature. This suggests that biologically mediated mechanisms are being employed in the service of high-order relationship patterns.

Stage 1: Engagement

The engagement stage forces consideration of issues involved along the emotional axis of sociability–withdrawal and to some extent along the trust–distrust dimension. The principal boundary being activated is the external group boundary. For patients with conflictual difficulties with affiliative processes, this stage provides a medium through which the difficulties can be addressed. Since many patients seeking psychotherapy have become sensitized to the real or imagined dangers of relationships, attempts to address the functional issues of this stage are accompanied by high degrees of affect. Because there is powerful pressure to join the forming group, members cannot avoid dealing with these affiliation issues.

The morale group of therapeutic factors is particularly useful in enhancing the development of this stage. The various aspects of universalization form the central interactional theme. The self-revelation factors are in evidence, although at a moderate and often rather superficial level. Indeed, it is amply demonstrated in the literature that too much self-disclosure too early is associated with premature drop out and negative therapeutic effects (Dies & Teleska, 1985). The above factors contribute to a process of positive identification with the group that will constitute a powerful sustaining force as the group moves into more confrontational activities. The information categories can form a central component in some groups. For example, brief groups, in-patient groups, and support groups may want to maintain an engagement stage atmosphere for their entire existence. Information and educational components form an excellent vehicle for this.

Those members occupying the sociable role position have an important function as the group begins. They provide the positive interpersonal "glue" that allows the process of identification to begin. Similarly, the task focus of the structural role members forms a cognitive and containing focus for the beginning of group work. The cautionary role members are generally less active during this stage or drop out early if the threat of group involvement is too great. The divergent role members are tolerated and to some extent ignored in the beginning unless they are overly active, in which case they too are at risk for isolation and premature termination. All of these effects can be seen to relate to the relative position of each behavioral role cluster along the affiliative and attachment–trust dimensions.

The powerful emotional process of becoming a member of a group may elicit deep fears regarding acceptability and likableness. Participation in the achievement of a cohesive group not only allays these fears but also is reflected in an enhanced sense of self-esteem. But there may also be an internal analogue to the engagement process. It is during this stage that a commitment is made to deal with personal material, often of a painful nature. The group process of universality may trigger a recognition of the need to come to grips with these issues.

Thus the group cohesive process may be paralleled by a more open relationship with self.

Stage 2: Differentiation

In this stage members must deal with negative interpersonal events, including anger, rejection, and polarization of opinion. This focus on difference of viewpoint constitutes a particular challenge for members who experience difficulty in finding a comfortable balance along the anger–fear or dominance–submissive dimension. In addition, the ability to tolerate and deal with negative interpersonal tone is tested. The boundary focus shifts from the external group boundary to that of the interpersonal one. The principal mechanism is the satisfactory negotiation of the sequence from polarization of differences to the development of a cooperative method of conflict resolution. Many psychotherapy patients are either highly fearful of a dissonant interpersonal atmosphere or are predisposed to an excessively angry and confrontational style. A successful outcome from this stage allows the members to appreciate that differences can be used constructively. This supplies the group with important skills in undertaking interpersonal psychological work, since issues can be addressed and not ignored. In addition, the challenges to the leader during this stage give the group a stronger sense of its own identity than present during the engagement stage.

During this stage, the morale factors will undoubtedly become weaker. That is why it is crucial that they be adequately developed during the engagement stage. The self-revelation factors play an important part during this stage. One effect of the confrontational atmosphere is that members must defend themselves and, in this process, reveal important aspects concerning themselves and their beliefs. This process aids in the consolidation of group norms. Because of the high level of emotion during this stage, the information categories cannot be effectively used. Groups emphasizing educational approaches are best advised to keep within an engagement style of interaction. The psychological work factors become more evident during this stage than in the engagement stage as the tempo of interaction increases.

The divergent role behaviors are particularly important during this stage. The emphasis on identifying differences and forcing their exploration enhances the differentiation process. Indeed, if these behaviors are not forthcoming from the members, the therapist may need to model them. The cautionary role members may contribute to the negative tone, believing that it is an inevitable component of attempts to achieve socialization. The structural role members may be helpful in this stage by struggling to make cognitive sense out of the conflict. The sociable role members will feel helpless and betrayed at seeing their "nice" group dissolving about them. They perhaps have the most to gain from experiencing a successful weathering of this stage.

At an internal level, the conflict of the differentiation process has the potential to create harmful effects. This is particularly likely for those without positive bonding with other members. Once this stage has been mastered, however, the satisfaction of realizing that one has stood up for personal beliefs and tolerated angry feelings can result in a substantial strengthening of self-confidence. In the confrontational process of this stage, previously rejected parts of self may come into the open and the anger at others may be directed at self as well. This is often begun with a process of projective identification with other members that then breaks down as the personal relevance is recognized.

Stage 3: Individuation

The central focus of this stage is on the active confronting of personal issues. The interactional process has the individual member as its main focus. The emphasis on understanding and self-investigation locates this stage on the control–dyscontrol dimension. The function of cognitive control falls into the same general emotional domain as exploration of the environment. While varying reactive emotional responses will emerge as issues are explored, the task is to move from these reactions into a sense of greater cognitive mastery of self. The members now appear to be involved in important collaborative explorations, often with a sharp and rapid transition from the turmoil of the differentiation stage. This "work" atmosphere is the result of successful accomplishment of the tasks of the first two stages. Positive and negative aspects can now be explored, and members feel more comfortable confronting issues in themselves and in others because they feel more competent to resolve them. This group atmosphere draws members into the introspective process in a manner that is distinctively more active than that which occurs in individual therapy. The boundary focus therefore shifts to internal boundaries where ambivalences, contradictions, and hidden material can be explored. There is a shift of material from "issues unknown to self" to "issues known to self." Feedback from "issues known to others" is an important mechanism. This is a consolidation stage, where material previously hinted at is explored and placed in perspective. The overall affective climate is less intense than during the differentiation stage.

Self-revelation dimensions are particularly important during this stage. There is a marked increase in the amount of information available to members about each other. This increase in interpersonal knowledge tends to bind the members closer together. Information categories are mainly represented by vicarious learning as members witness each other's efforts toward greater self-understanding. This stage offers an opportunity for deeper identification with each other than present during prior stages as members detect common developmental issues and similar defensive methods. Psychological work is clearly predominant, particularly "insight" events as members look for the motivations or antecedents of their behavioral patterns. The morale factors return to a higher level during this stage than in the differentiation stage. The sense of productive work characteristic of this stage is highly reinforcing to group cohesion.

Structural role members readily respond to the ''call to work'' of this stage. Divergent role members will also find this stage manageable because of the importance they place on identifying interpersonal issues. Sociable role members may have problems getting into introspective work since they often handle interpersonal issues by a reactive rather than a mastery response. The demand for further public revelation will be difficult for cautionary role members but it is essential that they participate or they will be unprepared for the demands of subsequent stages.

This stage involves further work on personal issues that may have been identified in a preliminary fashion during the preceding stage. As new awareness is achieved of the motivations behind problematic behaviors, or of the earlier roots of current difficulties, there is a danger of significant loss of self-esteem. The presence of a group atmosphere that can combine intrusive work with support is most helpful. As internal issues are worked through, there may be a surge of greater acceptance of self as a more complicated but understandable person.

Stage 4: Intimacy

The focus now shifts to the interpersonal boundary once again, especially as reflected in pairing phenomena. An exploration of the meaning of closeness will raise important issues on the sociability–withdrawal and trust–distrust dimensions. In the engagement stage these same issues were worked out in terms of the relationship between the individual member and the group. Now they take a more personalized form. The personal information that was revealed during the preceding stages has drawn the members into a close interactional network in which issues related to intimacy cannot be avoided. Intense attractions may occur, often with a romantic component. These may be compared and contrasted with previous or current relationships outside of the group. This process will activate fears associated with possible rejection. Difficulty in achieving intimacy is a common component of dysfunctional interpersonal patterns. It is therefore critical that the implications of such dysfunctional interpersonal patterns are carefully and thoughtfully explored. In particular, it is important that the emergence of themes of intimacy not be denigrated or criticized but rather understood. Echoes of earlier experiences and family of origin material may be expected.

The most important therapeutic factors at work are found in the psychological work categories of interpersonal action and insight. At this more advanced stage of group work, it becomes clear how inadequate these categories are to effectively describe group events. Of considerable more relevance are approaches that look at interpersonal perception and the constructs around which it is organized. During this stage, it is not unusual to find significant distortions in the attachment process. This often relates to childhood experiences in which the normal affection of a naive child becomes paired with contradictory issues of control, rejection, fear, or punishment. Such inhibiting fusions may emerge in the relationships between group members. At this stage it is to be expected that the most important work will focus on these here-and-now phenomena. Successful mastery of previous stage tasks will lay a base upon which this interpersonal focus can be sustained.

The sociable role members will find this stage to be of particular interest. Issues of intimacy and affiliation have motivated most of their efforts to encourage positive and friendly relations in the group. Thus, they will perceive the emerging themes of intimacy as a happy prognostic. Once developed, however, the work of understanding intimacy will prove difficult but thematically very important for these members. Structural role members will experience difficulty in dealing with this noncognitive material and their affective blindness will be very much in evidence. Divergent role members will feel more comfortable with this focus on delicate process issues even though they may handle them clumsily. Their tendency to "act out" conflictual issues may be a danger in terms of group romances. Cautionary role members imagine their worst fears are coming true as they witness liaisons forming between members.

All members stand to gain important knowledge from these group themes. The unrealistically positive evaluation of group relationships will provoke a reconsideration of other current and past intimacies. The recognition of lost opportunities or destroyed partnerships may produce sobering self-examination. At the same time, the group process experience of being of importance to someone else may result in an exhilarating increase in self-esteem. This stage offers an opportunity to examine the basic dimensions of bonding and attachment.

Stage 5: Mutuality

This stage embodies work of a more mature nature. The thematic focus is on the issue of responsibility in relationships. Thus, it builds upon the experience of closeness in the preceding stage. There are two competing emotional dimensions within this material. The first has to do with the dominance–submission axis. This power dimension is basic to an understanding of the question of dependency and exploitation in relationships. The second major dimension is trust, which is inextricably woven into the question of responsibility in relationships. Both of these dimensions have of course already been dealt with in the group's development, but here they undergo more advanced examination. Trust in particular has been a constant issue throughout the group's life but now it becomes a central issue. The focus therefore remains on the interpersonal boundary, but with an emphasis on personal autonomy in relationships. As in the intimacy stage, the therapeutic factor categories have marginal relevance to an understanding of the issues of this stage. One anticipates continuing psychological work with less emphasis on the other dimensions.

The cautionary role members may have a useful role to play in this stage. With their emphasis upon individual autonomy, they are able to polarize the issues through caution over uncritical acceptance of closeness as well as through resistance to overly committed involvement in the group process. This will lay a groundwork for eventual termination issues. Structural role members will welcome the opportunity to stand back and understand relationships and will help the group to address these issues. Divergent and sociable role members will have the most difficulty with the thematic material of this stage of the group. During the preceding stage and this one, it is to be expected that role-stereotypic patterns will give way to a broader range of interactions. Indeed, one might characterize the goal of therapy as the development of role flexibility. This equips the individual to respond to situations appropriately and not in an overdetermined fashion.

The emphasis on existential issues of personal autonomy and responsibility makes advanced demands on the members. The focus on the distribution of power in this stage, coupled with the preceding focus on intimacy, provides exposure to the two major dimensions of interpersonal functioning. There is a greater tendency to apply group learning to outside situations in preparation for termination.

Stage 6: Termination

The ending of the group should receive the same careful attention to group-level issues as the engagement stage. The double task of this stage is to disengage from the group and at the same time to incorporate the group experience as an enduring positive influence. This calls for a return to the external boundary of the group as the principal focus. Now the process goes in reverse to that of the engagement stage. Group learning must be purposefully applied to outside circumstances. The mourning process will involve the recapitulation of group events of particular importance to each member and a review of personal changes since the beginning. Reactions involving depression and anger are to be expected. Sociable role members find termination most difficult and may experience a transient return of symptoms. Cautionary role members may welcome the chance to be free of the obligations of the group.

This last stage forces a consideration of loss and separation. This grief work must be directly addressed and not avoided by euphemisms that all is going well. By adequately dealing with the sadness, the member is able to accept that he can function without the group. It is particularly critical that the group memory be positively retained while acceptance of responsibility for one's self allows optimism for the future. Table 7.4 summarizes the focal dimensions of each stage of group development discussed here.

TABLE 7.4

SYSTEM AND EMOTIONAL DIMENSIONS MOST IN FOCUS DURING EACH STAGE[a]

Stage	Role	Boundary	Therapeutic factors	Emotional dimensions
1. Engagement	Sociable, structural	External	Morale, self-revelation, information	Sociable–withdrawr, trust–distrust
2. Differentation	Divergent	Interpersonal	Self-revelation, psychological work	Anger–fear, dominance–submission
3. Individuation	Structural	Internal	Psychological work, self-revelation, information	Control–dyscontrol
4. Intimacy	Sociable	Interpersonal	Psychological work	Sociable–withdrawn, trust–distrust
5. Mutuality	Cautionary	Interpersonal	Psychological work	Dominance–submission
6. Termination	Cautionary	External	Morale	Joy–sadness

[a] The dimensions represent trends emerging from the complexity of group interaction.

SUMMARY

The material reviewed in this chapter offers challenging opportunities for clinical practice and research. The stage and role descriptions offer a functional perspective for understanding the relationship between group phenomena and individual behavior. This provides useful guidelines for therapeutic interventions. The dimensions are couched in language from a common system of interpersonal dimensions. Thus each can be plotted in the hypothetical space circumscribed by these basic axes. The therapy group offers a unique setting in which to observe a multifaceted interactional field. The intersecting stage–role theoretical material presented in this chapter places emotion in the central role of both driving the group to resolve issues as well as providing role figures to assist in this process. The same dimensions can be used to track internal change in patterns of interpersonal construal. One pressing task is to translate these theoretical ideas into suitable measurement methods.

REFERENCES

Bales, R. F., & Cohen, S. P. (1979). *SYMLOG: A system for the multiple level observation of groups*. New York: Free Press.

Beck, A. P. (1974). Phases in the development of structure in therapy and encounter groups. In D. A. Wexler & L. N. Rice (Eds.), *Innovations in client-centered therapy*. New York: Wiley.

Bion, W. (1961). *Experiences in groups*. New York: Basic Books.

Bloch, S., & Crouch, E. (1985). *Therapeutic factors in group psychotherapy*. London & New York: Oxford University Press.

Dies, R. R., & Teleska, P. A. (1985). Negative outcome in group psychotherapy. In D. T. Mays & C. M. Franks (Eds.), *Negative outcome in psychotherapy*. New York: Springer.

Durkin, J. E. (1981). *Living groups: Group psychotherapy and general system theory*. New York: Brunner/Mazel.

Ezriel, H. (1950). A psychoanalytic approach to group treatment. *British Journal of Medical Psychology*, **23**, 59–74.

Foulkes, S. H. (1964). *Therapeutic group analysis*. London: Allen & Unwin.

Frank, J. D. (1973). *Persuasion and healing: A comparative study of psychotherapy*. Baltimore, MD: Johns Hopkins University Press.

French, T. M. (1954). *The integration of behavior*. Chicago, IL: University of Chicago Press.

Freud, S. 1955. Totem and taboo. In J. Strachey (Ed. and Trans.), *The standard edition of the complete psychological works of Sigmund Freud* (Vol. 13). London: Hogarth Press. (Original work published 1913)

Freud, S. (1955). Group psychology and the analysis of the ego. In J. Strachey (Ed. and Trans.), *The standard edition of the complete psychological works of Sigmund Freud* (Vol. 18). London: Hogarth Press. (Original work published 1921)

Horowitz, M. (1979). *States of mind: Analysis of change in psychotherapy*. New York: Plenum.

Kellerman, H. (1981). The Deep Structures of group cohesion. In H. Kellerman (Ed.), *Group cohesion: Theoretical and clinical perspectives*. New York: Grune & Stratton.

Lacoursiere, R. (1980). *The life cycle of groups*. New York: Human Sciences Press.

LeBon, G. (1920). *The crowd: A study of the popular mind*. New York: Fisher Unwin.

Lieberman, M. A., Yalom, I. D.,& Miles, M. B. (1973). *Encounter groups: First facts*. New York: Basic Books.

Livesley, W. J., & MacKenzie, K. R. (1983). Social roles in psychotherapy groups. In R. R. Dies & K. R. MacKenzie (Eds.), *Advances in group psychotherapy: Integrating research and practice*. New York: International Universities Press.

Luborsky, L. (1984). *Principles of psychoanalytic psychotherapy: A manual for supportive-expressive treatment*. New York: Basic Books.

MacKenzie, K. R. (1979). Group norms: Importance and measurement. *International Journal of Group Psychotherapy*, **29**, 471–480.

MacKenzie, K. R. (1983). The clinical application of a group climate measure. In R. R. Dies & K. R. MacKenzie (Eds.), *Advances in group psychotherapy: Integrating research and practice*. New York: International Universities Press.

MacKenzie, K. R. (1987). Therapeutic factors in group psychotherapy: A contemporary view. *Group*, **11**, 26–34.

MacKenzie, K. R. (1990). *Introduction to time—limited group psychotherapy*. Washington D. C.: American Psychiatric Press, Inc.

MacKenzie, K. R., & Livesley, W. J. (1983). A developmental model for brief group therapy. In R. R. Dies & K. R. MacKenzie (Eds.), *Advances in group psychotherapy: Integrating research and practice*. New York: International Universities Press.

McDougall, W. (1920). *The group mind*. New York: Putnam.

Plutchik, R. (1980a). *Emotion: A psychoevolutionary synthesis*. New York: Harper & Row.

Plutchik, R. (1980b). A general psychoevolutionary theory of emotion. In R. Plutchik & H. Kellerman (Eds.), *Emotion: Theory, research, and experience: Vol. 1. Theories of emotion*. New York: Academic Press.

Rogers, C. R. (1951). *Client-centered therapy*. London: Constable.

Schutz, W. (1966). *The interpersonal underworld*. Palo Alto, CA: Science & Behavior Books.

Scott, W. A. (1965). *Values and organizations*. Chicago, IL: Rand McNally.

Slavson, S. R. (1979). In M. Schiffer (Ed.), *Dynamics of group psychotherapy*. New York: Jason Aronson.

Strupp, H. H., & Binder, J. L. (1984). *Psychotherapy in a new key: A guide to time-limited dynamic psychotherapy*. New York: Basic Books.

Sullivan, H. S. (1953). *The interpersonal theory of psychiatry*. New York: Norton.

Tuckman, B. W. (1965). Developmental sequence in small groups. *Psychological Bulletin, 63*, 384–399.

Whitaker, D. S. (1985). *Using groups to help people*. London: Routledge and Kegan Paul.

Whitaker, D. S., & Lieberman, M. A. (1964). *Psychotherapy through the group process*. New York: Atherton.

Yalom, I. D. (1985). *The theory and practice of group psychotherapy* (3rd ed.). New York: Basic Books.

Part III

COGNITIVE, BEHAVIORAL, AND DYNAMIC FOCUS

Chapter 8

COGNITIVE APPROACHES TO PSYCHOTHERAPY: THEORY AND THERAPY

MICHAEL S. GREENBERG AND AARON T. BECK

ABSTRACT

According to the cognitive model of emotional disorders, individuals suffering from a variety of emotional disorders can be characterized as possessing enduring and maladaptive cognitive organizations or "schemas" that have a strong impact upon affective and behavioral responses. These schemas become activated as the psychological disturbance begins and lead to systematically biased conclusions about the self, the world, and the future. This process, in turn, is hypothesized to maintain and exacerbate the existing psychological disturbance. Further, it is proposed that different psychological disorders can be distinguished on the basis of their ideation, with depressive schemas typically containing themes of failure, worthlessness, incompetence, and rejection, whereas anxiety disorders often contain themes of threat, danger, and uncertainty. Cognitive therapy is an active and structured approach to the treatment of depression and anxiety that is based upon the cognitive model of psychopathology. Patients are trained to systematically identify, evaluate, and test the reality of their biased or distorted cognitions. The patient in cognitive therapy is encouraged to view negative cognitions as hypotheses to be tested in relation to facts about the self, the world, and the future. This goal is achieved by a variety of cognitive and behavioral methods designed ultimately to reduce the symptoms of depression and anxiety and minimize the probability of relapse. Outcome studies have generally shown cognitive therapy to be an effective treatment, with the strongest evidence indicating cognitive therapy to be superior to nondirective and behavior therapies and at least as effective as chemotherapy.

177

THE COGNITIVE MODEL OF DEPRESSION

The cognitive model of depression and therapy is based upon a set of assumptions about the interaction of cognition, affect, and behavior (Beck, 1964, 1967, 1976; Beck, Rush, Shaw, & Emery, 1979). Individuals are conceptualized as active perceivers who are constantly engaged in the cognitive processing of internal and external information. Consequently, they may selectively attend to, modify, categorize, and transform information prior to a behavioral response. An examination of an individual's "automatic thoughts" (Beck, 1963) can often indicate how he or she has appraised and evaluated a specific set of input data. Further, these cognitions represent an individual's phenomenal field and reveal his or her attributions of causality. Changes and modifications in the processing of information can result in corresponding changes in affect and behavior.

For example, a depressed individual who is unemployed and searching for suitable employment may think "I'm a failure and incompetent, no one will ever hire me and there is no use in applying for a job or going to an interview." Further, such individuals are likely to consider themselves failures as spouses and as parents and incapable of carrying out relatively simple tasks. This negative view of the self and the future, centering on thoughts of failure and incompetence, may result in not looking for a job and becoming generally inactive in this area. This process may involve a self-fulfilling prophecy so that initial expectations of being unhirable are confirmed by the inactivity, thereby resulting in an increase in depression, thoughts of failure and incompetence, and consequently an increase in the other symptoms of depression.

It would be misleading and simplistic to assume that changes in cognitions are unidirectional, without affect and behavior subsequently influencing cognitions. Thus, a reciprocal interactional model appears more in accord with clinical and empirical observations (Bandura, 1977; Coyne, 1982; Isen, Shalker, Clark, & Karp, 1978). Beck et al. (1979) expanded the unit of observation to important aspects of the patient's environment, including family, friends, peers, and employer. A person who is becoming increasingly depressed may withdraw from significant others. Individuals within the depressed person's social network may respond by rejection or criticism, which then leads to a vicious cycle of social alienation and withdrawal.

In contrast, maintenance of harmonious interpersonal relationships may cushion or buffer the development of a severe depressive episode. While the cognitive model explicitly acknowledges the influence of these other domains upon the generation of psychopathology, it also proposes that cognitive factors occupy a position of primacy in the sequence of symptom development (Beck et al., 1979). A patient's negative view of reality is hypothesized to be the initial link in a sequence of symptoms that include deficits in motivation, reduced voluntary responding, social withdrawal, and neurovegetative changes. Beck et al. (1979) has proposed that a patient's negative view of reality frequently arises from cognitive structures originating in childhood. Childhood events hypothesized to lead to the development of negative cognitive structures include early parental loss or rejection, parental discouragement of autonomy and independence, physical defects and abnormalities, and learning that one's worth as an individual is primarily contingent on successful performance. This formulation also has the advantage of leading to testable hypotheses. While the cognitive model rests on the assumption of the primacy of cognitive events, it does not deny the influence of biochemical and genetic factors on the development of depression.

According to Ingram and Hollon (1986), the development of a unified and consistent theory of depression has been hindered by variation in the types of cognitive variables that have been hypothesized to be central to an understanding of depression. For example, cognitive variables such as self-schemas, self-statements, attributional styles, and irrational beliefs have all been proposed as central to the genesis and maintenance of depression. In order to provide a consistent framework in which to view these and other cognitive variables, Ingram and Hollon proposed a taxonomy that categorizes the basic mechanisms of cognition into four classes: (1) cognitive structures, (2) cognitive propositions, (3) cognitive operations, and (4) cognitive products. This schema is relatively consistent with Meichenbaum and Gilmore's (1984) discussion of "cognitive structures, cognitive processes, and cognitive events." Classifying cognitions within a coherent framework will facilitate the following discussion of important cognitive processes in depression and may reduce some of the inconsistent usages of terms such as "schemas" and "cognitive distortions" that have been observed in the literature.

COGNITIVE STRUCTURES

The term "cognitive structures" refers to relatively enduring representations of prior knowledge and experience in memory. Further, cognitive structures are used to process information and to predict future courses of behavior by selective encoding, evaluation, and retrieval of information from memory (Neimeyer, 1985). Memories are typically organized in hierarchical and network form, are linked to other memory structures, and contain both conceptual and factual information (Ingram & Hollon, 1986).

From the standpoint of the cognitive model, the most important cognitive structure is the "schema," which acts as a pattern for selecting, encoding, retrieving, and interpreting the stimuli that confront an individual. Cognitive schemas enable an individual to break down and filter the vast array of stimuli impinging upon him or her at any given moment and serve a function of "cognitive economy" and efficient processing of information (Neisser, 1976; Rosch, 1975). Information that is inconsistent with the general organization is often ignored or forgotten; other aspects of the information are elaborated in ways that make them consistent with the activated schema (Bobrow & Norman, 1975; Bower, Black, & Turner, 1979; Minsky, 1975; Owens, Bower, & Black, 1979). Thus, although schemas facilitate perception, comprehension, recall, and problem solving (Taylor & Crocker, 1980), an important consequence of the continuous operation of schemas is biased and distorted information processing (e.g., selective attention and recall).

SELF-SCHEMAS

The concept of a negative self-schema has been central to the cognitive model of depression. Derry and Kuiper (1981) and Kuiper and Derry (1982) proposed a "content specificity hypothesis," which suggested that the self-schemas of clinical depressives consists primarily of pathological or depressive content, whereas the schemas of nondepressives contain primarily positive or nonpathological content. This hypothesis predicts relatively clear-cut differences in the processing styles of nondepressed and depressed individuals. In a "depth-of-processing," incidental free-recall paradigm, Derry and Kuiper presented trait adjectives with depressed and nondepressed content to clinical depressives, psychiatric controls, and normal subjects during an initial "orienting task" and subsequently asked subjects to recall the same trait adjectives. They found that depressed subjects recalled self-referent depressive items at higher levels than they recalled depressive items initially encoded in a non-self-referent orienting task. In addition, depressed subjects recalled the self-referent stimuli to a greater extent than did either the psychiatric or normal control groups. Further, the opposite pattern of results was found for the recall of nondepressed trait adjectives.

Derry and Kuiper concluded that depressed individuals have self-schemas that play an important role in the processing of self-referent information and that these schemas differ in content from the self-schemas of nondepressed individuals. If cognitive processes influence affective responses, it can be seen how a negative self-schema, with content including ideas of personal worthlessness and incompetence, can prolong dysphoria and other symptoms of depression by excluding the processing of potential positive stimuli and entrapping the individual in an increasingly negative spiral of cognitions, affect, and negative memories (Isen et al., 1978).

An important question may be raised as to whether the "strong version" of the content specificity hypothesis can account for differences between mildly depressed and nondepressed persons. In a depth-of-processing study, Kuiper and Derry (1982) found that, as expected, normals recalled more nondepressed than depressed items, but mildly depressed subjects recalled an equal number of depressed and nondepressed stimuli. This suggested that the schemas of mildly depressed individuals may contain both positive and negative content about the self. Similarly, Davis (1979) reported that the ratio of self to non-self items recalled was significantly correlated with severity of depression. Lloyd and Lishman (1975) found that severity of depression was associated with a progressively diminishing ratio between latency of recall for pleasant versus unpleasant events. In a trait-rating task, Ingram, Smith, and Brehm (1983) found that while nondepressed subjects endorsed many more positive items than negative items as self-descriptive, mildly depressed subjects were more "even-handed" in the relative number of positive and negative items judged as self-descriptive. This was further supported by a similar effect in a depth of processing paradigm. Other studies indicating that mildly depressed and clinically depressed subjects may have important differences in information-processing styles have been reported by Alloy and Greenberg (1983) and Kuiper and MacDonald (1982). These studies have also found that mild depressives have enhanced recall for both positive and negative information in depth-of-processing paradigms.

Thus, biased processing of negative information appears to be related to the severity of depression. The literature suggests that clinical depressives process negative depression-relevant information more efficiently than positive information. However, mild depressives seem to process negative and positive information with equal efficiency. This suggests that clinical and mild depressives may differ in the content of their underlying self-schemas.

WORLD AND FUTURE SCHEMAS

Most of the investigations of schemas in depression have focused on schemas about the self. However, the cognitive model of depression also suggests that depressed individuals have negative schemas about the world and the future, the "cognitive triad" of depression. In a depth-of-processing paradigm, Alloy and Greenberg (1983) reported that mildly depressed college students recalled more negative than positive world-relevant trait adjectives, whereas nondepressed subjects did not show a preference for either type of stimuli. In addition, subjects' future-oriented cognitions were also studied within the depth-of-processing paradigm, although consistent group differences were not found.

The construct of hopelessness has played an important role in the cognitive theory of the emotional disorders and of depression in particular. Hopelessness is a future-oriented construct that has been associated with increasing risk of suicide. For example, in a long-term prospective study, Beck, Steer, Kovacs, and Garrison (1985) were able to predict 90% of eventual suicides from a sample of hospitalized suicidal patients by use of the Hopelessness Scale (Beck, Weissman, Lester, & Trexler, 1974). The mean score of suicide completers was significantly higher than noncompleters. In order to determine the predictive power of the Hopelessness Scale, the sample was dichotomized according to low and high scores. A cutoff score of 9 was found to clearly separate suicide completers from noncompleters. Only 1 (9.1%) of the completers had a score of 9 or less, whereas 90.9% had obtained a score of 10 or more. The number of true positives was 10 out of 86 cases (11.6%), and the number of false positive was 76 out of 86 cases (88.4%). Below the cutoff point were 1 false negative (1.3%) and 78 true negatives (98.7%). In sum, the cognitive therapist is always on the alert for increased or sever hopelessness in the depressed patient as reduction of hopelessness and suicide risk becomes of paramount importance.

DEPRESSOGENIC ASSUMPTIONS

Another type of cognitive structure that has been hypothesized to play an important role in the development and maintenance of depression is the individual's underlying assumptions. According to Beck et al. (1979), these are the basic beliefs and personal rules that predispose an individual to depression and are activated when the depressive episode begins. A depressive episode is typically triggered by a negative environmental event or stressor, which subsequently interacts with the individual's cognitive structures. These rules are frequently rigid, are in all-or-none form, and are highly maladaptive. For example, a depressed individual may believe that, "If I don't have love I am worthless" or "I must be accepted by all people at all times to be happy" or "I must be successful in all my actions or else I am a failure." As long as these favorable conditions exist, the individual will probably not experience depression or dysphoria. However, when the person experiences a severe defeat or deprivation (i.e., stressor), as in the case of a perceived failure or of the loss of a loved person, then the negative schemas can become activated and propel the individual into an increasingly downward spiral of depression. According to Ingram and Hollon (in press), underlying assumptions probably represent "higher order" schemas that are typically inferred by the therapist after repeated presentations of negative cognitions by the patient. Thus, one of the critical tasks of cognitive therapy is to help the individual identify and modify his underlying assumptions.

An instrument that has been developed to investigate a wide variety of underlying assumptions is the Dysfunctional Attitude Scale (DAS; Weissman & Beck, 1978). Work in our own laboratory has indicated that the DAS has high internal consistency and test–retest reliability. Further, a principal factor analysis with 765 subjects yielded the following eight resultant factors, in order of variance accounted for: *Vulnerability* ("If a person asks for help it is a sign of a weakness"); *Attraction–Rejection* ("I am nothing if a person doesn't love me"); *Perfectionism* ("My life is wasted unless I am a success"); *Imperatives* ("I should be happy all of the time"); *Approval* ("I need others' approval in order to be happy"); *Dependence* ("A person cannot survive without the help of other people"); *Autonomous Attitudes* ("My own opinions of myself are more important than others' opinion of me"); and *Cognitive Philosophy* ("Even though a person may not be able to control what happens to him, he can control how he thinks"). Our work has also indicated that clinical samples score higher than nonclinical samples, and DAS scores are correlated with other measures of dysfunctional cognitions. The DAS has also been shown to have discriminant validity as it correlates more highly with measures of depression than it does with anxiety. Further, studies using the DAS as a pre-to-posttreatment outcome measure suggests that it measures relatively stable cognitive schemas that change less than measures of cognitive products such as the Automatic Thoughts Questionnaire (Hollon & Kendall, 1980).

The DAS has also been used to investigate the question of whether dysfunctional attitudes are state dependent rather than more enduring cognitions that persist during remission of clinical symptoms. Several studies (Dobson & Shaw, 1986; Eaves & Rush, 1984) have shown that dysfunctional attitudes persist in remitted depressives, while another found that high levels of dysfunctional attitudes were associated with eventual relapse (Simons, Murphy, Levine, & Wetzel, in press). These studies suggest that dysfunctional attitudes may be vulnerability markers that are of predictive value with respect to prognosis and relapse into symptomatic depression.

COGNITIVE PROPOSITIONS

According to Ingram and Hollon (1986), cognitive propositions are the actual content that is represented in various cognitive structures. In the case of depression, the content typically consists of negative beliefs about the self, the world, and the future. For example, Alloy and Greenberg (1983) developed a Self-Schema Questionnaire (SSQ) consisting of 53 semantic, differential-type scales on which three groups of subjects were asked to rate their self-concepts. The bipolar scales were constructed to reflect cognitive beliefs about the self theoretically related to depression (e.g., worthless–worthy; unmotivated–motivated; lovable–unlovable). The three groups that were studied were drawn from an undergraduate subject pool and were selected on the basis of their scores on the Beck Depression Inventory and the Trait Anxiety Inventory: Depressed, Anxious, and Nondepressed–Nonanxious. A reliability analysis indicated that his questionnaire was a highly reliable (alpha = .93) index of cognitive dimensions about the self. Further, the scales were factor analyzed, and the factor that accounted for the greatest amount of variance was conceptualized as a "Self-evaluation" factor. Items on this factor included "worthless–worthy, unvaluable–valuable, impotent–potent, unlovable–lovable, and shameful–praiseworthy." Further, the Self-evaluation factor discriminated between the depressed and nondepressed subjects, with the depressed group scoring most negatively and the two nondepressed groups not differing from one another. In addition, the same subjects were also presented with a World Schema Questionnaire and a Future Schema Questionnaire that also indicated that depressed individuals can be discriminated from nondepressed individuals on the basis of their beliefs about the world and future.

COGNITIVE OPERATIONS

Cognitive operations are the mechanisms responsible for the active manipulation of information through the processing system (Ingram & Hollon, 1986) and are hypothesized to be products of the schemas. These processes include rules and heuristics, attentional processes, encoding processes, control processes, and the concept of spreading activation in memory networks. Beck (1967; Beck et al., 1979) has outlined a number of cognitive operations, derived from clinical observations, that may result in the maintenance of dysphoric moods and symptoms of depression. The following are the most prominent mechanisms observed in clinical settings: arbitrary inferences (drawing conclusions in the absence of supporting evidence), selective abstraction (focusing on a detail taken out of context), overgeneralization (drawing a general rule on the basis of one or more isolated events), magnification and minimization (distorting the significance or magnitude of an event), personalization (relating external events to the self in the absence of data), and dichotomous thinking (tendencies to evaluate events in terms of one of two mutually exclusive categories such as winners and losers and competent and incompetent). Cognitive therapy teaches the patient to recognize these processes as maladaptive distortions of experience and to subsequently draw conclusions on the basis of empirically verifiable observations.

The cognitive model of depression has also led to empirical studies of information-processing differences between depressed and nondepressed individuals.

For example, Buchwald (1977) attempted to determine whether a depressed mood was related to a tendency to underestimate the frequency of successful experiences. Depressed and nondepressed college students were presented with a multiple-choice learning task and were then presented with feedback information indicating right and wrong answers. After this task, the subjects were asked to estimate the percentage of correct responses they had made. The results indicated that depressed subjects tended to underestimate the number of correct responses they had given (see also Werner & Rehm, 1975). Similarly, Nelson and Craighead (1977) reported that depressed subjects recalled being reinforced on fewer trials than nondepressed subjects when given high rates of reinforcement and recalled being punished on a greater number of trials than nondepressed subjects when presented with low rates of punishment (see also DeMonbreun & Craighead, 1977). Thus, it appears that depressed individuals may, indeed, be less positive and more negative in their perceptions of feedback information than nondepressed individuals.

Another cognitive operation variable that is central to the cognitive model is the notion of "automatic negative thoughts" (Beck, 1963; Ingram & Hollon, 1986). For example, this type of processing might occur when a depressed individual is at work and greets the boss first thing in the morning, but the boss responds in a curt or gruff fashion. If trained to observe the thoughts experienced prior to the dysphoria, he may recognize a thought such as "I've done something wrong, the boss is going to chew me out or fire me." This series of thoughts may occur in split-second time, usually without full awareness on the part of the depressive, and have an immediate impact on the level of dysphoria. This dysphoria, in turn, may lead to other automatic thoughts, including beliefs about personal incompetence and selective recall of past perceived failures. Since memories of past failures can also include negative affective components, the depressed individual is caught in an increasingly depressive downward spiral.

The cognitive therapist trains the depressive to examine the validity of conclusions such as "The boss is mad at me" by testing their empirical and logical basis. In many instances, the negative conclusion does not have a basis in reality, and the patient is typically relieved that "things were not nearly as bad" as imagined. The model of helping the patient become aware of automatic thoughts and subsequently testing them out in a scientific fashion is an important cornerstone of cognitive therapy. In cases where the negative automatic thoughts are true, cognitive therapy helps the patient cope and reduce depression by assisting in the generation of coping strategies and by "decatastrophizing" the perceived negative consequences. These interventions have been demonstrated to reduce depression and to provide the patient with a model of coping with negative events.

COGNITIVE PRODUCTS

Cognitive products have been viewed by Ingram and Hollon (1986) as cognitions that result from information input and the interaction of cognitive structures and operations Cognitive products relevant to the study of depression include self-statements, attributions, causal inferences, and images. These cognitions frequently contain themes of failure, rejection, incompetence, and hopelessness. They are relatively accessible to awareness, constitute the cognitions that are subjected to empirical validation by the patient and therapist, and eventually lead to the discovery of the underlying assumptions and schemas.

At the Center for Cognitive Therapy, we have developed the Cognition Checklist to measure the frequency with which depressive and anxious cognitions occur in depression and anxiety (Beck, Brown, Steer, Eidelson, & Riskind, 1987). The checklist is based on the assumption that depressed and anxious patients differentially select those items that most characterize the underlying cognitive themes of each disorder. Items on the checklist are grouped into three hypothetical situations: (1) "When I have to attend a social occasion I think," (2) "When I am with a friend I think," and (3) "When I feel pain or physical discomfort I think." Under each situation the scale presents several thoughts or cognitions (e.g., "I am a social failure") that are relevant to depression and anxiety. The subject is asked to rate how often he or she has each of the included thoughts, with response alternatives ranging from "never" to "always." In addition, subjects are also asked to rate the frequency of various thoughts (e.g., "Life isn't worth living") regardless of the situation. In one study, the depression and anxiety subscales were able to discriminate ($p < .025$, all comparisons) a sample of individuals with major depressive disorder from a group of generalized anxiety disorder patients. Further, scores on the depression factor were highly correlated with the Beck Depression Inventory and the Hamilton Rating Scale for Depression, two widely used depression measures.

The concept of hopelessness is a central construct in the cognitive model and treatment of depression. When individuals become hopeless and are unable to perceive solutions to their problems, the risk of suicide increases. In view of the major public health concern of suicide, the assessment and understanding of the relationship between suicide and hopelessness is of critical importance (Beck, Steer, & McElroy, 1982). The Hopelessness Scale (Beck et al., 1974) was developed to assess negative views of the future. Three tentative factors comprising the scale are Feelings about the Future, Loss of Motivation, and Negative Expectations. We have also found that the Hopelessness Scale can discriminate between depressed and anxious individuals and that the correlation between depression and suicidal ideation is nonsignificant when hopelessness is partialed out of depression (Minkoff, Bergman, Beck, & Beck, 1973).

For the suicidal patient, the reduction of hopelessness becomes of paramount importance during the course of therapy. This can be accomplished by use of behavioral and cognitive task assignments. Homework assignments can serve to reduce depression and hopelessness by providing positive feedback and undermining negative expectations and predictions. Patients are also instructed on how to recognize, monitor, and label specific cognitive distortions; become aware of the tendencies to view themselves in a negative fashion; help themselves become more aware of their positive attributes; and help generate the cognitive data that can be subjected to empirical testing.

COGNITIVE VULNERABILITY

The preceding discussion of the cognitive model attempted to classify specific types of cognitive processes into categories in order to facilitate an understanding of how information is processed by the depressed individual. However, this formulation does not address the critical question of why some individuals develop either major depressions or chronic depression at various times in their lives, why there is a high rate of relapse among people who have suffered serious depressions, and why some individuals appear to be susceptible to the development of depression across many years. The issue of cognitive vulnerability attempts to address these questions from the standpoint of the cognitive model of depression.

A current controversy in the cognitive theory of depression is whether negative cognitions and distortions function as traits and endure even in the absence of symptomatic depression or are state dependent and can only be observed when an individual is depressed. Cognitive theory assumes that depressive schemas are latent during nondepressed periods and then are activated during depression. Once activated (most likely by psychosocial stressors) the schemas give rise to distorted interpretations about the self, the world, and the future. Thus, the cognitive model hypothesizes that negative schemas are present but inactive during nondepressed states. In contrast, an alternative view suggests that dysfunctional cognitions are essentially consequences of dysphoria and depressive moods. This view proposes that negative cognitive structures do not predate the onset of depression, and that after remission of symptoms, the cognitions of depressed individuals resemble those of nondepressed individuals.

Lewinsohn (1974) presented a reinforcement model of depression where cognitive phenomena are seen as consequences of dysphoric moods. Dysphoric moods, in turn, were hypothesized to arise from low rates of response-contingent positive reinforcement. However, Lewinsohn's model has not been supported by adequate empirical evidence and reviews of the relevant literature indicate that this "theory" is essentially a tautology (Blaney, 1977; Greenberg & Silverstein, 1983). More recently, Bower (1981) has suggested that being in a depressed mood facilitates the accessibility of negative memories and their associated affects, while others (Hammen, 1985; Teasdale, 1983) have suggested that mood and affect have a reciprocal relationship. Thus, the issue is still the subject of much speculation and debate and awaits additional research.

The question of cognitive vulnerability has been explored relatively recently, with most investigations being conducted in the past 5 years. The most frequently cited studies have typically compared remitted depressives with non-depressives and currently depressed individuals. This paradigm assumes that if cognitive vulnerability markers are present, then the remitted depressives should still manifest negative schemas, although possibly in attenuated form. While remitted depressives should still show evidence of latent schemas and dysfunctional attitudes (i.e., cognitive structures), cognitive theory also predicts that differences between remitted depressives and nondepressives on cognitive-product variables such as automatic thoughts should not be observed (Eaves & Rush, 1984; Simons et al., 1986). Since depressive schemas are not *activated during remission,* the remitted individuals would not be expected to manifest negative cognitions that are the surface derivatives of the schemas.

Hammen, Marks, deMayo, and Mayol (1985) have described this approach to cognitive vulnerability as a "main effects" model of stable and active cognitive-vulnerability factors. Another approach, the interaction model, which will be discussed at greater length shortly, assumes that cognitive-vulnerability markers may not be observable until latent schemas become activated, sometimes by environmental stressors or negative life events, and sometimes by as yet poorly elucidated neurochemical factors.

In general, the evidence in favor of cognitive vulnerability from the main effects paradigm has been mixed, as several investigations have not found elevations on various cognitive measures in remitted depressives, particularly on the Dysfunctional Attitude Scale (Billings & Moos, 1985; Hamilton & Abramson, 1983; Lewinsohn, Steinmetz, Larson, & Franklin, 1981; Silverman, Silverman, & Eardley, 1984). In contrast, several other studies have found that dysfunctional attitudes remain residually elevated in remitted depressives (Eaves & Rush, 1984; Reda, 1984). The main effects model may be an oversimplified approach to cognitive vulnerability and it will be argued that the cognitive diathesis-stress approach, where cognitions interact with life stressors to produce depression, may be a more fruitful paradigm in which to search for cognitive vulnerability.

Investigations examining the interaction of cognitive phenomena with stressful life events are more consistent with the cognitive model of depression (Beck et al., 1979) than with the main effects paradigm. For example, marital separation or divorce may activate an early childhood schema of loss that was formed after the death of a parent and thereby produce a severe depression. Similarly, a business failure by a high-pressure executive may activate a schema of incompetence, failure, and loss of self-esteem that was developed during childhood when that individual learned that self-worth was dependent upon tangible achievements.

Alloy, Clements, and Kolden (1985) presented a cognitive diathesis-stress theory of depression in which attributional styles were conceptualized as a vulnerability factor that can produce depression when an individual is confronted with negative life events. In a study of depressive reactions in the classroom, Alloy et al. summarized a study using path analyses to compare the adequacy of the main effects and interaction models in explaining changes in depression. In this study, subjects attributional styles and level of depression were assessed at the beginning of the semester. After receiving the grades on a midterm examination, the subjects' depression levels were reassessed. The interaction between attributional styles and receiving a poor grade was a better predictor of poststress depression than either factor alone. This interaction also predicted depression over and above an individual's initial level of depression. Thus, the interaction model was able to demonstrate greater predictive validity than the main effects model.

The notion of an interaction between cognitive processes and environmental stressors as a basic model for predicting depression is an improvement over a main effects model. However, the interaction model needs considerable refinement in order for it to be a model with comprehensive explanatory power. A comprehensive cognitive model needs to address the question of what types of specific stressors interact with specific cognitive schemas to produce depression. This is a question of individual differences in vulnerability to depression.

A fruitful area to search for specific vulnerabilities to depression is individual differences in stable personality structures. For example, Hammen, Marks, Mayol, and deMayo (1985) initially identified individuals who were "schematic" for either interpersonal or achievement-oriented themes and then followed these subjects over an extended period of time. They found that depressive reactions were more associated with subsequent schema-congruent than schema-incongruent negative life events.

Beck and his colleagues have also identified two major personality characteristics that appear to be individual-difference factors in vulnerability to depression (Beck, Epstein, Harrison, & Emery, 1983). He has suggested that these are associated with different patterns of precipitation, symptomatology, and treatment response. The socially dependent or sociotropic individual values positive interactions with others, intimacy, support, nurturance, and guidance. The autonomous individual is mainly concerned with achievement and independent functioning, choice, mobility, and personal integrity. It can be seen that these domains are relatively compatible with Hammen, Marks, Mayol, & deMayo's (1985) specific factors of vulnerability. In order to assess these individual differences, the Sociotropy–Autonomy Scale was developed, and initial investigations found acceptable levels of reliability and validity (Beck et al., 1983). Individuals who are relatively sociotropic or autonomous are hypothesized to be susceptible to specific types of stressors. Thus, the same stressor may affect each type of individual in an entirely different fashion. Investigations are currently being conducted to confirm the hypothesized relationship between the two personality styles and susceptibility to specific types of stressors.

FUTURE DIRECTIONS: TOWARD AN INTEGRATED THEORY OF THE EMOTIONAL DISORDERS

To this point, the focus of discussion has been on depressive disorders. However, depression and anxiety are two phenomena that have been closely related in clinical, empirical, and theoretical investigations. Despite their close association, there have been very few attempts to formulate an integrated theory of depression and anxiety. This is somewhat enigmatic since clinicians have long recognized that depression and anxiety coexist not only in affective disorders but in a wide variety of psychiatric disorders, medical conditions, and nonclinical mood fluctuations.

The critical questions are whether depression and anxiety can be discriminated on the basis of symptomatology, and whether an integrated cognitive theory can account for both the differences and overlap between depressive and anxiety disorders. With respect to the question of reliably diagnosing and discriminating depressive and anxiety disorders, evidence from our laboratory and independent investigations (Gurney, Roth, & Garside, 1970; Mathew, Swihart, & Weinman, 1982; Murray & Blackburn, 1974) indicates that depressive and anxiety disorders can be reliably discriminated and constitute separate syndromes. However, there has been a dearth of research investigating cognitive differences in depression and anxiety, and intensive study of these differences is required for purposes of theoretical relevance and discriminant validity.

According to the cognitive model of the emotional disorders (Beck, 1967, 1976; Beck & Emery, 1985), each of the emotional disorders can be distinguished from the others on the basis of the specific content of cognitions about self, world, and future; attributions of causality; and selective processing of schema-relevant material. Depressed individuals are hypothesized to possess distorted schemas that typically involve depressive themes and contents. The depressive believes that he or she is unworthy, interaction with the environment is characterized by defeat and deprivations, and the future is considered hopeless. Anxious individuals also possess negative beliefs about the self, world, and future, but their schemas are organized around the themes of threat, danger, vulnerability, and uncertainty. The critical aspect of the theory suggests that the beliefs of depressed and anxious people are organized into content-specific schemas that guide the processing of current experiences in a biased fashion because available information is assimilated into the schema. Thus, the cognitive theory of the emotional disorders predicts that depressed and anxious people will evidence similar schema-based processes differing in content and, thus, in the direction of cognitive bias.

Despite the current interest in the cognitive theory of the emotional disorders, few studies have attempted to test out this formulation. With a college sample, Alloy and Greenberg (1983) employed the depth-of-processing methodology to investigate self, world, and future schemas in depressed, anxious, and non-depressed–nonanxious subjects. Subject groups were formed on the basis of cutoff scores on the Beck Depression Inventory and Trait-Anxiety Inventory. They included trait adjectives that were selected to represent items relevant to depression, anxiety, and neutral items. These types of adjectives were included as a recognition that specific groups of subjects may selectively process only those adjectives for which they have specific vulnerabilities. This series of investigations was able to demonstrate that depressed, anxious, and nondepressed–nonanxious individuals could be discriminated on the basis of their self, world, and future cognitions. However, this study was limited by virtue of it being conducted with a college sample in contrast to clinical samples, which differ from college samples in terms of quality and quantity of psychopathology and the extent to which careful diagnoses have been made.

Preliminary evidence suggests that the concept of hopelessness is an important variable that may discriminate depression and anxiety. With a college sample, Alloy and Greenberg (1983) found that mildly depressed subjects had significantly higher Hopelessness Scale scores ($p < .01$) than a sample of anxious subjects. Recently, we have replicated these findings with clinically depressed and anxious patients classified on the basis of DSM-III (*Diagnostic and statistical manual of mental disorders*, 3rd ed.) diagnoses (Spitzer & Williams, 1985).

We are also conducting a large-scale longitudinal study of depression and anxiety that will attempt to address many of the questions that have been raised. We are examining cognitive differences in carefully diagnosed groups of individuals with major depressive disorder (both primary and secondary), generalized anxiety disorder (primary and secondary), dysthymia, phobias, panic disorder, and several appropriate control groups. These subjects will be assessed throughout their treatment with cognitive therapy and at a 1-year follow-up, a time that will permit questions of cognitive vulnerability to be addressed. These subjects will be presented with a wide variety of cognitive-assessment instruments that can be classified into the multilevel scheme described earlier. For example, the depth-of-processing paradigm and Dysfunctional Attitude Scale will be employed as measures of cognitive structures, and the Cognition Checklist and Hopelessness Scale will assess more surface manifestations of cognitive products. The ultimate goal of this study is to provide evidence for an integrated theory of the emotional disorders by means of a multilevel cognitive assessment of individuals suffering from specific emotional disorders.

REFERENCES

Alloy, L. B., Clements, C., & Kolden, G. (1985). The cognitive diathesis-stress theories of depression: Therapeutic implications. In S. Reiss & R. Bootzin (Eds.), *Theoretical issues in behavior therapy*. Orlando, FL: Academic Press.

Alloy, L. B., & Greenberg, M. S. (1983). *Depression, anxiety, and self-schemata: A test of Beck's theory*. Paper presented at the 91st annual convention of the American Psychological Association, Anaheim, CA.

Bandura, A. (1977). *Social learning theory*. Englewood Cliffs, NJ: Prentice-Hall.

Beck, A. T. (1963). Thinking and depression: 1. Idiosyncratic content and cognitive distortions. *Archives of General Psychiatry, 9*, 324–333.

Beck, A. T. (1964). Thinking and depression: 2. Theory and therapy. *Archives of General Psychiatry, 10*, 561–571.

Beck, A. T. (1967). *Depression: Clinical, experimental, and theoretical aspects*. New York: Harper & Row.

Beck, A. T. (1976). *Cognitive theory and the emotional disorders*. New York: International Press.

Beck, A. T., Brown, G., Steer, R. A., Eidelson, J. I., & Riskind, J. N. (1987). Differentiating anxiety and depression utilizing the Cognition Checklist. *Journal of Abnormal Psychology, 96*, 179–186.

Beck, A. T., & Emery, G. (1985). *Anxiety disorders and phobias: A cognitive perspective*. New York: Basic Books.

Beck, A. T., Epstein, N., Harrison, R., & Emery, G. (1983). *Development of the Sociotropy–Autonomy Scale: A measure of personality factors in psychopathology*. Unpublished manuscript, University of Pennsylvania.

Beck, A. T., Rush, A. J., Shaw, B. F., & Emery, G. (1979). *Cognitive therapy of depression*. New York: Guilford Press.

Beck, A. T., Steer, R. A., Kovacs, M., & Garrison, B. E. (1985). Hopelessness and eventual suicide: A 10-year prospective study of patients hospitalized with suicidal ideation. *American Journal of Psychiatry, 142*, 559–563.

Beck, A. T., Steer, R. A., & McElroy, M. G. (1982). Relationship of hopelessness, depression, and previous suicide attempts to suicidal ideation in alcoholics. *Journal of Studies on Alcohol, 43*, 1042–1046.

Beck, A. T., Weissman, A., Lester, D., & Trexler, L. (1974). The measure of pessimism: The Hopelessness Scale. *Journal of Consulting and Clinical Psychology, 42*, 861–865.

Billings, A., & Moos, R. (1985). Psychosocial processes of remission in unipolar depression: Comparing depressed patients with matched community controls. *Journal of Consulting and Clinical Psychology, 53*, 314–325.

Blaney, P. (1977). Contemporary theories of depression: Critique and comparison. *Journal of Abnormal Psychology, 86*, 203–223.

Bobrow, D. G., & Norman, D. A. (1975). Some principles of memory schemata. In D. G. Bobrow

& A. M. Collins (Eds.), *Representation and understanding: Studies in cognitive science.* New York: Academic Press.

Bower, G. H. (1981). Mood and memory. *American Psychologist,* **36,** 129–148.

Bower, G. H., Black, J. B., & Turner, T. J. (1979). Scripts in memory for text. *Cognitive Psychology,* **11,** 177–220.

Buchwald, A. (1977). Depressive mood and estimates of reinforcement frequency. *Journal of Abnormal Psychology,* **86,** 443–446.

Coyne, J. C. (1982). A critique of cognitions as causal entities with particular reference to depression. *Cognitive Therapy and Research,* **6,** 3–13.

Davis, H. (1979). Self-reference and the encoding of personal information in depression. *Cognitive Therapy and Research,* **3,** 415–426.

DeMonbreun, B. G., & Craighead, W. E. (1977). Distortion of perception and recall of positive and neutral feedback in depression. *Cognitive Therapy and Research,* **1,** 311–329.

Derry, P. A., & Kuiper, N. A. (1981). Schematic processing and self-reference in clinical depression. *Journal of Abnormal Psychology,* **90,** 286–297.

Dobson, K. S., & Shaw, B. (1986). Cognitive assessment with major depressive disorders. *Cognitive Therapy and Research,* **10,** 13–30.

Eaves, G., & Rush, A. J. (1984). Cognitive patterns in symptomatic and remitted unipolar and major depression. *Journal of Abnormal Psychology,* **93,** 31–40.

Greenberg, M., & Silverstein, M. (1983). Cognitive and behavioral treatments of depressive disorders: Interventions with adults. In H. L. Morrison (Ed.), *Children of depressed parents: Risk, identification, and intervention.* New York: Grune & Stratton.

Gurney, C., Roth, M., & Garside, R. E. (1970). Use of statistical techniques in the classification of affective disorders. *Proceedings of the Royal Society of Medicine,* **63,** 6–12.

Hamilton, E. W., & Abramson, L. Y. (1983). Cognitive patterns and major depressive disorder: A longitudinal study. *Journal of Abnormal Psychology,* **92,** 185–195.

Hammen, C. (1985). Predicting depression: A cognitive-behavioral perspective. In P. C. Kendall (Ed.), *Advances in Cognitive Therapy* (Vol. 4). Orlando, FL: Academic Press.

Hammen, C., Marks, T., deMayo, R., & Mayol, A. (1985). Self-schemas and risk for depression: A prospective study. *Journal of Personality and Social Psychology,* **49,** 1147–1159.

Hammen, C., Marks, T., Mayol, A., & deMayo, R. (1985). Depressive self-schemas, life stress and vulnerability to depression. *Journal of Abnormal Psychology,* **94,** 308–319.

Hollon, S. D., & Kendall, P. C. (1980). Cognitive self-statements in depression: Development of an automatic thoughts questionnaire. *Cognitive Therapy and Research,* **4,** 383–395.

Ingram, R. E., & Hollon, S. D. (1986). Cognitive therapy of depression from an information processing perspective. In R. E. Ingram (Ed.), *Information processing approaches to psychopathology and clinical psychology.* Orlando, FL: Academic Press.

Ingram, R. E., Smith, T. W., & Brehm, S. S. (1983). Depression and information processing: Self-schemata and the encoding of self-referent information. *Journal of Personality and Social Psychology,* **45,** 412–420.

Isen, A., Shalker, T. E., Clark, M., & Karp, L. (1978). Affect, accessibility of material in memory and behavior: A cognitive loop? *Journal of Personality and Social Psychology,* **36,** 1–12.

Kuiper, N. A., & Derry, P. (1982). Depressed and nondepressed content self-reference in mild depressives. *Journal of Personality,* **50,** 67–69.

Kuiper, N. A., & MacDonald, M. R. (1982). Self and other perception in mild depressives. *Social Cognition,* **1,** 223–229.

Lewinsohn, P. (1974). A behavioral approach to depression. In R. Friedman & M. Katz (Eds.), *Progress in behavior modification.* New York: Academic Press.

Lewinsohn, P., Steinmetz, J., Larson, D., & Franklin, J. (1981). Depression-related cognitions: Antecedent or consequence? *Journal of Abnormal Psychology,* **90,** 213–219.

Lloyd, G. G., & Lishman, W. A. (1975). Effect of depression on the speed of recall of pleasant and unpleasant experiences. *Psychosomatic Medicine*, **5**, 173–180.

Mathew, R. S., Swihart, A., & Weinman, M. L. (1982). Vegetative symptoms in anxiety and depression. *British Journal of Psychiatry*, **141**, 161–165.

Meichenbaum, D., & Gilmore, J. (1984). The nature of unconscious processes: A cognitive-behavioral perspective. in K. Bowers & D. Meichenbaum (Eds.), *The unconscious reconsidered*. New York: Wiley.

Minkoff, K., Bergman, E., Beck, A. T., & Beck, R. (1973). Hopelessness, depression and attempted suicide. *American Journal of Psychiatry*, **130**, 455–459.

Minsky, M. (1975). The framework for representing knowledge. In P. H. Winston (Ed.), *The psychology of computer vision*. New York: McGraw-Hill.

Murray, L. G., & Blackburn, I. M. (1974). Personality differences in patients with depressive illnesses and anxiety neuroses. *Acta Psychiatrica Scandinavica*, **50**, 189–190.

Neimeyer, R. A. (1985). Personal constructs in clinical practice. In P. C. Kendall (Ed.), *Advances in cognitive-behavioral research and therapy* (Vol. 4). Orlando, FL: Academic Press.

Neisser, U. (1976). *Cognition and reality: Principles and implications of cognitive psychology*. San Francisco, CA: Freeman Press.

Nelson, R., & Craighead, W. (1977). Selective recall of positive and negative feedback, self-control behaviors, and depression. *Journal of Abnormal Psychology*, **86**, 379–388.

Owens, J., Bower, G., & Black, J. (1979). The "soap opera" effect in story recall. *Memory and Cognition*, **7**, 185–191.

Reda, M. A. (1984). Cognitive organization and antidepressants: Attitude modification during amitriptyline treatment on severely depressed individuals. In M. A. Reda & M. J. Mahoney (Eds.), *Cognitive psychotherapies: Recent developments in theory, research, and practice*. Cambridge, MA: Ballinger.

Rosch, E. (1975). Cognitive representation of semantic categories. *Journal of Experimental Psychology: General*, **104**, 192–233.

Silverman, J. S., Silverman, J. A., & Eardley, D. A. (1984). Do maladaptive attitudes cause depression? *Archives of General Psychiatry*, **41**, 45–51.

Simons, A. D., Murphy, G. E.,Levine, J. L., & Wetzel, R. D. (1986). Cognitive therapy and pharmacotherapy of depression: Sustained improvement over one fear. *Archives of General Psychiatry*, **43**, 43–48.

Spitzer, R. L., & Williams, J. B. (1985). *Instrumental manual for the structured clinical interview for DSM-III (SCID)*. New York: Biometrics Research Department, New York State Psychiatric Institute.

Taylor, S., & Crocker, J. (1980). Schematic bases of social information processing. in E. Higgens, P. Hermann, & M. Zarra (Eds.), *The Ontario symposium on personality and social psychology* (Vol. 1). Hillside, NJ: Erlbaum.

Teasdale, J. D. (1983). Negative thinking in depression: Cause, effect, or reciprocal relationship? *Advances in Behaviour Research and Therapy*, **5**, 3–25.

Weissman, A. W., & Beck, A. T. (1978). *Development and validation of the Dysfunctional Attitude Scale*. Paper presented at the annual meeting of the Association for Advancement of Behavior Therapy, Chicago, IL.

Werner, A., & Rehm, L. (1975). Depressive affect: A test of behavioral hypotheses. *Journal of Abnormal Psychology*, **84**, 221–227.

Chapter 9

EMOTIONS: A MULTIMODAL THERAPY PERSPECTIVE

ARNOLD A. LAZARUS AND CLIFFORD N. LAZARUS

ABSTRACT

It is argued that in humans, the expressions of affect and cognition are inextricable and that the views put forth by Zajonc (1980, 1984) concerning the primacy of affect are highly questionable. The multimodal position is that no single factor can account for all emotionality at the human level. It is postulated that affect is the product of the reciprocal interaction of behavior, sensation, imagery, cognitive factors, and biological inputs, usually within an interpersonal context. The foregoing schema results in an assessment (diagnostic) template that underscores the necessity of investigating each of these functions (e.g., cognitive, behavioral, phenomenological, perceptual, biochemical, and neurophysiological). Practitioners who limit the focus of their attention to a restricted range of affect-related factors are likely to compromise their overall effectiveness. In multimodal therapy, the use of Modality Profiles tends to foster greater specificity and comprehensiveness. The chapter also challenges the view that "means must be found for modifying affect directly" (Wilson, 1984). It is submitted that affects can be worked with only indirectly. This calls for a serious reconsideration of the necessary and sufficient conditions for durable treatment outcomes.

EMOTION
Theory, Research, and Experience
Volume 5

INTRODUCTION

According to the *Encyclopedia of Psychology* (Corsini, 1984), "Emotions are a basic component of human experience, but their exact nature has been elusive and difficult to specify" (p. 427). *Webster's Ninth New Collegiate Dictionary* (1984) defines emotion as "a psychic and physical reaction (as anger or fear) subjectively experienced as strong feeling and physiologically involving changes that prepare the body for immediate vigorous action." Plutchik (1980a) listed 28 definitions of the word *emotion*. The psychological literature usually refers to three interlocking components that constitute emotion: (1) the subjective experience, (2) the physiological responses, and (3) the overt or expressive reactions. Lang (1977) proposed a tripartite conception of *fear* consisting of verbal, physiological, and behavioral components, these three modes being only loosely correlated. In other words, reports of fear, visceral reactions, and avoidance behaviors may converge, diverge, or remain independent of each other. Emotions provide much leeway for different patterns of action, physiology, and thought; there appears to be no predetermined linkage across all conditions.

The wide ranges, forms, intensities, and varieties of emotion make classification extremely difficult. While no universal agreement on any single classificatory schema exists, Plutchik (1980a, 1980b) has provided a model that is perhaps the most widely accepted. In essence, he has postulated eight primary emotions—fear, surprise, sadness, disgust, anger, anticipation, joy, and acceptance—with each one varying in intensity. Thus, fear can range from mild apprehension to pervasive terror; sadness extends from pensiveness to abject grief. Plutchik also considers the positive-to-negative spectrum of emotions, as well as mixed emotions (e.g., disappointment may be considered a mixture of sadness and surprise).

In discussing the vicissitudes of emotion, the present chapter will first examine the debate between Zajonc and R. S. Lazarus regarding the relation between cognition and emotion, followed by the multimodal viewpoint of affective processes as a product of the reciprocal interaction of six "modalities." Thereafter, the main features of multimodal assessments and diagnostic processes will be reviewed. Finally, the modification of affect will be addressed, and the multimodal position will be compared with behavioral and cognitive–behavioral perspectives.

THE COGNITION–EMOTION DEBATE

Over the past century, psychologists have debated how physiological (autonomic) arousal interacts with emotion-provoking events to produce the subjective reactions we call "affective responses." To this very day, the theories of William James (1890) and Carl Lange (1887) are cited, and the virtues and limitations of the James–Lange theory of emotion still receive prominent coverage, even in modern and sophisticated introductory textbooks (e.g., Crider, Goethals, Kavanaugh, & Solomon, 1986). James contended that bodily changes precede the feeling state. His sequencing of events was perception–bodily changes–action–feeling. As Plutchik (1985) points out, "this chicken-and-egg problem posed by William James has never been fully resolved" (p. 197). Nevertheless, the psychotherapeutic implications of this theory are that a combination of cognitive therapy (perception) biofeedback (sensation), and behavior therapy (action) are necessary for the thorough treatment of emotional disturbance. This point will be expanded in the sections dealing with multimodal assessment and therapy.

More recently, the relation between cognition and emotion has been hotly debated in the literature (R. S. Lazarus, 1982; Zajonc, 1980). Zajonc asserts that cognition and emotion are under the control of separate and partially independent psychological systems, and that emotions can occur prior to and independently of cognitive processes. R. S. Lazarus contends that all emotional responses are preceded by some basic cognitive processing (appraisal), and he implies that emotions are postcognitive.

Zajonc (1980) implies that emotional responses are synonymous with irrational, automatic, and uncontrollable behaviors. He stated: "People do not get married or divorced, commit murder or suicide, or lay down their lives for freedom upon a detailed analysis of the pros and cons of their actions" (p. 1972). It seems, therefore, that his view of cognitions is that they are necessarily rational, deliberate, and controllable. In arguing for the primacy of affect, Zajonc appears to have overlooked the difference between cognitive content and cognitive process. The latter operates outside of awareness (cf. Nisbett & Wilson, 1977). In essence, cognitive psychologists have demonstrated that personal meaning (semantic knowledge) influences perception, that the larger cognitive structure of semantic-network associations may be divided into subcomponents (schemas), and that the activation of schematic processing is automatic and uncontrollable (cf. Bower, 1981; Collins & Loftus, 1975). Furthermore, the cognitive domain includes both explicit and implicit learning. Implicit learning is the acquisition and usage of formal rules through exposure to examples without being able to verbalize them.

More recently, Zajonc (1984) has suggested that emotional reactions are directly triggered by pure sensory inputs. With respect to this supposition, Bandura (1986) remarked: "The notion that emotional reactions are triggered directly by pure sensory input requires decisive evidence that sensory experiences undergo no interpretation whatsoever. People select and process sensory information, rather than simply react to whatever impinges on their sense organs" (p. 198).

To a large extent, it can be argued that the debate between Zajonc and R. S. Lazarus is partially a question of semantics, and that they both embrace limited definitions of cognition and emotion (cf. Watts, 1983). Nevertheless, from a clinical standpoint, Zajonc's (1980) assertion that people cannot voluntarily control the emergence of emotion in response to affectively valent stimuli casts a pall on the psychotherapeutic endeavor. If this were indeed the case, how could even the most skillful therapists ever hope to alleviate depression or eliminate phobic responses? Zajonc's claim is essentially that once an object or situation (automatically and holistically) elicits an affective response (e.g., anxiety) it will always do so. In the face of such compelling evidence directly supporting the effectiveness of specific therapies in treating affective disturbances such as anxiety (e.g., Bandura, 1977, 1986) and depression (e.g., Rush, Beck, Kovacs, & Hollan, 1977), Zajonc's supposition of emotional inescapability is highly suspect.

A more serious problem for the clinician is posed by Zajonc's (1980) claim that "affective judgments tend to be irrevocable" (p. 157). Again, by virtue of the unquestionable success of specific treatment techniques in remediating emotional disturbance—such as guided exposure (Matthews, Gelder, & Johnston, 1981) and participant modeling (Bandura, Adams, & Beyer, 1977) for anxiety— Zajonc's assertion does not appear to be correct. By and large, the literature (e.g., Bandura, 1986; Gordon & Holyoak, 1983) tends to support R. S. Lazarus's position. As Plutchik (1985) underscored:

> One can put an electrode into the brain of a cat, or of a human being, and produce emotional reactions without a cognitive evaluation of an external event, and even without arousal. In such unusual cases, cognitive events are not primary, but such cases rarely occur in the course of life. . . . When emotions are conceptualized as complex chains of events with feedback loops, it is obviously possible to focus attention on any of the elements of the chain. One can then produce theories that emphasize, for example, the primacy of arousal, or the primacy of expressive behavior. (p. 199)

PSYCHOTHERAPY AND EMOTION

In the clinical arena, each therapist's conceptualization of emotion will dictate the particular subset of the client's past and present activities that are viewed as significant and relevant, or as incidental and unimportant. Whereas current theory suggests that emotional phenomena are a product of complex interactions among several organismic systems—cognitive, behavioral, perceptual, and neurophysiological/biochemical—few therapists are apt to invoke each of the foregoing in their understanding or treatment of emotional disturbance. Evidence of bias and selectivity are clearly apparent in the psychoanalytic, narrow behavioral, and rational–emotive perspectives. A brief critique of each will be presented.

The psychoanalytic model of emotion had its origins in the "cathartic technique" developed by Breuer and Freud (1895/1955), which led them to postulate that neurotic symptoms are based on buried conflictual feelings. In this context, affect was associated with the resurrection of traumatic memories; therapeutic reminiscences usually resulted in some emotional release. However, as Nichols and Efran (1985) pointed out, Freud "was never really an emotivist—he was a seeker after memories, who saw affect as a signal that critical memories were being uncovered" (p. 48).

The earlier Freudian view of emotions had a distinctly hydraulic flavor. Feelings were conceptualized as entities that could be stored up and then drained off. Subsequently, in revising his theories, Freud presented affective responses in a totally different light. They were regarded as dispositions to action, calling for recognition and appropriate expression. Freud (1912/1959) emphasized that buried feelings must be made manifest, so that they could be dealt with directly (see section on "Modifying Affect"). These views have permeated the entire field of psychodynamic thinking. Thus, Davanloo (1980) in his modern, short-term dynamic psychotherapy places primary importance on "releasing hidden feelings by actively working on and interpreting resistance or defenses" (p. 45).

The linguistic construction of psychoanalytic or psychodynamic viewpoints seems to eschew operational definitions, so we are provided with no specific ingredients that point to the essence of affective processes. All we have are generalizations to the effect that human behavior and feelings are motivated from within by various drives, impulses, needs, and instincts. Moreover, the interplay of these dynamic forces usually operates below the level of consciousness. Thus, the closest one can get to a definition of emotion is that it is somehow associated with blocked drives. In short, circular explanations abound within this model. For example, a hostile impulse is inferred from the individual's overt (irascible) behavior and thereupon attributed to the influence of an underlying hostile impulse. Basically, the main criticism of this type of theorizing is that its "explanations" have no predictive value and end up being pseudoexplanations at best (Bandura, 1986).

The kinds of techniques employed by different schools of therapy are usually consistent with their specific or implicit theories of emotion. Thus, for Wolpe (1958, 1982), anxiety (sympathetic nervous arousal) is the cornerstone of "unadaptive behavior" and the therapist's primary task is to ferret out the stimuli to which needless fear has been conditioned and, subsequently, to break the stimulus—response connection by "reciprocal inhibition" or counterconditioning at the level of the autonomic nervous system. In this system, cognitive factors are regarded as secondary, if not irrelevant, to the understanding and treatment of anxiety. By contrast, rational–emotive therapy (Ellis, 1962; Ellis & Bernard, 1985) regards thought and emotion as inextricably intertwined, with *thinking* as the trigger of emotional states. Without denying the biochemical or physiological substrate, Ellis regards virtually all emoting as the result of the individual's internal monologue of his or her beliefs: "Much of our emoting takes the form of self-talk or internalized sentences. . . . Then for all practical purposes the phrases and sentences that we keep telling ourselves frequently *are* or *become* our thoughts and emotions" (Ellis, 1962, p. 50).

THE AFFECTIVE MODALITY: THE MULTIMODAL VIEW

We have alluded to the current viewpoint that emotional phenomena rest upon complex interactions among cognitive, behavioral, phenomenological, perceptual, biochemical, and neurophysiological functions. We have also stated that few approaches to psychotherapy invoke each of the foregoing in understanding or treating emotional disturbance. The multimodal approach (e.g., Brunell & Young, 1982; A. A. Lazarus, 1976, 1985, 1986, 1987, 1989, 1989a) endeavors to cover this entire spectrum in assessment, and in treatment if indicated.

For example, to generate the emotion of anxiety most effectively (powerfully), you would do something, act in a certain way (behavior); you would conjure up negative thoughts and images pertaining to yourself (cognition and imagery) and to significant others (interpersonal); you would observe various unpleasant sensory concomitants (sensation); and all of this would, of course, rest on the substrate of your neurophysiological and biochemical processes (biology). For illustrative purposes, we have confined ourselves to one negative emotion, anxiety, but the same holds for any emotional reaction (affective response). Hence: "The multimodal position is that *affect is the product of the reciprocal interaction of behavior, sensation, imagery, cognitive factors, and biological inputs, usually within an interpersonal context*" (A. A. Lazarus, 1986, p. 68). Of course, not all behaviors, sensations, images, and cognitions produce emotions. As Plutchik (1985) stated, "The whole complex process begins with a significant stimulus in the life of the individual" (p. 198). R. S. Lazarus (1982) ties emotion into a transaction between the individual and the environment that involves a cognitive evaluation about central life agendas related to survival.

Multimodal assessment employs the mnemonic BASIC I.D. as a template to ensure thoroughness and comprehensiveness by serving as a constant reminder that each of the seven modalities calls for equal attention during the diagnostic process: B = behavior, A = affect, S = sensation, I = imagery, C = cognition, I. = interpersonal, and D. = drugs–biology. The acronym BASIC I.B. is less compelling than BASIC I.D., and since most psychiatric interventions in the biological modality involve the use of *drugs* (mainly neuroleptics, antidepressants, and anxiolytic agents), neurophysiological–biochemical processes are subsumed under the convenient "drugs–biology" rubric. Nevertheless, it cannot be overemphasized that the "D." modality addresses *all* medical–physiological issues such as diet, sleep habits, exercise, central nervous system (CNS) pathology, and endocrine and metabolic disorders, in addition to the use of prescribed medications and recreational drugs.

A BRIEF DESCRIPTION OF THE BASIC I.D.

1. *Behavior* refers mainly to overt responses, acts, habits, gestures, and reactions that are observable and measurable.

2. *Affect* refers to emotions, moods, and strong feelings.

3. *Sensation* simply covers the five basic senses—seeing, hearing, touching, tasting, and smelling. (Clinically, we are usually required to correct negative sensations—tension, dizziness, pain, blushing, etc.)

4. *Imagery* includes dreams, fantasies, and vivid memories; mental pictures; and the way people view themselves (self-image). "Auditory images," recurring tunes or sounds, also fall into this category.

5. *Cognition* refers to attitudes, values, opinions, and ideas (self-talk). (Clinically, in this modality, the main task is to identify and modify dysfunctional beliefs.)

6. *Interpersonal relationships* include all significant interactions with other people (relatives, friends, lovers, acquaintances, etc.).

7. *Drugs–Biology* includes drugs (self- or physician prescribed) in addition to nutrition, hygiene, exercise, and all basic physiological and pathological inputs. It involves the panoply of neurophysiological–biochemical factors that affect personality.

In addition to providing a template for comprehensive assessment, the BASIC I.D. represents the fundamental vectors of personality just as ABCDEFG represent the notes in music. Combinations of ABCDEFG (with some sharps and flats) will yield everything from "Chopsticks" to Beethoven. Or consider the primary colors (red, yellow, and blue) and how secondary colors (green, purple, orange, etc.) are derived from various combinations thereof. Thus, our hypothesis is that virtually every human condition can be related to the BASIC I.D.— love, faith, ambition, hope, joy, optimism, pessimism, anticipation, disappointment, surprise, failure, awe, boredom, ecstasy, grief, assertiveness, and so on. Let us discuss, for instance, how pessimism would be characterized multimodally.

Pessimism tends to result in restricted, somewhat withdrawn behaviors, similar to that often seen when depression is present. Sensations that feed into an aura of pessimism include muscle tension and many of the responses associated with anxiety, suggesting that pessimism combines certain aspects of anxiety and depression. (When depression predominates, hope is all but abandoned, whereas pessimism implies that hope has merely been attenuated.) The imagery modality clearly reveals a spate of pictures involving disappointment, failure, or significant loss, which ties into negative cognitive appraisals, often typified by approach–avoidance conflicts. When the pessimism involves interpersonal reactions, these will be characterized by reluctance, hesitancy, and the manifestations of discouragement. At the biological level, pessimism would be indistinguishable from mild anxiety and minor mood disturbances.

Clinically speaking, patients seek therapy because of disturbances in one or more areas of their BASIC I.D. Presenting complaints may be confined to one modality: "I want to stop the bad habit of biting my nails" (behavior) or "I feel depressed" (affect). The stated problem may involve two or more modalities: "My shoulders and jaws feel tense" (sensation) and "I also have these recurring nightmares and fantasies" (imagery); "I can't decide what to do about my marriage" (cognitive and interpersonal) and "My diabetes is out of control" (biological). Regardless of the entry point(s), the multimodal therapist will conduct a thorough assessment of the discrete yet interactive aspects of the entire BASIC I.D. While it is clinically expedient to divide the reciprocal interactive flux that typifies actual life events into the seemingly separate dimensions of the BASIC I.D., it must be underscored that we are always confronted by a recursive, continuous, multileveled living process. What we have outlined should not be viewed as a flat, static, linear representation.

By viewing *affect* as involving reciprocal interactions of behavior, sensation, imagery, cognition, interpersonal factors and biological processes, the multimodal clinician invokes a systematic and interactive modus operandi. For example, a patient states, "I am anxious." Most scientifically minded therapists would thereupon endeavor to obtain specific information about the so-called anxiety. What exactly is the patient experiencing? What appears to trigger these reactions? When did the problem start? What are the most relevant antecedents? What are the main physiological and behavioral concomitants? Who or what appears to be reinforcing (maintaining) the problem? What solutions have been sought? What has helped to ameliorate the problem? What is apt to exacerbate it? What are its main consequences?

A multimodal assessment would be more comprehensive than the foregoing. It would examine a wider range of the salient behaviors that seem to precipitate, accompany, and follow the affective state. Moreover, apart from the presenting complaint (anxiety), a systematic and detailed inquiry would be conducted into other emotional reactions that may also be playing a role (e.g., depression, guilt, and anger). The accompanying sensory responses would receive detailed attention (e.g., tension triggers and palpitations), as would the associated imagery and cognitive factors. The interpersonal network (e.g., family systems) would be closely scrutinized to determine to what extent the patient's significant others were deliberately or inadvertently nurturing the problem, and to what extent there were social-skill deficits. The D. modality (medicine–physiology) is, of course, fundamental. Indeed, in certain instances, most of the variance vis-a-vis a given individual's complaint of anxiety, depression, or rage may be a function of a space-occupying intracranial lesion, endocrinological imbalance, simple caffeinism, or a host of other medical disorders. Nevertheless, the multimodal position is that since we are unified dynamic entities, the entire BASIC I.D. is implicated in almost every situation.

The Modality Profile of a patient who complains of depression might contain the following interactive items:

1. Behavior: Inertia, statements of self-denigration, fitful sleep pattern, and weepy and tearful.
2. Affect: Depression (the presenting complaint), guilt, and self-hate.
3. Sensation: Diminished pleasure from food, sex, and other sensory inputs; various somatic discomforts (aches and pains); easy fatigability.
4. Imagery: Pictures of gloom and doom (past, present, and future).
5. Cognition: Considers self unworthy and deficient globally and particularly in specific areas (negative self-appraisal), anticipates indefinite suffering.
6. Interpersonal: Sullen and uncommunicative.
7. Drugs–Biology: Fatigue possibly related to anemia or hypothyroidism (many medical conditions can result in depression, and a complete physical examination is recommended prior to the possible administration of anti-depressants or other drug treatments).

Even when the diagnosis is predominantly organic, a multimodal inquiry will traverse the entire spectrum of the BASIC I.D. lest some crucial "stone" be left unturned. Let us assume that a man is informed by his physician that he has diabetes and will require a special diet as well as injections of insulin. A multimodal practitioner would not simply let it go at that but would ask the following questions:

1. Behavior: How is this going to change his day-to-day activities? What will he do more of and less of? What will he stop doing? What will he start doing?
2. Affect: What affective impact will this have on him? Will he become anxious, depressed, or angry?
3. Sensation: Will his sensory pleasures be compromised, especially when having to avoid foods that he had enjoyed and looked forward to in the past?
4. Imagery: Will his self-image or his body-image change significantly? What sorts of fantasies will he entertain about his bodily functioning? Will he dwell on images pertaining to his premature demise?

5. Cognition: How much factual information should he acquire about diabetes and its management? What implications will he apply to himself? What sorts of inferences will he draw? Will he be concerned about his potency?
6. Interpersonal: Will his interpersonal interactions be affected? Will others accept his condition? Will he become more gregarious, more withdrawn, or will there be no interpersonal consequences?
7. Drugs–Biology: Will he comply with his doctor's prescriptions vis-a-vis his dietary habits, insulin injections, exercise regimen, rest and relaxation, and so forth?

The first published report of multimodal therapy (A. A. Lazarus, 1973) argued that in the treatment of schizophrenia, once the florid symptoms are controlled by medication, the other six modalities should be addressed. The case history of a woman with a diagnosis of chronic undifferentiated schizophrenia was presented. Thirty-one interrelated problems were treated by the same number of specific techniques. It is hypothesized that, in addition to biological treatments, unless all significant problems in behavior, sensation, imagery, cognition, and the interpersonal sphere are remedied, optimal recovery and durability of change are unlikely. Compliance with the medical regimen itself is likely to be compromised unless the other modalities are addressed (Fay, 1976). This is the essence of the multimodal treatment rationale and leads to an important question: how can one deal *directly* with affects or emotions?

MODIFYING AFFECT

Wilson (1984), in commenting on Rachman's (1981) paper on the primacy of affect, stated: "If the affective or emotional system is largely inaccessible to cognitive influences, then means must be found for modifying affect directly" (p. 114). *We submit that one cannot deal with affects or emotions directly; this modality can be worked with only indirectly.* If asked to deal directly with behavior, we can readily show someone how to act, what to say, what to do, what not to do, and so on. The sensory modality is also open to direct stimulation—hear that, see this, touch that, smell this, taste that. In the interpersonal modality, direct interventions such as imitation, role playing, and modeling are among the most common. The biological modality lends itself to numerous direct interventions, drugs and surgery being the most obvious. Even inferred constructs such as cognitions and images are amenable to direct intervention: "Think about it this way," "Dispute that false belief," "Imagine yourself sitting on a sandy beach," and "Picture a big tiger running through the jungle." But affect can only be reached through behavior, sensation, imagery, cognition, interpersonal relationships, and biological processes.

One therapist declared: "I arouse emotions directly by getting my patients to get in touch with their childhood agonies and then scream out loud." Our answer was that loud screaming (behavior) coupled with painful memories (images and cognitions) could probably stimulate affective responses in many people, but that this was still a matter of generating emotion via the other modalities. Another therapist stated that she evoked powerful emotional reactions by encouraging her patients to pound foam rubber cushions while yelling at the top of their lungs. We pointed out that pounding and yelling are specific behaviors, not emotions. Even if emotions are specifically generated by electrodes implanted into the brain, this is still *indirect* (i.e., via stimulation at the biological level). While many people seek the counsel of professional psychotherapists because they *feel* bad (i.e., they are experiencing negative affective states such as anxiety, depression, and guilt), the multimodal position is that the most elegant and thorough way of reducing anxiety, lifting depression, and assuaging guilt is to eliminate the specific and interrelated dysfunctional patterns of behavior, sensation, imagery, cognition, interpersonal relationships, and possible biological processes.

FINAL COMMENTARY

As alluded to earlier in this chapter, each therapist's explicit or implicit theory of emotions will determine which methods and techniques he or she employs in clinical practice. Carl Rogers did not regard emotion as the reciprocal interaction of the six modalities specified throughout this chapter, and his treatment arsenal rested exclusively upon a single technique—genuine, concrete, empathic reflection of the client's affective reactions and emotionally charged statements. This stands in sharp contrast to the training, shaping, modeling, rehearsing, disputing, and restructuring that typifies most multimodal interventions or, for that matter, the more limited cognitive–behavioral strategies.

To cite another example, Eysenck (1986), in the face of all evidence to the contrary, insists that "Pavlovian conditioning . . . is the principal causal factor in neurotic disorders, and that Pavlovian extinction is the basis of all curative efforts" (p. 378). Thus, by downplaying cognitive factors while underscoring the role of hypothalamic, subcortical reflexes, he subsequently claims that "flooding and response prevention" (Rachman & Hodgson, 1980) achieve an 80–90% cure in people suffering from compulsive handwashing. Follow-up data are not provided. Indeed, our own follow-ups suggest that unimodal treatment is seldom durable. While response prevention and flooding may be necessary treatments for compulsive handwashers, we find that they are often insufficient and are best supplemented with additional interventions that tend to prevent relapse (e.g., family-systems interventions and communication training, the modification of dysfunctional beliefs, the acquisition of sensory skills—such as relaxation—to offset future stresses, coping imagery techniques to enhance a sense of self-confidence, and social-skills training whenever specific person-to-person deficits are in evidence).

To reiterate a significant point, even if certain conditions (e.g., some schizophrenias and depressive conditions) tend to emanate primarily from the genetic diathesis and fall under the rubric of neurophysiological–biochemical processes, the multimodal position on emotion is that an assessment of behavior, sensation, imagery, cognition, and interpersonal relationships will nevertheless play an integral role in any holistic understanding and therapy of the afflicted individual. Emotional pain and dysfunction is likely to be durably assuaged and improved to the extent that salient problems in each discrete but interactive modality are addressed.

This is the essence of the multimodal position vis-a-vis emotions and the resolution of emotional dysfunction. It stands in marked contrast to the more limited views espoused by Freud, Wolpe, Ellis, Rogers, and Eysenck. Its major hypothesis is that durable results are in direct proportion to the number of specific modalities deliberately invoked by any therapeutic system. Thus, in pointing to the necessary and sufficient conditions or stable treatment outcomes, the major thesis is that comprehensive therapy at the very least calls for the correction of irrational beliefs, deviant behaviors, unpleasant feelings, intrusive images, stressful relationships, negative sensations, and possible biochemical imbalance. To the extent that problem identification (diagnosis–assessment) systematically explores each of these modalities, whereupon therapeutic intervention remedies whatever deficits and maladaptive patterns emerge, treatment outcomes will be positive and long lasting.

ACKNOWLEDGMENTS

We appreciate the incisive criticisms of Dr. Windy Dryden, Dr. Allen Fay, and Dr. Robert Plutchik.

REFERENCES

Bandura, A. (1977). *Social learning theory*. Englewood Cliffs, NJ: Prentice-Hall.
Bandura, A. (1986). *Social foundations of thought and action: A social cognitive theory*. Englewood Cliffs, NJ: Prentice-Hall.
Bandura, A., Adams, N. E., & Beyer, J. (1977). Cognitive processes mediating behavioral change. *Journal of Personality and Social Psychology*, **35**, 125–139.
Bower, G. H. (1981). Mood and memory. *American Psychologist*, **36**, 129–148.

Breuer, J., & Freud, S. (1955). *Studies on hysteria.* In J. Strachey (Ed. and Trans.), *The standard edition of the complete works of Sigmund Freud* (Vol. 2). London: Hogarth Press. (Original work published 1895)

Brunell, L. F., & Young, W. T. (Eds.). (1982). *Multimodal handbook for a mental hospital: Designing specific treatments for specific problems.* New York: Springer.

Collins, A. M., & Loftus, E. F. (1975). A spreading-activation theory of semantic processing. *Psychological Review,* **82,** 407–428.

Corsini, R. J. (Ed.). (1984). *Encyclopedia of psychology.* New York: Wiley.

Crider, A. B., Goethals, G. R., Kavanaugh, R. D., & Solomon, P. R. (1986). *Psychology* (2nd ed.). Glenview, IL: Scott, Foresman.

Davanloo, H. (1980). A method of short-term dynamic psychotherapy. In H. Davanloo (Ed.), *Short-term dynamic psychotherapy.* New York: Jason Aronson.

Ellis, A. (1962). *Reason and emotion in psychotherapy.* Secaucus, NJ: Lyle Stuart.

Ellis, A., & Bernard, M. E. (Eds.). (1985). *Clinical applications of rational emotive therapy.* New York: Plenum.

Eysenck, H. J. (1986). Consensus and controversy: Two types of science. In S. Modgil & C. Modgil (Eds.), *Hans Eysenck: Consensus and controversy* (pp. 375–398). London: Falmer.

Fay, A. (1976). The drug modality. In A. A. Lazarus (Ed.), *Multimodal behavior therapy* (pp. 65–85) New York: Springer.

Freud, S. (1959). The dynamics of transference. In J. Riviere (Ed.), *Collected papers* (Vol. 2). New York: Basic Books. (Original work published 1912)

Gordon, P. C., & Holyoak, K. J. (1983). Implicit learning and generalization of the "mere exposure" effect. *Journal of Personality and Social Psychology,* **45,** 492–500.

James, W. (1890). *Principles of psychology.* New York: Holt.

Lang, P. J. (1977). Physiological assessment of anxiety and fear. In J. D. Cone & R. P. Hawkins (Eds.), *Behavioral assessment: New directions in clinical psychology* (pp. 178–195). New York: Brunner/Mazel.

Lange, C. (1887). *Uber gemutsbewegungen: Eine psycho-physiologische studie.* Leipzig: Thomas.

Lazarus, A. A. (1973). Multimodal behavior therapy: Treating the BASIC ID. *Journal of Nervous and Mental Disease,* **156,** 404–411.

Lazarus, A. A. (1976). *Multimodal behavior therapy.* New York: Springer.

Lazarus, A. A. (Ed.). (1985). *Casebook of multimodal therapy.* New York: Guilford Press.

Lazarus, A. A. (1986). Multimodal therapy. In J. C. Norcross (Ed.), *Handbook of eclectic psychotherapy* (pp. 65–93). New York: Brunner/Mazel.

Lazarus, A. A. (1987). The multimodal approach with adult outpatients. In N. S. Jacobson (Ed.), *Psychotherapists in clinical practice* (pp. 286–326). New York: Guilford Press.

Lazarus, A. A. (1989). *The practice of multimodal therapy.* Baltimore: The Johns Hopkins University Press.

Lazarus, A. A. (1989a). Multimodal therapy. In R. J. Corsini & D. Wedding (Eds.), *Current psychotherapies* (pp. 503–544). Itasca, IL: Peacock.

Lazarus, R. S. (1982). Thoughts on the relation between emotion and cognition. *American Psychologist,* **37,** 1019–1024.

Matthews, A. M., Gelder, M. G., & Johnston, D. W. (1981). *Agoraphobia: Nature and treatment.* New York: Guilford Press.

Nichols, M. P., & Efran, J. S. (1985). Catharsis in psychotherapy: A new perspective. *Psychotherapy,* **22,** 46–58.

Nisbett, R. E., & Wilson, T. D. (1977). Telling more than we can know: Verbal reports on mental processes. *Psychological Review,* **84,** 231–259.

Plutchik, R. (1980a). *Emotion: A psycho-evolutionary synthesis.* New York: Harper & Row.

Plutchik, R. (1980b). A language for the emotions. *Psychology Today,* 68–78.

Plutchik, R. (1985). On emotion: The chicken-and-egg problem revisited. *Motivation and Emotion,* **9,** 197–200.

Rachman, S. J. (1981). The primacy of affect: Some theoretical implications. *Behaviour Research and Therapy,* **19,** 279–290.

Rachman, S. J., & Hodgson, R. (1980). *Obsessions and compulsions.* Englewood Cliffs, NJ: Prentice-Hall.

Rush, A. J., Beck, A. T., Kovacs, M., & Hollan, S. D. (1977). Comparative efficacy of cognitive therapy and pharmacotherapy in the treatment of depressed outpatients. *Cognitive Therapy and Research,* **1,** 17–31.

Watts, F. N. (1983). Affective cognition: A sequel to Zajonc and Rachman. *Behaviour Research and Therapy,* **21,** 89–90.

Wilson, G. T. (1984). Fear reduction and the treatment of anxiety disorders. In G. T. Wilson, C. M. Franks, K. D. Brownell, & P. C. Kendall (Eds.), *Annual review of behavior therapy* (Vol. 9, pp. 95–131). New York: Guilford Press.

Wolpe, J. (1958). *Psychotherapy by reciprocal inhibition.* Stanford; CA: Stanford University Press.

Wolpe, J. (1982). *The practice of behavior therapy* (3rd ed.). New York: Pergamon.

Zajonc, R. B. (1980). Feeling and thinking: Preferences need no inferences. *American Psychologist,* **35,** 151–175.

Zajonc, R. B. (1984). On the primacy of affect. *American Psychologist,* **39,** 117–123.

Chapter 10

INTERPERSONAL ANALYSIS OF THE CATHARTIC MODEL

LORNA SMITH BENJAMIN

ABSTRACT

The cathartic model proposes that psychopathology results from blocked mental energy, and the treatment implication is that the obstructed energy should be released. Using the cathartic model, Freud suggested that depression is the result of blocked anger, and so therapists very frequently encourage depressed patients to "get out their anger." Therapist facilitation of anger as an end in itself can, however, be iatrogenic. Five examples of harmful uses of the cathartic model are presented. Harmfulness is defined as reinforcement of, rather than change in, the patient's destructive interpersonal patterns as described by Structural Analysis of Social Behavior (SASB). It is proposed that instead of routinely encouraging expression of anger, therapists identify and confront the interpersonal purpose of the anger. Only if the expression of anger is consistent with a constructive interpersonal purpose and pattern, should it be encouraged.

INTRODUCTION

In 1880 Joseph Breuer discovered that when an hysterical girl under hypnosis was induced to speak freely, she expressed profound emotion and experienced relief from her symptoms. . . . In conjunction with Freud, in 1895, the two men published their conclusions that . . . hysterical symptoms developed as a result of experiences so traumatic to the individual that they were repressed. The mental energy associated with the experiences was

209

EMOTION
Theory, Research, and Experience
Volume 5

blocked off, and not being able to reach consciousness was converted into bodily innerva-
tions. The discharge of strangulated emotions (abreaction), through normal channels
during hypnosis, would relieve the necessity of diverting the energy into symptoms. This
method was termed "catharsis."

Wolberg (1954, p. 54)

Wolberg's description of the cathartic model summarizes the historical reason for the widespread practice of encouraging, indeed, sometimes exhorting patients to "get out your feelings." Speaking somewhat informally about the psychoanalytic theory underlying the cathartic model, the idea of catharsis is that energy is tied up in the struggle between the id and the superego, and the conflictual issue in question has been repressed or blocked from consciousness by the ego; the anxiety associated with threatened breakthrough of the repressed conflict keeps the individual unconsciously tied up with these unresolved issues from the past. The cathartic treatment plan is to release the blocked energies.

The practice of releasing affective energy is prevalent in psychoanalytic treatment to this day and is accompanied by substantial justification in the literature, ranging from the original cathartic treatments described by Freud and Breuer through many variations on the psychoanalytic cathartic theme and culminating most recently in the emergence of brief therapies. For example, Shea, Elkin, and Hirschfeld (1988, p. 237) report that important techniques in one well-researched brief therapy, interpersonal therapy as developed by Klerman, Weissman, and associates, include: "Clarification (restructuring and feeding back the patient's communication); encouragement of affect (helping the patient recognize and accept painful affects, and to express suppressed affects); and communication analysis (identifying maladaptive communication patterns and increasing effective communication)."

The identification and expression of affect clearly is an important part of psychotherapy in general as well as of psychoanalysis in particular.

Unfortunately, in practice it not difficult for supervisors, consultants, and research analysts to find examples where there appears to be little rationale for the therapist's behavior other than an apparent belief in the importance of "getting out" the affect as an end in itself. As with any good thing, indiscriminant and universal use of catharsis is not good. In fact, there are times when expression of affect seems iatrogenic. A crucial psychotherapist skill is to be able to tell when the expression of affect is helpful, when it is irrelevant, and when it is harmful.

Evaluation of the effectiveness of an intervention is dependent upon the therapist's theoretical framework. There are over 150 varieties of psychotherapy in practice today (Parloff, London, & Wolfe, 1986), so it is not easy to agree on a "gold standard." Nonetheless, the purpose of this chapter is to offer a theoretical framework that is capable of making operational the interpersonal consequences of interventions made from different schools of psychotherapy. The approach provides guidelines to the therapist about whether use of the cathartic model in a given instance will likely be constructive, irrelevant, or harmful. The exposition will be confined to the common problem of the expression of anger and will follow this outline: (1) Prototypic examples of irrelevant and of harmful applications of the cathartic model. (2) The proposed theoretical framework for evaluating the effect of a cathartic intervention, called Structural Analysis of Social Behavior (SASB), will be illustrated by applying this model to Freud's interpretation of the role of the expression of anger in depression. The SASB model was developed from the work of many others, including Sullivan, Murray, Leary, and Schaefer; the reader interested in historical and other details is referred to Benjamin (1974, 1984). (3) Reanalysis of the prototypic examples of harmful or irrelevant interventions from the point of view of a developmental learning approach called SASB-directed Reconstructive Learning (SASB-RL). (4) Statement of general principles for use of the cathartic model, illustrated by the use of SASB-RL in the treatment of a borderline and multiple personality.

IRRELEVANT OR HARMFUL USE OF THE CATHARTIC MODEL

The following examples are prototypic in the sense that the patterns are easy to find in supervisory, consulting, and clinic settings. The reasons for viewing these cathartic interventions as irrelevant or harmful will be detailed in the section "Reanalysis of the Prototypic Examples." In all five examples, "P" indicates the patient, and "T" the therapist.

Example 1

P: Well, in fourth grade, actually, I would come home and my mother would say, "Your report card came today," and I could really feel the chill run through my spine, and would go down and look at it, and I would see straight Cs and Ds in penmanship, and my handwriting hasn't improved one lick since then. But um, there would be about 15 to 20 seconds after which my mother would scream, "If I had those grades, I'd be in there studying right now." And I just felt tremendous tensions, tremendous anxiety, tremendous fear. . . . What was going to happen when Dad gets home?

T: How did you react when your mother would scream?

P: Basically I would just take it. I wouldn't answer back to her.

T: It must have been awful painful for you as a child, to see your parents reacting like that. So you had a lot of fear.

P: My father would come home, yeah, there was a lot of, you know, when my mother tells my dad, un, first anger was just boiling out of him and after about 15 minutes he would just sort of tone down into a, I remember a couple of times sitting with my dad and he would be in the living room talking for at least a half hour or 45 minutes, the tension on my part was just unbearable. I would get massive headaches, sitting there, and uh, just wanted, had to get out of the room immediately. But that was not acceptable. "Where are you going?" "I have a headache." "What do you mean, you have a headache?" It was not believed.

> T: What was he telling you during all this?
> P: I really don't know. Just that I had to do better.
> T: Must have been, for 45 minutes, awful painful stuff for him to be doing.
> P: Well I would basically sort of zone out.
> T: How do you feel about that, as you talk about it?
> P: It pisses me off just to think about it.
> T: You get angry.
> P: Yeah, it does, sitting here recounting it very concretely, brings a lot boiling up to the surface. Yeah it's ridiculous to put a ten-year-old kid's mind through.
> T: It must have felt, it sounds like from your description there was an awful lot of pain at the time that you were a boy.
> P: Yeah.
> T: It sounds like you swallowed it. It was something that was very difficult about yelling back at them. Somehow expressing that you were in pain in some way or form.
> P: Uh, it was just not something kids were supposed to do to their parents.
> T: How was that expressing bad feelings or anger?
> P: Yelling at your parents was like, you know, original sin.

In this example, there was great therapist interest in and empathy for pain and anger; the excerpt characterizes the session in general—the therapist skillfully elicited and acknowledged specific memories of the patient's feelings in reaction to parental demandingness. It became unequivocally clear that, in relation to his parents' expectations for him, the patient was uncomfortable and angry and that he had not felt free to disclose his feelings to his parents. The potential therapeutic value of the intense and continued focus on expressing and sharing pain and anger rested on faith in the cathartic model.

Example 2

A psychiatric resident used the expressive model to counsel a patient to speak up to her abusive alcoholic father. The patient, in her mid-20s, had visited her father in another city during spring break, and during that visit the father had initiated a number of vicious verbal attacks on the patient. Having a long history of such abuse from him, the patient decided to say nothing and had withdrawn in silence.

> T: That's fine if you decided to say nothing about it, but the part I have trouble with is whether you might have felt better about yourself if you had been able to speak up and let him know how you felt.
> P: But I have such trouble feeling warmth for him, it is very hard to want to speak up. I know that I should.

The patient then became self-critical about her lack of expressive abilities and her inability to care for her father. The therapist's invitation for the patient to express herself to her father only increased the patient's sense of guilt and inadequacy.

Example 3

A young therapist, confident of his use of the cathartic–expressive model, conducted a series of family sessions between a socially isolated male student in his mid-30s and the student's mother (M) who was dying of cancer.

> T: What P needs is, I think, to be understood by you, as far as I can tell.
> M: Ya.
> T: But we haven't talked much about what you need from P.
> M: That doesn't matter so much anymore.
> T: You get very teary eyed when you say that. Why doesn't it matter?
> M: 'Cause my days are numbered.
> T: Why doesn't it matter if your days are numbered?
> M: Well, because I don't want to impose on family and friends. I'd like to cope with it myself if I could.

A discussion followed during which the therapist tried to communicate to the mother that the patient should be responsible for himself, and she could be responsible for herself. The patient interrupted to complain that his mother felt too responsible for him.

> P: I kind of feel the opposite thing. I feel almost smothered by her because she's so damned concerned about me.
> M: Ya, I know.
> P: Well no matter, I can't jump either way, but I'm worrying about how she's going to react to it.

Then there was a series of exchanges in which the therapist asked the mother for examples to illustrate her smothering. The mother provided examples that showed concern, but some of them included attempts to encourage the son to be more independent.

> T: Well, what is this smothering concern, then? What—how is that an example of smothering?
> M: Well, if he was—for example—had somebody else in his life, maybe a girlfriend or somebody else that I knew he was very close to, then I would feel that there was somebody else, but I just never see that friendship develop with anybody else, and I think everybody needs that special person in their life.
> T: And how does that lead you to smothering?
> M: I don't know really. I guess the whole thing—the fact that different things have—I really don't know. I just don't really feel that I was smothering—it's not how I see it, it's how he sees it. I tried not to. I tried to let him make decisions and stuff. I don't know.
> T: But you're not sure what you did—
> M: [unintelligible]

> T: Okay, well maybe we can find out.
> M: Yeah, okay.

Without acknowledging the mother's protest that she didn't think she had smothered her son, the therapist then conducted an investigation that established two ways the mother had smothered the son.

> T (to P): So what you're saying is one of the ways that you felt you were kept in a childish role is that when you say something that it's not taken as valuable.
> P: And not treated as an adult.
> T: And the second example you gave was when you were humored. So you're basically saying your feeling—your opinion is not respected. And the second example you gave was that growing up you were very secure, so secure that like you never went out and got a job when the other kids did or something like that. So I guess those are two examples. What's your response to this, M?

This and other sessions continued in this vein, with the therapist consistently facilitating the patient's expressions of dissatisfaction with the mother and confronting her on the patient's behalf. The mother sometimes agreed with the complaints and sometimes defended or tried to explain herself. One would have to conclude that the main therapeutic rationale was for the patient to "get it out" in relation to the presumed source of the psychopathology, the mother.

Example 4

Sometimes adherence to the cathartic model presses the outer limits of therapist ability to withstand negative transference! The hospitalized patient had been listing symptoms, and the therapist was extremely empathic in reflecting the discomfort.

> T: So it feels pretty hopeless to try and talk about these things.
> P: I already told you what's wrong—sleep, pain, eating.
> T: And what about those things? I don't know very much about them. Tell me about the sleeping.
> P: I'm waking up every hour. Not because of the pain. I don't know why. I just feel like giving up.
> T: It's been quite a battle. You've been fighting a long time.
> P: What do you mean?
> T: First the (medical illness), to make you different from the other kids, at a time when it's important to be the same as the others. So you can't (fit in).
> P: It wasn't like that. It wasn't any problem. There wasn't any struggle. I'm just tired of being in here the last seven weeks and having no one help me.
> T: And you are angry with us.
> P: Well, wouldn't you be? You're the doctors, that's why I'm paying you for this. I'm paying for this room and I don't even get to spend time in it.
> T: So you are angry at me and feeling helpless.
> P: Yeah, I'm giving up (defiantly).

It is hard to imagine a therapist being more empathic; there are few ways the patient's expression of feelings could have been better accepted and facilitated. Despite this the patient's rageful attacks upon everyone in sight continued unabated for weeks, with no change suggestive of interpersonal growth that might lead to a decrease in suicidality and to a discharge from the hospital. The therapist and the staff were approaching "total burn-out."

Example 5

Some patients "get high" on rage.

> P: A big fight is exciting. . . . It's so hard to let those feelings sit. Wheels churn if I feel wronged. I thrive on retaliation. I have to get control. I have to stop myself.
>
> T: You describe resisting anger as an alcoholic might resist a drink.
>
> P: It is an addiction. Physiological. The adrenalin, excitement, winning, arguing, fighting. I try to get my mind off of it. I sweat, my heart beats. The wheels start. I think I am going to stick it to them. It is not for control. It is to PUNISH. It's jumping the gun. I am so punitive that way.

STRUCTURAL ANALYSIS OF SOCIAL BEHAVIOR (SASB)

The SASB model, presented in simplified cluster form in Figure 10.1, is based on the three dimensions shown in Figure 10.2. The model will be explained by application to Freud's (1917/1953) discussion of the role of anger in depression in "Mourning and Melancholia."

Rereading Freud is like exploring an old mine and finding new veins again and again. In some passages Freud's model appears to be mechanical, describing a fixed universe of energy that must be safely placed. However, his clinical observations are nonetheless often quite interpersonal, even when writing about implied transactions between the id and its derivatives. The explicit and implicit interpersonal aspects of Freud's analysis, loosely called object relations here, will be the focus of the SASB analysis. Two excerpts from Freud (1917/1953, pp. 158–159) comprise the exercise:

> If one listens patiently to the many and various self-accusations of the melancholiac, *one cannot in the end avoid the impression that often the most violent of them are hardly at all applicable to the patient himself but that with insignificant modifications they do fit someone else, some person whom the patient loves, has loved or ought to love.* . . . So we get the key to the clinical picture—by perceiving that the self-reproaches are reproaches against a loved object which have been shifted on to the patient's own ego. . . . It is because everything derogatory that they say of themselves at bottom relates to someone else that they are not ashamed and do not hide their heads.

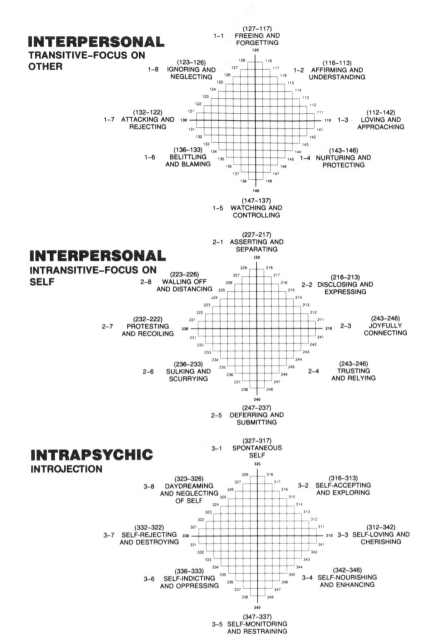

FIGURE 10.1. Cluster version of the SASB model. Interpersonal and intrapsychic events can be classified on the model in terms of three judgments: focus (which selects one of the three diamonds), love–hate (which positions the event on the horizontal axis), and enmeshment–differentiation (which positions the event on the vertical axis). If the interpersonal and intrapsychic antecedents and consequences of a cathartic therapy event are classified on the model, it will be clear whether the catharsis was helpful or harmful to the therapy goal of changing maladaptive patterns. From Benjamin (1987).

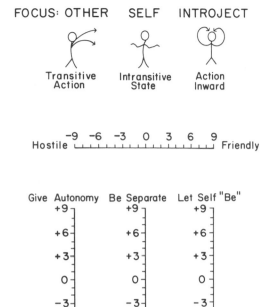

FIGURE 10.2. Dimensions of the interpersonal space shown in Figure 10.1. Object relational process (what is happening in the here-and-now) and content (what is being talked about) are coded in terms of focus (the diamonds in Figure 10.1), love–hate (the horizontal axis in both figures), and enmeshment–differentiation (the vertical axis in both figures). These three dimensional judgments determine the precise code in Figure 10.1. From Benjamin (1986).

> First there existed an object-choice, the libido had attached itself to a certain person; then, owing to a real injury or disappointment concerned with the loved person, this object-relationship was undermined . . . [there was] an *identification* of the ego with the abandoned object. Thus the shadow of the object fell upon the ego, so that . . . the loss of the object became transformed into a loss in the ego, and the conflict between the ego and the loved person transformed into a cleavage between the criticizing faculty of the ego, and the ego as altered by the identification.

The implied interpersonal elements of the first excerpt are (1) reproaches against a loved object, and (2) everything derogatory they say about themselves. The implied interpersonal elements of the second excerpt are (3) injury or disappointment concerned with the loved object, and (4) the loss of the object became transformed into a loss in the ego. These four elements appear in Table 10.1 along with their SASB codes, which were derived as follows.

TABLE 10.1

SASB Dimensional Analysis of Freud's Explanation of the Dynamics of Depression[a]

Element	Ref	Focus	Affiliation	Interdependence	Cluster
1. Reproaches against a loved object	PO	Transitive	Hostile	Controlling	1–6
2. Derogate self	PP	Introject	Hostile	Controlling	3–6
3. Loved object injures	OP	Transitive	Hostile	Controlling	1–8
Loved object disappoints	OP	Transitive	Hostile	Autonomy giving	1–8
4. Loved object unavailable (lost)	OP	Transitive	Hostile	Autonomy giving	1–8
Ego is unavailable (lost)	EP	Introject	Hostile	Autonomy giving	3–8

[a]P = Patient; O = loved object; E = ego; Ref = referents; Cluster 1–6 = belittling and blaming; Cluster 3– = self-indicating and oppressing; Cluster 1–8 = ignoring and neglecting; Cluster 3–8 = daydreaming an neglecting of self.

SASB (Benjamin, 1974, 1984) is a model for describing interpersonal interactions in terms of three dimensions: (1) interpersonal focus (other, self, introjection); (2) love or hate; (3) enmeshment or differentiation. SASB coding begins with the identification of referents, which in this analysis are P = patient; O = loved other person; and E = ego. Each element to be coded must identify one referent (called X) in relation to another (called Y). The requirement that there be an X and a Y means that elements must be object relational in order to be SASB codable. Once referents are identified, coding is made from the point of view of X. For example, Element 1, reproaches against a loved object, has the referents PO, meaning it is about an implicit transaction from the patient to the loved object. Coding is from the point of view of P.

The first coding decision is whether X's transaction is transitive, intransitive, or introjected; these possibilities are sketched by the stick figures at the top of Figure 10.2. If X's position is transitive, which characterizes reproach (an action is passing over and toward the direct object, Y), then the SASB code will be on the top diamond in Figure 10.1, the surface that represents transitive actions. That first decision eliminates two thirds of the possible codes (the middle and bottom diamonds). The rule for deciding upon focus is simple: if the transaction between X and Y is about what is happening to Y, it is transitive; if it is about what is happening to X, the transaction is intransitive. If the referents are X and X (that is, if X = Y), then the transaction is an introjective event.

The second coding decision is about affiliation, with the "loving friendly" points occuring on the right-hand side of the model, and the "hateful hostile" points appearing on the left-hand side. This dimension is shown by the horizontal scale in Figure 10.2, and a decision about love versus hate eliminates half of the remaining possibilities. Reproach is hostile, say about halfway (-4 or -5) on the scale in Figure 10.2.

The final coding decision is about enmeshment versus differentiation and is represented by the vertical dimension on the scales in Figure 10.2 and on the model in Figure 10.1. The anchor points on the vertical scale are different for each type of focus, and the appropriate three scales are respectively located in Figure 10.2 under the three possible types of focus. Independent or differentiated positions are represented on the top half while enmeshed positions are represented on the bottom half, and this last decision eliminates half of the remaining possibilities. Reproach, which is transitive, is judged on the leftmost scale in Figure 10.2, and it is controlling, say −4 or −5.

In sum, the dimensional analysis of reproach from the patient toward the loved object leads to the conclusion that it is transitive (−4,−4). Using principles of ordinary geometry, the vector (−4,−4) [horizontal value, vertical value] is located at about 7:30 on the transitive surface in Figure 10.1, at the cluster named "1–6 Belittling and Blaming." The full SASB model, not shown here, uses the numbers in the vector (H,V) to more exactly locate the code with finer degrees of resolution. The cluster version, shown in Figure 10.1, suffices for many purposes, including the present context.

Cluster numbers in Figure 10.1 begin with a 1 if they appear on the first or top surface, a 2 for the middle or second, and a 3 for the bottom or third surface. The second part of the cluster number ranges from 1 to 8, starting with 1 at 12:00 and proceeding clockwise. Cluster 1–6 is on the top surface, and is the 6th cluster counting from 12:00.

The decisions shown in Figure 10.2—focus, love–hate, enmeshment–differentiation—are the quintessence of a SASB dimensional analysis. The final words for the code, whether in terms of the cluster model or the full model, are only convenient for communication and are less important than the dimensional dissection into focus, love–hate, and enmeshment–differentiation.

Inspection of Table 10.1 shows that the dimensional analysis of Freud's description of the dynamics of depression involves the following SASB codes: 1–6 Belittling and Blaming (X puts Y down, blames Y, and punishes Y), and its internalization, 3–6 Self-indicting and Oppressing (X punishes himself or herself by blaming and putting self down); 1–8 Ignoring and Neglecting (without giving it a thought, X uncaringly ignores, neglects, and abandons Y), and its internalization, 3–8 Daydreaming and Neglecting of Self (X is recklessly neglectful of himself or herself, sometimes completely "spacing out"). The descriptions within parentheses are items from the SASB short form (Benjamin, 1988), which can be used to have patients rate their object relations in terms of the SASB model.

One could use these SASB dimensional analyses to reframe, in interpersonal terms, a simple sequence for the creation of a depression according to Freud. Loved other belittles (1–6) and neglects (1–8) the patient. Patient responds by reproach (1–6), which he or she dares not express for fear of consequential neglect (1–8) (SASB code for inhibition of expression is 3–5 Self-monitoring and Restraining). The patient then reproaches the self (3–6) instead of the other. In SASB terms, the patient substitutes the self, X, for the referent Y. The patient also internalizes the other's neglect, 1–8, to neglect the self (3–8).

This SASB dimensional analysis of Freud's passages makes explicit two possible interpersonal mechanisms for self attack. (1) *Redirected reproach.* "You degrade and neglect me, but I dare not tell you that I blame you for that, so I blame myself for the whole thing."(2) *Internalized reproach.* "You hold me in contempt, and so I do too."

Freud's explanation for self-attack in depression follows the first of these two alternatives, and that alternative implies that the cathartic model would be an appropriate treatment intervention. If the self-attack results from attack that should be directed at the loved other, then expression of that anger (as in Example 3 above) should be helpful. There have been many attempts to research the Freudian (Alternative 1) interpretation of depression, but the idea that depressed individuals would be inhibited in aggressiveness has been contradicted by findings that during depression, some people become more hostile toward the self and toward others, especially loved ones (e.g., Weissman, Klerman, & Paykel, 1971).

The second alternative is simpler and conforms to Sullivan's (1953) concept of introjection, which is concretized by the third surface of the SASB model. If self-attack in depression represents doing to the self what important others have done, then the cathartic model does not have direct treatment relevance. The patient is not suffering from a wish to attack that has been deflected. Quite the contrary, the mechanism "If you hold me in contempt, I hold myself in contempt" suggests imitation of the loved other, and imitators respect and love those they imitate. Attacking a respected loved one is neither a natural nor an adaptive response. If, then, the second alternative is operative, rather than encouraging attack of the loved other, the treatment should help the patient differentiate from this destructive internalization. The key concept in this case would be to help the patient separate psychologically from the one who is treating him or her so badly; patients need to develop their own view of themselves individually. This separation might be facilitated by the expression of anger, but differentation rather than anger is the treatment goal; there are alternatives other than expression of anger for differentiating.

Freud's analysis of the loved object's neglect, SASB coded as transitive hostile autonomy giving (1–8), is consistent with the second alternative and SASB introject theory. The loved other abandons the patient (1–8) and so the patient abandons the self (3–8). This SASB translation of Freud requires viewing the ego (E) as equivalent to patient (P) in order to generate the 3–8 code that states, in effect: "If you don't care about me, I don't care about me. I will just let myself go unattended. I will not 'be' in this world." It is not clear why Freud uses the first alternative to account for self-attack, but the second alternative to account for self-neglect in depression.

Whether self-attack in depression arises from redirected or from internalized reproach could be studied by SASB technology that includes questionnaires, a formal coding system, and software (Benjamin, 1984). The SASB methods for operationalizing object relations could be used to identify variables involved in determining whether the self-attack is redirected reproach or internalized reproach. It seems most reasonable to assume that in some cases, self-attack is mounted by redirected reproach and, in others, by internalized reproach. Identification of the parameters of each process is an important and resolvable research question. For the present, the SASB analysis serves only to identify specifically the interpersonal nature of the Freudian hypothesis about the dynamics of depression, and to show how his first alternative implies that the cathartic model would be appropriate to alleviate depression. It is also of more than passing interest to note that Freud started his analysis of depression with observations about hostile input from a loved other person. Despite the clear interpersonal implications of his description, the traditional psychoanalytic literature does not include the loved other in formulations about either the diagnosis or the treatment of depression.

REANALYSIS OF THE PROTOTYPIC EXAMPLES

SASB codes of the interpersonal context for each of the prototypic examples can determine whether the cathartic intervention is helpful or not. The assessment of the value of the interventions in the examples requires the following two assumptions. (1) Therapy is helpful if it facilitates change in destructive, currently maladaptive ways of seeing the self and interacting with others. Therapy is harmful if it enhances or fails to change currently maladaptive ways of seeing the self and interacting with others. (2) Constructive ways of seeing the self and interacting with others consist of three factors. The first is a balance of focus; the person must skillfully engage in as much focus on others as on the self. The second is some degree of attachment to others (the extreme of which is shown on the SASB model by Clusters 1–3, 2–3, and 3–3). The third is some degree of self-definition (the extreme of which is shown on the SASB model by Clusters 1–1, 2–1, and 3–1). Therapy that is guided by these factors, that decodes content and process in psychotherapy in terms of the three SASB dimensions, and that helps the patient learn about interactive patterns—where they came from, what they are for, and whether to change them—is called SASB-directed Reconstructive Learning (SASB-RL).

In the earlier analysis of the five examples, the SASB codes are not included, but the reader is invited to make particular note of comments having to do with enmeshment versus differentiation.

In Example 1, the therapist facilitated the young man's recall of his pain and anger over his parent's coercive intrusion into his performance at school. Ruminating over the injustice of it all, and wishing they had been different, served to keep the patient engaged in hostile enmeshment with his parents. Their harsh demands about his school performance had made it hard for him to learn that the acquisition of cognitive skills was supposed to be for him, not for them. The resulting confusion about whose successes and whose failures belonged to whom was manifest in the patient's current difficulties with completing college.

Rather than faciliating the expression of anger and pain as a primary therapeutic goal, as an apparent end in itself, the SASB-RL analysis suggests the more important goal would be to facilitate differentiation from parents. Under the alternative interpersonal formulation, rather than enhancing the expression of his pain and anger about the past and the associated wishes that his parents had been different, the patient would be helped more if he could discover that his adult procrastinations were residuals from the ancient battle with his parents. Such a reframing could help him decide whether to live his own life for himself in the present, that is, become differentiated, or whether to continue being focused on and angry about what happened 15 years ago.

It is important to note that cathartic theory assumes that releasing the feelings will free the patient to live in the present. Too often, however, the cathartic practice unfolds toward an intensification of concern about and with the past.

For Example 2, the SASB-RL formulation is that the father's long-standing alcoholism was very unlikely to change during the patient's brief visit, no matter what she did. If the patient had told her father how she felt, there probably would have been further abuse. Under the present, alternative interpersonal formulation, the patient's decision to be silent and stay out of the way was framed as self-protective and adaptive. The more central therapeutic issue was that the patient needed to give up the fantasy that she could or should take care of her father. The therapeutic task was to learn to acknowledge the reality that without other intervention (e.g., father joins AA, and/or starts an effective psychotherapy), her father will always be relentlessly critical, and that she was right to conclude there was no point in exposing herself to certain abuse. Therapist comments designed to enhance psychological separateness from such a destructive parent and his internalizations would have been more helpful than the cathartic–expressive recommendation that increased the patient's guilt about and enmeshment with a powerful and destructive parental figure.

For Example 3, the SASB-RL alternative formulation is that in trying, albeit ambivalently, to please and do a good job with her son, the mother was indeed too nurturant, too self-sacrificing, masochistic, and compliant, just as she was during the interview. As a result of exposure to this indulgent, appeasing mother, the son felt entitled and demanding. Nobody could please him, including himself. Having been taught that a major solution to life's dilemmas is to become mad at somebody else who will then try to take care of things, the patient has little reality-based sense of his own potential for efficacy. This session, during which his demanding, complaining, and blaming stance was enhanced by the therapist, exacerbated his major problem of angry entitlement. It would have been more constructive to help him learn that nobody but a masochistic mother (or her stand-in) would respond to his accusations by trying to figure out what would make him feel better, and by trying to "make it up to him." In searching for a replication of that indulgent pattern, he stays stuck in ways that do not work well for him or for those who might be close to him. If he could develop more empathy for others and learn about the impact of his blaming and expectations of entitlement, he might become truly strong and more likely to develop a mature love relationship and a self-determined work identity. In sum, the cathartic model, as implemented in Example 3, exacerbated the presenting problems of malaise, poor self-esteem, and difficulty in forming a love relationship.

For Example 4, the alternative formulation is that this patient believed that if she suffered enough, the therapist would finally stop witholding the magic and would fix everything. The therapist needed to take a highly differentiated but friendly stance and help the patient learn that her signal "My misery is your command" did not work because it could not work. The problem was not, as the patient believed, that the staff refused to help but rather that they could not do what the patient had in mind. The patient needed to learn that, in reality, others cannot respond to the escalation of misery by magically bestowing happiness and comfort. If she, the patient, would like to learn more about how she came to believe that increased suffering is the pathway to happiness, the staff would help her do that, and then, if she wished, the staff could be quite helpful in teaching more adaptive ways of interpersonal action in the adult world. The approach eventually led to better patient–therapist collaboration and to a deescalation of symptoms.

For example 5, the SASB-RL interpersonal formulation is that the patient had been raised in a chaotic household where expressions of anger, indeed cruelty, were rampant. She had learned that the person who strikes first, strikes best. If her dreams of a stable, reliable, emotionally satisfying relationship and of an important work identity were to be realized, she would need to learn an entirely different, more modulated way of relating to others than previously achieved. She developed a strong, idealizing attachment to the therapist, who was very steady in modeling and in reinforcing a higher level of functioning. Using this support well, the patient learned to inhibit her chaotic impulses. Being nicely endowed with looks, intelligence, and other talents, she soon succeeded both in choosing a succession of progressively kinder and better functioning partners than before, and in better modulating her own affect. Her greatest problem, one which took a long time to resolve, was to decide whether she could allow herself to be happy and successful. "Getting better" required detaching psychologically from her family's devotion to trouble and chaos (unbridled expression of affect), a step that was sure to lead to rejection by them. Abandoning her attachment to them and to their interesting soap opera lifestyle was not easy.

The preceding five examples illustrate how implementation of the cathartic model to encourage the expression of anger as an end in itself can at times be harmful or even irrelevant. The next example shows how it can be helpful to accept and encourage the patient's wish to express anger. The difference between this implementation and the preceding five examples is that the interpersonal purpose of the anger is identified and that interpersonal need rather than anger per se is addressed.

The patient thought of herself as "bitchy," and her husband (H) agreed with that assessment. In the following quoted therapy segment, the interpersonal purpose of the "bitchiness" was identified, and the interventions were focused on the interpersonal roots and goals of the anger.

> P: I get hostile when H takes to his bed. Though he doesn't demand anything from me then, and just wants to withdraw, I feel put upon. I focus on him and don't think about where *my* responses are coming from. I'd like to yell, to attack. I'd like to yell, I don't want to take care of you. Handle your stuff. I feel I am the most responsible one. I have to pick up the pieces always. His being ill is a command, an expectation.
>
> T: What is the purpose of your yelling. What would you like?
>
> P: Him to change. It becomes clear when he's sick, I can't count on him anyway. [Long pause] I wonder what I'm fighting anyway. How do I get stuck with these needy people who can't function? I'm panicky that this is the way it always will be. I'll never know when I'll have to take the bottom line.

There was a discussion about when the husband did take the bottom line, and the idea was that it only happened when the patient was absolutely overwhelmed and unable to function herself, as revealed in the following segment. It is also important to note that the patient had been an exploited child, taking care of younger siblings in a large family.

> P: I have feelings like when I was a child. I feel alone. Not reciprocated. To be a child is to be vulnerable, need caring, and to be an adult is to be not vulnerable. So if he is vulnerable, he is a child and I am the adult, alone and abandoned. My needs won't be met. Just as it was when I was a kid. Which is why I'm not free to be vulnerable.

Next, the patient explored her relationship with a daughter.

> P: I see it is not natural for a child to be either exclusively dependent or not.
>
> T: [Encourages exploration of whether the wife could take a dependent position with her husband.]
>
> P: I am not good at it! When I was young, my brothers and sisters would gang up on me, and that was the time my mother told me never to cry. Someone else was always needier. My brothers and sisters saw me as just a mean bitch with bad intentions. Always. That's how they saw me.

The passage shows how the patient was helped to see that her "bitchiness" and angry moodiness were in the service of control, which in turn was importantly related to early roles that were not relevant or adaptive in her adult situation. The husband also worked in his own therapy on how to assert and be responsible rather than withdraw. After a while, he affirmed that she was far less controlling, demanding, and irritable, and, as he withdrew less and took charge more, she saw him as becoming more potent and involved. Their marital satisfaction improved markedly.

GUIDELINES FOR KNOWING WHEN EXPRESSION OF ANGER IS HELPFUL AND WHEN IT IS HARMFUL

In SASB-RL, when the patient expresses an affect, the therapist acknowledges, reflects, and consolidates that affect and then helps the patient find the interpersonal parallel to that affect. Discussions of affect are transformed to discussions of the object relations relevant to that affect. In the case of angry affect, the SASB analyses have suggested that the parallel interpersonal issues always are that the patient wishes to have control over or distance from the person or issue being discussed (or both).

As shown earlier, the assumptions of SASB-RL are that healthy persons (1) can focus equally as well on others as on themselves; (2) are able to show attachment that is, have warm bonds with other human beings; and (3) have a clearly articulated sense of self or separateness. The therapeutic guidelines associated with these assumptions are that expressions of affect that facilitate a sense of *differentiated self in a context of bondedness* are helpful and should be facilitated by the therapist. Affects that do not meet this standard are more likely to interfere with therapeutic growth.

The idea of encouraging the expression of affect in some stages of therapy and not in others is illustrated in the following brief sketch of the treatment of a woman with borderline and multiple personality. The patient, who was in her early 20s, languished in college, unable to complete any semester's work because of a debilitating depression. She also was vulnerable to cutting on her abdomen and upper legs with a razor and to "losing time." She had no memory for the time lost, but other people would tell her that she had been acting like a very different person during the periods in question. Close to her family, particularly to her father, she was married to a man whom she periodically would abuse both verbally and physically. Occasionally, after monumental provocation, he would lose his temper and become inordinately violent with her.

She began this therapy (not her first) very worried about whether the therapist would care enough about her to be available as often as she might need to be in contact. Instead of promises of extended availability, she was offered a therapy contract to help her learn about her interactive patterns, where they came from and what they were for. She was told that once she understood her unconscious goals and patterns, she would need to decide if she wanted to change them. If she did decide to change, the therapist would help her develop new patterns that could work better in the here and now. After some discussion and clarification, the patient accepted this contract, acknowledging that learning about and giving up old patterns has little to do with measures of therapist caring in terms of availability for extra appointments and long telephone contacts. In this therapy-structuring interview, the patient's anger about therapists who do not care was ignored because it was an attempt to control the therapy in ways that, if successful, would only recapitulate old family patterns of reckless intimidation on the theme of love and caring.

Not long after therapy began, a very angry and threatening woman (this patient) left a message on the therapist's answering machine to the effect that the therapist had better watch her step because she was venturing into forbidden territory. If the therapist did not back off, there would be dire consequences, the voice warned. This episode, which the patient did not remember, was resolved by the therapist's acknowledgment that part of the patient may be reluctant to change. The therapist, who was quite active in ferreting out and reflecting ego-alien material in order to encourage exploration of difficult topics, decided that the proper response to that phone call was to go slower in therapy. To avoid such episodes in the future, the patient was encouraged to say during sessions when she was uncomfortable about the pace. Instead of encouraging the patient to vent her anger at the therapist, there was a direct and effective response to the interpersonal issue causing the anger.

In the next phase, the patient became angry with her father, who was angry with her for being in therapy. Therapy creates unhealthy dependency, he maintained, and he refused to keep his promise to pay the therapy bill. A family session was held during which the father's concerns were heard and his questions answered. In this phase, encouragement of expression of anger at the father would have served to increase the already intense, hostile enmeshment between father and daughter.

Therapy progressed well for a number of weeks, and gradually it became clear that, as a very young child, the patient had been a victim of chronic and severe sexual abuse. The identity of the abuser was not known, but an unwelcome possibility was that it was her father. The patient was supported through this suicidal phase, and she was reassured that there need not be any overt confrontations with her father if she did not want them. It was noted that if she ultimately decided to "divorce" her father, and if that devastated him as she expected, he could be referred for his own therapy.

Anger at the therapist came next, "for confronting me with a reality I do not want or like." The patient said she "could not go back"; she could no longer "pretend the incest had not happened." "Things will never be the same, even if I terminate therapy now." In this stage, the therapist simply let her vent the anger, interpreting it as a need to distance herself from the therapy process. She needed time to accommodate this new and starkly unacceptable information, and, after the anger subsided, she was reassured that it was okay to just chitchat in sessions and not "push" for a while. There was empathy with how difficult it is to uncover and work through old injuries.

Finally, murderous, intense rage toward the father appeared. At this point, there was some attention to setting limits on physical acting-out of that rage, but the verbal expressions of anger, fear, and despair and tears during sessions were encouraged. The cathartic model was given full rein. The expression of rage at her father, as well as the enhancement of other affects such a fear and pain, was very appropriate to the task of reclaiming reality so that she could differentiate from a destructive parental figure.

In conclusion, the patient's expressions of anger early in therapy were to control and/or distance herself from engaging with the therapy process, and they were circumvented or ignored by constructive reframing. By contrast, the expression of affect was encouraged as the patient reexamined her own memories in a setting where she was not told what to think and to feel, and where her own feelings and sense of reality were affirmed (e.g., "It did hurt even though you were told it felt good").

The assumption is that affect and behavior evolved together, and if there is an affect, there must be an accompanying interpersonal issue. Therefore, affective expressions associated with old, maladaptive interpersonal patterns are discouraged, and, instead, the interpersonal meaning of the anger is addressed directly. In the case of anger, that meaning can be identified if the clinician applies the hypothesis that anger usually has the purpose of achieving control and/or distance. On the other hand, expressions of affect that lead to realistic appraisals of maladaptive situations are facilitated and supported. Cognitive and affective experiencing of "how it really was" helps the patient gain the perspective needed to "betray" old maladaptive contracts and views and to replace them with new and better patterns.

SUMMARY

Five examples of therapist use of the cathartic model in psychotherapy were given that were interpreted as irrelevant or destructive. The frame of reference for evaluating what is helpful is the following. (1) Decode the content and process of therapy in terms of three dimensions defined by the SASB model—focus, love–hate, and enmeshment–differentiation. (2) Assume that whatever the school of therapy, the main task is for the patient to learn about his or her interactive patterns (SASB coded), where they came from and what they were for, and to decide whether and how to change them. (3) Assume that everyone must accomplish the fundamental developmental tasks of learning to focus on others as often as on self, of developing bondedness, and of developing a sense of differentiated self (these respectively representing the three SASB dimensions). Organize the selection of therapeutic approaches around the task of helping the patient learn any deficient skills in balancing focus, in capacity for love, or in connection with differentiation. When the cathartic model is clearly relevant to these interpersonal and intrapsychic goals, it will be helpful. When the expression of affect merely recapitualates ancient patterns, it is ineffective. To the extent that implementation of the cathartic model strengthens old patterns, it is harmful. Each time the expression of affect is at issue, the clinician should reflect upon its interpersonal purpose, and on how the interpersonal consequences of affect expression relate to the patient's specific learning goals at that particular stage of therapy.

ACKNOWLEDGMENTS

I would like to thank Steve Wonderlich, Marianne Gerber, and the editors for their helpful comments on an earlier draft of this paper. Appreciation also is expressed to the supervisees and patients who provided the examples.

REFERENCES

Benjamin, L. S. (1974). Structural analysis of social behavior. *Psychological Review, 81,* 392–425.
Benjamin, L. S. (1984). Principles of prediction using structural analysis of social behavior. In R. A. Zucker, J. Aronoff, & A. I. Rabin (Eds.), *Personality and the prediction of behavior* (Vol. 1, pp. 121–174). New York: Academic Press.
Benjamin, L. S. (1986). Adding social and intrapsychic decriptors to Axis I of DSM-III. In T. Millon & G. L. Klerman (Eds.), *Contemporary directions in psychopathology.* New York: Guilford Press.
Benjamin, L. S. (1987). Use of the SASB Dimensional Model to develop treatment plans for personality disorders. I. Narcissism. *Journal of Personality Disorders, 1,* 43–70.
Benjamin, L. S. (1988). *Intrex shortform users manual.* Madison, WI: Intrex Interpersonal Institute.
Freud, S. (1953). Mourning and melancholia. In E. Jones (Ed.) & J. Riviere (Trans.), *Sigmund Freud collected papers* (Vol. 4, pp. 152–172). New York: Basic Books. (Original work published 1917)
Parloff, M. B., London, P., & Wolfe, B. (1986). Individual psychotherapy and behavior change. In M. R. Rosenzweig & L. W. Porter (Eds.), *Annual review of psychology* (pp. 321–350). Palo Alto, CA: Annual Reviews.

Shea, M. T., Elkin, I., & Hirschfeld, R. M. A. (1988). Psychotherapeutic treatment of depression. In A. J. Frances & R. E. Hale (Eds.), *Review of psychiatry* (Vol. 7, pp. 235–255). Washington, DC: American Psychiatric Press.

Sullivan, H. S. (1953). *The interpersonal theory of psychiatry*. Washington, DC: William Alanson White Psychiatric Foundation.

Weissman, M. M., Klerman, G. L., & Paykel, E. S. (1971). Clinical evaluation of hostility in depression. *American Journal of Psychiatry, 128,* 41–46.

Wolberg, L. R. (1954). *Technique of psychotherapy*. New York: Grune & Stratton.

Chapter 11

EMOTION AND RULES OF LIVING

RICHARD L. WESSLER AND SHEENAH HANKIN-WESSLER

ABSTRACT

Personal rules of living (PRLs) are algorithms the person uses to process social information and are implicated in affect and action. One type of PRL is mainly descriptive and represents the person's conception of the natural regularities among events in the world. A second type of PRL is primarily prescriptive and is based on moral principles and social values as internalized by the person. PRLs may be articulated by the person, but more likely they are inferred from observations of behavior and are, therefore, nonconscious algorithms. PRLs serve as mediators of affect and action. The derivation of the PRL construct and other concepts from Ellis's rational–emotive therapy and Beck's cognitive therapy is traced, and their application to the psychological treatment of neurotic disturbance is discussed.

The aim of this chapter is to show some relationships among certain cognitions and emotions and a cognition-oriented approach to psychotherapy. The central theme is that certain cognitions are predictably implicated in emotional experiences, and that psychological treatment for some forms of psychopathology can be derived from a theoretical account of the interrelations among cognition, emotion, and behavior. The cognitions involved in this discussion, personal rules of living (PRLs), are implicit and explicit guides for personal conduct and for the appraisal of one's own and others' actions. The psychological treatment approach of the authors, developed using the concepts and principles outlined in this chapter, has been labeled cognitive-appraisal therapy in order to underscore

EMOTION
Theory, Research, and Experience
Volume 5

the importance of evaluations or appraisals in emotional process and in psycho-logical therapy (R. L. Wessler & Hankin-Wessler, 1986).

COGNITION-ORIENTED PSYCHOTHERAPIES

Several approaches to psychological treatment of disturbance share an as-sumption that "learned misconceptions (or faulty beliefs, or mistaken ideas) are the crucial variables which must be modified or eliminated before psychotherapy can be successful" (Raimy, 1975, p. 186). The works of Albert Ellis and Aaron T. Beck are prominent examples of cognitive hypotheses of disturbance and treatment and have directly influenced the development of the points discussed in this chapter.

Ellis's rational–emotive therapy (RET) has had considerable influence on psychotherapy and counseling in America. His early publication *Reason and Emotion in Psychotherapy* (Ellis, 1962) was one of the first discussions of the effects of thought on emotional disturbance and of the therapeutic potential for cognitive change to result in emotional change. From its inception, RET has given a prominent place to perceptions, semantic meanings, appraisals, and philosophies of living as mediators of experiences and actions. Although Ellis never stated that beliefs are the sole cause of emotions, his emphasis on cognitive change as the essential ingredient of successful psychotherapy easily gave the impression that cognitions are primary and controlling variables in emotional processes. His statements about the interdependence of psychological processes, of which cognition is but one, have been overshadowed by the cognitive media-tional theory he proclaimed along with techniques for modifying the cognitive mediators of experience and action.

The central assumption of RET and other cognition-oriented psychotherapies is that "cognitions control emotions and feelings; disruptive affect is the result of faulty perceptions, beliefs, and convictions. . . . The alternative point of view, that emotion or affect is somehow an independent entity which can be modified or eliminated only by expressing it, is an outmoded doctrine" (Raimy, 1975, pp. 195–196). The main task of the cognition-oriented psychotherapies is to identify and modify dysfunctional cognitions. In particular, Ellis's RET, Beck's cog-nitive therapy, and the authors' cognitive-appraisal therapy hold that cognitive evaluations or appraisals are crucial to emotional processes, a point of view found in several contemporary theories of emotion (Arnold, 1960; Beck, 1976; R. S. Lazarus & Folkman, 1984; Mandler, 1984; Plutchik, 1980).

Ellis called his theory of emotions and of disturbance the ABC theory. The letter *A* stands for activating event or experience, that is, one's observations of what has happened and/or thoughts and images about what might happen. The letter *B* stands for beliefs, that is, cognitions about A or the evaluative implications one makes about A. The letter *C* stands for emotional and behavioral consequences of cognitively evaluating A and/or the implications of such evaluation. While emotion is conceived of as part of an ongoing process of perceiving, thinking, evaluating, and behaving, the key to emotional change in RET is clearly the modification of beliefs.

As a nonspecific account of emotion, ABC theory is consistent with other theories of emotion that assume the primacy of cognition (R. S. Lazarus, 1984) over the primacy of affect (Zajonc, 1984) and with other cognition-oriented models of emotion and disturbance, especially that of Beck (1976). However, ABC theory is, in addition, specific and speculative about the relationships between cognitive content and psychopathology. The critical issue concerns the content of the belief system.

There are two major categories within the belief system. Ellis defined so-called rational beliefs as accurate cognitions and evaluations that express a preference, desire, wish, want, or liking for someone, something, or oneself. They may lead to either positive or negative emotional experiences, depending on whether or not one's desires are fulfilled. They are by definition nondebilitating, even when negative, and contribute to the individual's survival and happiness. For example, a negative emotion might motivate a person to take actions toward attaining some personal goals.

Irrational beliefs, again by definition, are those that do not promote the individual's survival and happiness. Here Ellis's idea matches one of Erich Fromm: "I propose to call rational any thought, feeling, or act that promotes the adequate functioning and growth of the whole of which it is part, and irrational that which tends to weaken or destroy the whole" (Fromm, 1977, p. 352). Irrational beliefs are, according to Ellis, absolute shoulds, oughts, musts, demands, and commands. These must-statements are the basis of other irrational conclusions. For example, people who say, "I must not feel a high degree of anxiety," make themselves very anxious about their anxiety and thus create a secondary symptom when they conclude that it is catastrophic to feel high levels of anxiety. Irrational thinking causes neurotic pathology, according to ABC theory.

The assumption that must-statements and their irrational conclusions determine inappropriate emotional and behavioral consequences distinguishes RET from other cognition-oriented psychotherapies and from Ellis's initial propositions about neurosis and treatment. In *Reason and Emotion in Psychotherapy*, Ellis closely linked emoting with "strongly evaluative thinking" and did not so definitively characterize irrational beliefs as must-statements. While there is evidence that perceptions, evaluations, and other cognitions can influence human emotional experience and correlate with neurotic disturbance, there is none that supports the central hypothesis of RET about the relationship between psychopathology and irrational thinking as Ellis defines it. Ellis continues to take ABC theory seriously (Dryden & Ellis, 1986) and considers it a theory of personality as well as a theory of psychopathology (Ellis, 1979).

The ABC model is, obviously, phenomenological and mediational and clearly excludes the possibility of emotional experiences that have not been cognitively processed. Ellis has repeatedly stated that A (event) does not cause C (emotional and behavioral consequences); rather, beliefs about A cause C. Even without the problem created by making must-statements primary in an account of emotion and psychopathology, the ABC model is very sketchy and does not account for other factors in emotional processes, for example, reinforcers from the environment and decisions about one's actions.

AN EXPANDED MODEL

R. A. Wessler and Wessler (1980) presented an expanded version of the basic ABC model. A revised and further extended model has been adapted for the author's cognitive-appraisal therapy (R. L. Wessler, 1986b). It makes two significant departures from Ellis's ABC theory. First, it does not assume that exaggerated evaluations are necessarily derived from must-statements; must-statements may show the strength or extreme degree of appraisal but are not necessarily the source of appraisals. Second, the dichotomy between rational and irrational has been eliminated in favor of a single continuum of appraisal and is closer in spirit than RET to contemporary, predominantly cognitive theories of emotion (Wessler, 1984).

The present version, termed the cognitive–emotive–behavioral episode (CEBE), has eight steps. An episode begins with a stimulus and concludes with reinforcing consequences. Although the steps are arranged sequentially, the arrangement is not rigid. The model resembles Plutchik's (1980) theory of emotions, but it was developed independently. It was derived from the clinical theories of Ellis (1962) and Beck (1976), with additions from social learning theory and attribution theory. The model contains an interpersonal dimension in its account of reinforcers and incorporates Wood's (1985) taxonomy of instrumental conditioning. The mediating steps include stimulus detection and four types of cognitive content.

CEBE consists of the following steps, arranged in a loosely sequential order: (1) stimulus, (2) detection of stimulus, (3) descriptive report of stimulus, (4) inferences based on descriptive reports, (5) appraisals of reports and inferences, (6) affect, (7) decisions and action, and (8) reinforcing consequences of action.

Stimulus

A specific CEBE starts with a stimulus in the external physical and/or social environment, or in the internal environment of one's thoughts and feelings. An overt, external stimulus might be other people's actions, an object or situation, or the loss of something tangible. Examples of covert stimuli are one's own thoughts and feelings, including bodily sensations, for example, nausea or autonomic arousal, or any of the cognitive steps in the model.

Detection

Stimuli, in order to have an effect, must be detected and discriminated from other available stimuli. However, stimuli need not be the central focus of attention or awareness and indeed can be accurately described as nonconscious in the sense that the person has no direct introspective access to the process (Kihlström, 1984). The failure to detect stimuli can be conceived of as defensive or may simply be owing to the lack of conceptual categories to pick up information (Neisser, 1976).

Description

Stimuli of which one is aware can be categorized and defined. This step can be divided into observations and symbolic representations of observations. Observations are temporally contiguous with stimuli, but descriptions need not be; they can occur after the fact or be about images that have no overt stimulus. Descriptions are overt or covert reports of one's observations. Therapists do not deal with people's observations but with their reports of observations; such reports are taken as statements about people's phenomenological awareness.

Mahoney (1977) provided a rationale for cognitive-behavior therapy when he argued that environments do not directly affect people and thereby create behavioral responses. Words and images, that is, symbolic representations of the environment, are the proximal causes of behavior. Mahoney described a shift from concern with the environment as the focus of interventions (as is the case in behavior modification) to concern with cognitions about the environment as the focus of interventions (and thus cognitive-behavior modification, or the modification of "cognitive behaviors" as Meichenbaum [1977] called it).

Independently of the emerging cognitive-behavior therapy movement that Mahoney chronicled, Raimy (1975) presented his own statement of the cognitive-misconception hypothesis: "If those ideas or conceptions of a client or patient which are relevant to his psychological problems can be changed in the direction of greater accuracy where his reality is concerned, his maladjustments are likely to be eliminated" (p. 7). Neither Mahoney nor Raimy implicated inaccurate symbolic representations of a nonsubjective reality in emotional disorders, although they clearly stated that distortions of reality affect both behavior and adjustment.

Inferences

This step includes such logical operations as reasoning, generating forecasts and expectations, making causal and motivational attributions, and other non-evaluative meanings and interpretations ascribed to one's observations. For example, the loss of a job might be interpreted to mean that one will never get another. The conclusions one reaches might be tested empirically or they might be supported by consensus, the validation of agreement from significant others, or by paralogical superstition. Accurate symbolic representations can be distorted by errors in logic. Beck (1976) has discussed how false and arbitrary conclusions may be involved in emotional disturbance. The cognitive errors he discussed—overgeneralization, selective abstraction, arbitrary interpretation, etc.—are logical errors of inference.

Predictive conclusions are the results of logical and paralogical operations and play an important part in several theories. In George Kelly's (1955) personal-construct theory, the person's forecasts or anticipations direct behavior, and anxiety results from becoming aware that one is making wrong predictions about events but has no alternatives within one's set of personal constructs to take their place. Rotter's (1954) version of social learning theory says that expectancies about reinforcement and not necessarily reinforcement per se influence behavior. Woods (1985) has proposed a scheme to show how expectancies can be acquired and how they relate to instrumentally obtained reinforcement. Bandura's (1977, 1986) account of social cognitive theory likewise emphasizes the behavior-regulating function of predictions based on the individual's knowledge of actions and outcomes of actions.

Postdictive conclusions are explanations for events that have already occurred. Attribution theory is the study of personally conceived causal explanations for one's own and others' behavior. Attributions that emphasize variability rather than stability of causes (e.g., effort rather than ability), and internal rather than external causes (the former under one's control), are associated with favorable changes in reattributional retraining programs (Försterling, 1985, 1986).

Both Heider (1958), who introduced attribution theory, and Kelly (1955) assume that humans function as lay scientists who strive to understand themselves, other people, and the world in cause-and-effect terms. However, research in cognitive psychology raises doubts about the quality of personal science performed by laypersons; they often ignore objective data in favor of unscientific evidence and reach predictive and postdictive conclusions based on the source of information rather than on the methodologies used to secure the information (Nisbett & Ross, 1980; Tversky & Kahnemann, 1981).

New information must be assimilated into existing categories, or new categories created when such assimilation is not possible. The failure to have relevant categories for new experiences or to accommodate new experiences with new categories can seriously affect cognitive knowledge and hence overall psychological functioning (Guidano & Liotti, 1983). Stimuli may not only be missed owing to the lack of conceptual categories, but they may be distorted when no appropriate category is available.

Some personal rules of living are relatively enduring cognitive categories of knowledge about regularities in the physical and social world. They are statements about how things or people are, rather than how they should be. They allow forecasts of what will happen if certain conditions are fulfilled. Although they may lack objective support, they are the subjective set of natural laws the person understands and relies on when thinking about actions and their consequences.

Appraisals

Cognitive evaluations are emphasized in several theories of emotion as necessary in much of the human emotional experience. The term cognitive evaluation is perhaps a misnomer. The word *cognition* historically has meant what one consciously knows, while the word *evaluate* derives from the same source as the word *value*. Common usage in psychology has led to the blurring of distinctions between knowing and valuing (R. L. Wessler, 1986a).

It is useful to retain the distinction between knowing and appraising (or evaluating) for conceptual purposes. Appraisals, rather than cognitions-as-knowledge, are involved in the quality of affective experience. When one's appraisal of a stimulus is neutral, ambiguous, indecisive, or absent, no affective response occurs. When it is positive, positive affective experience is the likely result. A negative appraisal produces a negative feeling.

The specific appraisals activated in any given situation result from one's personal values and from one's description of and inferences about the situation. One's set of moral principles and social values are codified as one's personal rules of living with respect to proper conduct. Because personal philosophies prescribe what one ought to do, they are moral and ethical statements and are involved in what has been called the moral emotions (Sommers, 1981).

Appraisals may be implicit instead of explicit but can be discovered nonetheless by attending to the language one uses. Connotative meanings of words are particularly good clues. Such strongly evaluative cognitions have been called "hot cognitions" by Abelson (1963) in order to distinguish them from "cold cognitions," which are statements of facts and/or of nonevaluative conclusions.

The most significant cognitions in psychotherapy are those that pertain to the self. The self-concept, when stripped of its evaluative aspects, is a set of cold cognitions—inferences and hypotheses that make up a theory of oneself (Epstein, 1973; Guidano & Liotti, 1983; Raimy, 1975)—and properly belongs in the preceding step of this model. However, it is the hot cognitions about self that are important for psychological therapy because they form the realm of self-judgment and self-regard. Negative self-appraisals are the basis of several forms of anxiety and depression, as explained in a later part of this chapter.

Affect

Without attempting to specify the physiological mechanisms involved, we hypothesize that affect follows closely on the appraisals one makes. The relationship is temporal and coextensive; the stronger the appraisal, the stronger the affective experience. (Let us note that affect need not always be associated with appraisal and that autonomic nervous system arousal is possible without cognitive mediation, but these reservations play no part in this model. The purpose of the model is to present a coherent picture for therapeutic purposes rather than an elegant theory of emotion that is accurate in all particulars.)

Decisions and Action

Decisions form an integral part of the CEBE model. Without decisions, the original model was very mechanistic. Decisions are special cognitions in which the probable outcomes of one's actions are weighed. Of special therapeutic importance are decisions to think and to act in ways that are inconsistent with one's affective states, for example, acting in spite of anxiety in order to demonstrate self-efficacy and bring about changes in one's self-conceived competence (Bandura, 1977). The cognition-oriented psychotherapies stress thinking about one's actions (instead of unconsciously repeating dysfunctional actions) and making self-instructional statements to carry out decisions (Meichenbaum, 1977).

There is a general tendency for action to accompany appraisal, for example, a tendency to approach that which is positively appraised and to avoid, escape, modify, or freeze in the presence of stimuli appraised as highly negative. However, in this model, behavior is conceived of as controlled by decisions and self-directions. No corrective experience or therapeutic progress is possible unless one refuses to act in a way that brings immediate relief of discomfort and, in its place, pursues a course of action that brings a delayed gratifying outcome.

Reinforcement

Reinforcing consequences of one's actions affect subsequent actions, emotional experiences, and cognitions. Self-satisfactions are included at this step, but social reinforcers are probably more important, especially when other people's reactions provide the satisfaction of having one's expectations about self, others, and social situations confirmed. Some, perhaps most, neurotic behaviors can be viewed as distorted transactions between two or more persons. (The security of obtaining a predicted response to one's actions may outweigh the negative aspects of the interpersonal reaction; the security of restoring an old familiar feeling, however negative it might be, can be a significant source of self-satisfaction. Both of these seemingly maladaptive kinds of reinforcers are security-seeking manuevers, a central concept in the authors' approach to psychological therapy discussed later in this chapter.)

It is an oversimplification to speak only of punishments and rewards when discussing reinforcement. Woods (1974) presented a complex classification of instrumental behavior formed by combining the consequent events (desirable or undesirable), the operation performed on the consequent event (present or increase versus remove or decrease), and whether the consequent event is contingent on response emission or omission. The failure to obtain a reward is not the same as either a penalty or a punishment; a penalty involves giving up what one already has, and a punishment involves the presentation of an aversive event. Woods (1985) has expanded his taxonomy of instrumental behavior to include prior cognitive expectations regarding the consequences of behavior.

To illustrate the use of this model, consider the following analysis of public-speaking anxiety. The crucial steps from a cognitive perspective are not the fact of the speech (stimulus) or the person's knowledge that the speech will be given at a particular time (detection and descriptive report). The person may anticipate poor performance or adverse audience reaction (inferences) and appraise the anticipated outcome as highly negative (appraisal). The subsequent anxiety (affect) may be reduced by a decision to procrastinate (decision and action). Such avoidance brings immediate relief from anxiety and is reinforcing of procrastination, but it is a neurotic choice if the person's goal is to make the speech. (In this example, procrastination is a defense maneuver because it has the effect of reducing or avoiding a negatively appraised affect.)

The CEBE model does not include either parallel and interactive physiological processes or emotional or behavioral exchanges that can be analyzed at the level of interpersonal behavior. A comprehensive clinical model of emotional disorder should include biological and social factors if it is to serve the practical applications of diagnosis and treatment. A psychological account that does not allow for biological or social factors to be assessed can lead to mistreatment of patients. For example, depression can be understood in cognitive terms, in biological terms (endogenous depression), or as loss of social reinforcers; in all probability each form of depression is owing primarily to one of these, and in some cases two or all three may contribute to the psychiatric condition diagnosed as depression; clinically, each of these modalities should be assessed and treated.

The CEBE model is limited in scope but presents two advantages over other accounts of emotion and treatment found in the cognitive-psychotherapy literature. First, it acknowledges the operation of several different types of cognitions and suggests how each may contribute to disturbance. Second, by specifying various steps in the emotional process, each step can be identified as a target for therapeutic intervention. Disturbance can be assessed according to the source of disturbance and then treated using a wide range of cognitive and behavioral interventions. When the biological and interpersonal aspects of disturbance are added to the CEBE model, a framework for assessment results that is as comprehensive as A. A. Lazarus's (1981) multimodal therapy, but with additional details about the types of cognitions involved.

PERSONAL RULES OF LIVING

The CEBE model contains several types of cognitions. The distinction between cold and hot cognitions has already been discussed; it is the difference between what one "knows" about something and how one "feels" about it or appraises it. A second distinction is between accurate and inaccurate cognitions; a report or inference might be accurate, but one cannot verify its accuracy without obtaining additional information. One's cognitive knowledge can be verified, but one's appraisals cannot. Appraisals are based on moral principles and social values. Personalized as PRLs, these judgments can be subjected to tests of utility (i.e., by discovering whether one's values are helpful according to some standard) but cannot be submitted to tests of accuracy.

A third distinction is between general and specific cognitions. Abstractions about events and behavioral data are general; specific thoughts about particular situations are derived from general assumptions about the self, people in general, the world, and other abstract categories. A generalized PRL, for example, "people cannot be trusted," can lead to the specific thought that "Sam cannot be trusted." Further, generalized appraisals can influence specific nonevaluative cognitions. For example, a woman who spoke of her hatred for men (generalized appraisal) once falsely inferred that a man's faulty directions were the cause of her friend's late arrival for an appointment (specific inference), when in fact the friend had simply chosen to delay her departure.

Relatively enduring and generalized cognitions have been variously called schemas or cognitive structures. Guidano and Liotti (1983) have applied Piagetian concepts of worldview to cognitive therapy. The organizing assumptions about self, other people, and the world that account for consistencies of behavior are located outside one's awareness. At the core are schemas that have been formed during childhood and adolescence and are nonconsciously held as unquestionable assumptions about some important aspects of self and reality. Liotti (1986) cites the following factors as contributing to the impossibility for the individual to doubt the validity of already formed, organizing schemas: (1) the child has limited ability to think critically, (2) the child's emotional schemas that were formed during emotional family interaction are likely to be repeated and reconfirmed in subsequent interactions, (3) the child's modeling of significant figures is repeatedly reinforced and leaves little opportunity for alternative views of one's identity, and (4) dogmatic descriptions of the child's character and of reality can be forced on the child by parents and other significant persons so that the descriptions cannot help but be accepted as undoubtedly true. The core level of implicit assumptions is protected from change by an intermediate level of explicit descriptions of the self, other people, and the world. A peripheral level of cognitive organization reflects plans and strategies the person uses in everyday life and includes appraisals and evaluations of internal and external experiences.

A fourth distinction is the one between conscious and nonconscious cognitions. Although the word *cognition* refers to what is known and unconscious processes are by definition outside one's awareness, it has nonetheless become acceptable in psychology to speak of nonconscious cognitions. The use of the term *nonconscious* can be understood without Freudian theory's emphasis on hidden motives and complex ego-protecting mechanisms. It can refer to mindless or automatic thinking; thinking without awareness.

Tacit PRLs are nonconscious algorithms. Lewicki (1986) presented a series of experiments on cognitive algorithms that have become automatic through repetition to the point that they operate without the awareness of the actor. As he states: "Human processing of information involves at its various levels numerous such nonconscious algorithms: (1) that definitely have never been learned at the level of consciousness, (2) that operate totally beyond one's conscious control, and (3) that are available to a person who follows these algorithms in no other way than by an 'outsider's viewpoint' observation of how they operate" (Lewicki, 1986, p. 11). These algorithms develop early in one's experience and become self-perpetuating: "An initial tendency . . . increases the likelihood that a subsequent stimulus would be encoded (perceived) in a way that is consistent with and would support the initial tendency. . . . The next relevant stimulus would be encoded in an even more biased way. . . . [I]n small children there are expecially good conditions for the operation of this self-perpetuating process" (Lewicki, 1986, p. 35).

PRLs can also be understood as core organizing principles (Meichenbaum & Gilmore, 1984), that is, tacit knowledge that guides and influences thoughts, feelings, and behaviors without any conscious awareness of the person who acts on them but nonetheless can be inferred from behavior and used to predict and explain other behaviors. We prefer to speak of personal rules of living because clients easily understand the word *rule* as one from their everyday vocabulary.

The notion of rule comes from the writings of Beck (1976): "The person uses a kind of mental rule book to guide his actions and evaluate himself and others. He applies the rules in judging whether his own behavior or that of others is 'right' or 'wrong'. . . . We use rules not only as a guide for conduct but also to provide a framework for understanding life situations" (p. 42). Such rules are not always conscious and are usually more readily inferred from what people say and do than available as self-report data. Hogan (1973) described people as rule-governed beings who apply their rules to specific life situations, as they understand those situations, in order to adapt to those situations. PRLs fall roughly into two types: descriptive and prescriptive.

Descriptive PRLs are statements about one's understanding of the social and physical world. The belief that people are inherently good is an example of a descriptive PRL. The inference that one acts as though people cannot be trusted is another example of a descriptive PRL. This type of PRL seems similar to the "human-as-scientist theme" that runs through the work of several psychologists (e.g., Helder and Kelly) and cognitive psychotherapists (e.g., Beck, Mahoney, and Ellis). However, it is different in that the seeking of information about an orderly world does not divide the population into scientists and nonscientists; indeed, nonscientific forms of learning and understanding also seek certainty about their descriptions of reality. Some who use nonscientific forms of learning, such as managers and mechanics, must even act on their assumptions—as people do in everyday life—and not simply discuss and publish their thoughts (R. L. Wessler, 1986a). Descriptive PRLs are personal versions of natural law about the regularities people need to assume in order to predict events and take adaptive actions.

A prescriptive PRL specifies what should be, how one should act, and how others should conduct themselves. Hogan (1973) has characterized morality as a natural phenomenon and as an adaptive response to evolutionary pressures. Prescriptive PRLs dictate moral conduct and are personal versions of moral principles and social values as understood by the individual who holds them. Examples are "people should treat me kindly"; "no one should upset anyone else"; "it is wrong to cheat another person." Prescriptive PRLs are centrally involved in the cognitive aspects of the emotion process, especially in what have been called the moral emotions: anger, social anxiety, shame, guilt, jealousy, envy, and some forms of depression. Like morality, these emotions pertain to cognitions about human interrelations and conduct.

Some cognition-oriented approaches to psychological therapy, like phenomenological approaches before them, give special importance to the concept of self and assume that one's most significant PRLs pertain to oneself. Self-descriptions (i.e., self-image or self-concept) do not predict behavior without knowledge of the person's PRLs about what to do "if." Take, for example, the prescriptive PRL that "a weak person should avoid threatening confrontations";

this PRL will get activated in situations defined as threatening provided one defines oneself as weak. Self-descriptions can have several sources, including information gathered from other people or as a result of experiences of interacting with them.

Self-judgments (i.e., self-esteem or self-regard) differ from self-descriptions in that one makes an appraisal about oneself. Such appraisals are based on one's prescriptive PRLs. There seems to be a strong tendency among humans not only to appraise their own actions but to appraise themselves as well (Hogan, 1973), and this may be seen as the basis for the self-regulation of conduct. It is efficient for a human group to devote as little of its time and other resources as possible to the enforcement of its rules, and for members of the group to engage in self-enforcement of the rules (Plutchik, 1980). In order to assure self-enforcement of the rules, it would be best to breed an individual who readily learns to comply with rules. Affect, because it is a private experience, provides the power of reward and punishment for moral decisions that come from within and are not imposed by some external authority. The learning of rules and of appropriate affective rewards and punishments is a process of the internalization of authority—of learning, often vicariously, what is right and wrong, how to appraise oneself, and how to feel when acting morally or immorally.

Personal rules of living and the appraisals they generate can be illustrated in three emotional processes typically seen among patients diagnosed as neurotic: hostility, anxiety, and depression.

Hostility

In hostility, there is an inference that a PRL has been, could be, or will be broken (Beck, 1976). We speculate that some degree of anger will result from such an inference and that the degree of anger depends on the degree of the person's negative appraisal of the rule breaker. (The anger may not necessarily be overtly displayed or subjectively experienced; we propose that other PRLs govern the display or the personal awareness and acknowledgment of the anger. Further, individuals may choose not to act on either their angry cognitions or affects, and these too depend on other PRLs.) The inference (see CEBE model) sets the conditions for hostility, but the appraisal determines its extent. When the person can justify someone violating PRLs (e.g., "it was an accident"), little if any angry reaction is expected. If, then, a person holds a tolerant PRL (e.g., "I will not condemn people even though they do what I do not like," i.e., "break my rules"), the person will react with a degree of anger that falls short of rage. The greater the degree of tolerance for the rule breaker, the lesser the degree of anger.

The following explanation is given to clients in order to lead to the uncovering of PRLs. It also helps to show whether the person accurately observes other people's actions as either rule breaking or rule conforming. "Enraged anger begins when we create rules for other people to live by, observe that they break or transgress against our rules, and then invoke a rule that says they should be condemned for what they have done. Your anger at your friend (spouse, child, etc.) is based on your rules about how other people should act and on your own punative rather than forgiving attitude toward them for not acting that way. Now, what rule did your friend break that caused you to become so angry"?

While this instruction pertains to a specific episode, the same inference–appraisal–anger linkage can be found in more pervasive hostility. The cognition-oriented psychotherapies assume that information rather than external events are the important determinants of action and affect. Thus in the CEBE model, the cognitive appraisal that one has been offended is seen as the proximal cause of anger. Anger, as Beck (1976) has noted, results when one's self-conception is that of strength and adequacy in the face of the threat of danger; the mental calculation that one can prevail over the threat gives a sense of power—a fight response. Angry displays remain among the most relied upon methods of inter-personal influence. Since power requires a dependent other, anger is usually directed at persons seen as less powerful and/or less secure; if the other person does not fit this requirement, displaced or indirect expressions of anger result.

Anger directed toward oneself can be understood as resulting from the knowl-edge of the breaking of salient PRLs *and* of self-criticism (cognitive inference *and* appraisal). When the PRL has a moral direction to it, feelings of guilt result. Thus, accusatory self-statements involved in anger are of the "how could I be so stupid as to make that mistake" variety, while those involved in guilt are of the "how could I be so bad as to do what I did" type. Guilt requires one to define an act as a sin or a crime (inference) and to activate intolerant PRLs (self-appraisal). The CEBE model suggests that guilt may be alleviated by identifying the violated PRLs, followed by self-forgiveness and possibly making amends for one's errors and effecting plans to avoid future instances.

Anxiety

The process of generating anxiety begins with an inference about the threat of danger and an appraisal about the catastrophic nature of the danger. Anxiety results when people conceive of threats to their self-image and/or physical well-being *and* believe that they cannot cope with those threats. R. S. Lazarus and Folkman (1984) describe this process as one of primary and secondary ap-praisals, that is, the appraisal of an event as threatening and the appraisal of one's ability to cope with the threat. Both appraisals may be based on the person's self-image, or, as Beck (1976) suggests, anxiety results from a ratio of subjectively defined danger to one's subjectively defined inability to cope with the danger (when the individual feels adequate to overcome the danger, the resultant feeling is anger rather than anxiety).

It is presumed that when anxiety is cognitively mediated, self-definitions of personal inadequacy or of weakness are responsible. When the threat of danger is to one's physical well-being, one has an expectation of physical harm or damage. In its most extreme form, death or dying is inferred to be the outcome of harm or danger, and, when appraised in a highly negative way, anxiety is a result. When the threat is to one's psychological well-being, the danger is not posed from the physical environment but from the social environment.

Threats to self-image or self-regard do not arouse anticipations of physical harm but of psychological harm. Social anxiety can be seen as stemming from the anticipation that one will act in a manner that brings criticism from other people and causes one to make self-judgments of weakness and inadequacy. When a moral dimension is added, doubts about one's personal worth are raised; the accompanying feelings are labeled as guilt and shame. The statement "I am not good enough" might imply mere weakness and inadequacy, or it might imply worthlessness, possibly because of one's perceived weakness and inadequacies.

The key inference, that a situation or event is dangerous, is incorrect when dealing with stimuli that cannot be objectively verified as dangerous. However, the mere awareness of the wrongness of an inference is not enough to eliminate anxiety. People with phobias usually recognize that there is no factual basis for their fears but continue to fear and avoid the stimulus as though the danger were real. It is apparent that cognitions do not rest on evidence and logic alone and that evidence and logic are irrelevant to some beliefs.

Depression

Cognitively mediated depression involves definitions of loss and/or devaluation. The inferences are of actual, hypothetical, or anticipated loss from or devaluation of one's personal domain or anything that one identifies with (Beck, 1976), which are then appraised as extremely negative. As in the account of anxiety, self-definitions of weakness or of inadequacy are important and involved in themes of hopelessness owing to lack of ability to remedy the loss. People may retreat into depression when they find their feelings of anxiety, guilt, shame, and hostility to be overwhelmingly intolerable and they have the thought "I cannot stand these feelings anymore; life is not worth living."

Thoughts of deprivation and frustration are common in depression and may be perpetuated by negative self-appraisals that diminish people's efforts to reduce deprivation and frustration, thus continuing themes of hopelessness and helplessness. A typical PRL and a depressive conclusion might be the following: "People get what they deserve. I am deprived of so much that I cannot be very good." When the person focuses on worthlessness and self-condemnation for incurring a loss, a guilty depression results. When the person emphasizes deprivations, self-pity emerges. Angry depression is owing to frustration and to the blaming of people or of situations for causing the frustration.

Assessment

By employing these accounts of anger, anxiety, and depression in psychotherapy, one can make reasonable hypotheses about clients' cognitions and affective experiences even when clients cannot readily identify them. If some PRLs can be discovered, the feelings they are theoretically tied to can be inferred. Conversely, PRLs can be inferred when certain feelings are acknowledged. Further, future problems clients might encounter can be reasonably forecast using the hypothetical link between PRLs and feelings. For example, if a client defines financial wealth as a condition of psychological self-worth, one can hypothesize that potential problems of anxiety and depression will emerge when the person's financial net worth significantly decreases or threatens to decrease. In other words, PRLs form the data base for inferring and evaluating past, present, and future events in one's life. The link between inference, appraisal, and affect provides the hypotheses about behavior.

The notion of rules is easily understood by clients. Their importance in life is readily acknowledged. PRLs are learned, usually at an early age. The person(s) who was the source of the early learning may not be recalled as credible or even trustworthy, but, in the tradition of Nazi propaganda and American advertising, frequency of repetition leads to increased belief and influence. For instance, a client whose mother was psychotically disturbed recalled believing everything the mother said, especially about the client's inadequacies, and continues to do so even though she now acknowledges her mother's disturbance and the falseness of her statements. The message continues to be indelible even when the source is no longer held as credible.

PRLs can be easily discovered without any special tests or interview schedules. They are nonconscious algorithms and can be inferred from what people say and do. One speaks and acts "as if" he or she uses a certain rule to guide words and actions. The evidence is the recurring pattern of thoughts and actions expressed by the person.

Treatment

The modification of PRLs is not as easily accomplished as their identification. The basic strategy is to pose a question about a PRL's effect in one's life. Does holding and following a certain PRL consistently bring the results the person wants? If not, what would be a more adaptive version of the PRL? Because PRLs are informal codifications of a person's values, it is unlikely any PRL must be rejected entirely, and it is even less likely that the person would do so anyway. It is reasonable to consider more adaptive alternatives, since dysfunctional versions of PRLs are usually rigidly held or conflict with other PRLs.

However, cognitions do not change any more readily by stating their alternatives than by presenting contradictory evidence or exposing logical fallacies. If humans truly functioned as lay scientists, they would change their minds when presented good reasons to do so, the task of cognition-oriented psychological therapy would be easy, and cognition-oriented therapy could factually claim to be based on an educational model. The stating of an alternative version of one's PRL is a necessary beginning, inasmuch as one is more likely to change if a reasonable alternative is available.

The remaining steps are to become aware of the old PRL and its newer alternative and to act using the newer version instead of the older one. Frequently speaking about the differences and the results one expects to obtain by following the more adaptive alternative further fixes it in one's mental rule book.

EMOTION AND PSYCHOTHERAPY

Some PRLs are prescriptions about how one should feel and are tied to global, nonconscious self-descriptions. For example, a person who repeatedly engages in actions that result in feelings of shame does so because of a nonconscious PRL that a worthless, morally inferior person should feel shame. The last assertion is based on a realization of the limitations of purely cognitive approaches to understanding affect and action. One theoretical departure centers on the affective modality and broadens the account of causation typically found in the cognition-oriented psychotherapies, which have generally assumed that affect and action are the products of cognitive variables. However, affect influences cognitive processes as well (Isen, 1984), and a reciprocal model of affect and cognition seems to be an improvement over one that ascribes primacy to either cognition (R. S. Lazarus, 1984) or affect (Zajonc, 1984). For example, Greenberg and Safran (1984) have proposed to integrate affect and cognition by adopting Leventhal's (1979) perceptual–motor model of emotion.

In clinical work, the authors have found it useful to think of personotypic affects (PAs), which are emotional feelings that have been learned, usually during the early developmental years. In each person's family and other early socialization groups, certain emotional expressions occurred more frequently than others, especially in stressful circumstances. Thus, certain emotions were more available to learn through modeling and operant conditioning. Even in homes where overt emotional expression was not common, such as families where people sulked when angry, models were present to learn from, and the family rules about overt emotional behaviors differentially reinforced certain patterns over others.

A myriad of different influences are involved in the creation of a person's affective repertoire. These include wartime, personal, and family crises. For example, victims of physical and sexual abuse often describe a deep sense of shame. Churches and religious schools teach moral values but at the same time instill in some people feelings of guilt that invade all aspects of their lives, including issues to which moral values are not normally applied.

Affect can result from preattentive processes whose components lie outside focal awareness. Therefore, "conscious changes at the conceptual level will not necessarily produce changes at the affective level, since emotional experience is as much a function of changes that take place at a perceptual-motor, preconceptual level as it is a function of conceptual cognition" (Greenberg & Safran, 1984, p. 568).

There are several implications to draw from the assumption that not all affect is cognitively mediated. First, both affect and action may result from either (1) previously learned cognitive structures (PRLs) or (2) from previously learned affect (PA). One may later add cognitions in order to understand and justify the feelings. When neither client nor cognitive therapist can identify cognitions associated with emotional experiences, the concept of PA is useful.

Both PAs and PRLs can be discovered by raising affect. Among the means to do this are the use of self-disclosure, vivid language and imagery, hypnosis, sad stories, and requests for the client to look, act, and sound anxious, angry, or depressed. Feelings can be induced by asking the client to describe the predominant emotional state of their significant others, for example, "my father was very hostile." The insight that one acts and sounds just like one's parent can be as unpleasant for some people as it is surprising. Cognitions, especially PRLs, emerge during the affective arousal, which are then the target of therapeutic interventions.

A second implication concerns emotional states as motivation. PAs take on motivational status when people want to reexperience certain familiar feelings, including negative ones. They will act in ways that bring about consequences from the environment and responses from other people that tend to confirm their PRLs and self-concept and that stir familiar PAs. The authors call such actions security-seeking maneuvers (SMs). SMs are protective actions people nonconsciously implement in order to prevent the surrender of hypothetical notions that constitute the self-image. While other accounts of interpersonal behavior (e.g., Carson, 1969) have emphasized its purposeful nature in confirming the self-image, we propose that SMs are people's nonconscious tactics to reexperience certain familiar affect, and that the feelings provide confirmation of self and of the rightness of one's phenomenological world.

The most obvious SMs form observable aspects of the individual's personality. SMs have a long personal history of good service in protecting the individual's self-image and reducing the anxiety that comes from having one's self-image threatened by information that contradicts it and by deliberate attempts to modify it. Thus, SMs can be seen as significant barriers to therapeutic change, for in therapy it is necessary to adopt new actions in order to change behavioral patterns and to provide disconfirming evidence leading to cognitive change. The potential loss of identity generates anxiety; the retaining of negative attitudes generates depression. For change to occur in those instances where therapy stalls, SMs must be identified as to their nature and purpose and eroded by persistent awareness of them and by adoption of actions that work against them.

Finally, these assumptions lead to an emphasis on the person's past history as he or she reports it. This is necessary in order to trace the origins of PRLs and PAs as this information is often necessary before one can modify them. The term phenomenological developmental history (PDH) refers to the resultant personal narrative that seems so important to people as they try to understand themselves in cause-and-effect terms. The examination of past influences of parents, siblings, teachers, and peers allows clients to construct a personal narrative of how they came to view the self, other people, and the world in their present manner. When significant figures from one's past explicitly taught or implicitly modeled behavior, affect, or the correctness of a PRL, the individual will have more difficulty in reassessing and reevaluating the current internalized versions of them. Anything learned through modeling is likely to be mindlessly repeated and is therefore nonconscious.

The PDH is never very systematic or complete. It is an attempt to help clients construct a mosaic of self-portraiture so that they can anticipate their responses to new situations and plan to modify well-established habitual patterns of thinking, acting, and emoting. An examination of the past aids in the predicting of the future and in the understanding of the present. This point has not been emphasized in the cognition-oriented psychotherapies, although none would try to refute it. A notable exception is the work of Guidano and Liotti (1983), in which they incorporate some specific ideas about the individual's cognitive development and view of self and of the world into what they call structural cognitive therapy.

A case example illustrates these points. A 35-year-old man had sought treatment for a variety of interpersonal problems: few friends, fear of his boss, anger at peers, social anxiety, awkwardness around women, and little social life. One of his goals in therapy was to reduce anxiety, expecially anxiety he felt around women, as it was his expressed intention to marry and have a family, as most of his friends from college had already done. He could with difficulty make first dates but complained that women were disinterested when he attempted to see them again.

His description of an evening's encounter with a first date could not be understood by searching for his relevant conscious cognitions, but when some assumptions were made about nonconscious PRLs, PAs, and SMs, his experience was not only understood, but he also gained insight and began to effect changes he had previously resisted. His evening began by meeting her at her apartment and attempting conversation. He laughed and smiled as he recalled the inept way he conducted himself, expressions that seemed inappropriate to the failure and rejection he reported. It appeared that he wanted to fail and get rejected by her, which is what had happened. He attributed his poor performance to anxiety, and the search for anxiety-relevant cognitions revealed nothing he had not previously covered in cognitive psychotherapy. He had not modified either his cognitions or his behavior despite numerous discussions with his therapist.

His PDH revealed a recurring pattern of rejection and failure with women. The existence of a recurring pattern suggests the operation of a SM. The therapist postulated that the client did not court women so much as he courted rejection and failure and hypothesized that the client sought to reexperience some PA that was especially significant to him. In this instance, it emerged that self-pity was the predominant feeling in his life. Indeed, following his disasterous blind date, he spent the weekend alone, depressed and, in his own words, "feeling sorry for myself." He recalled frequently feeling sorry for himself as he was a child and adolescent. His father had volatile temper, and both parents avoided social contacts. They had openly discussed their inferiority to others in their community—"we're just dumb Pollacks," he recalled their saying. They remained isolated from people, and he remembered his mother being extremely anxious for several weeks when preparing to entertain close family members at Christmas. Thus, he grew up with a self-image of inferiority, learned to feel very anxious in the company of other people, and acted as though he was a failure when in fact he had received a great deal of recognition in his profession and was considered a success by others. He had learned to expect rejection from people he deemed better and felt most secure when nervously acting inappropriately and playing the fool for them. Though he expressed disappointment over his social failures, he also expressed relief that a first date did not become a second.

EMOTION AND PSYCHOPATHOLOGY

The view of psychopathology discussed in this chapter assumes that persons are motivated to reexperience certain affects that, because they have been familiar for so long, seem natural even when they are negative experiences. The reexperiencing of emotional states is a fundamental process; when emotional states are defined as negative, the label of pathology applies. Pathology becomes more evident when consciously held, explicit goals of enjoyment and fulfillment conflict with the implicit or tacit goal of security through familiarity of feelings.

We postulate an emotional setpoint, which acts like a thermostat: when affective experience deviates from the setpoint, a self-regulatory process begins to return individuals' feelings to where their nonconscious personal rules say they should be. Justifying cognitions furnish people with plausible reasons for feeling as they do. These are cognitions that people may uncritically assume as correct or may not truly believe. For example, a man once reported anxiously dwelling on the thought that his business would fail even though he knew that all objective evidence contradicted such a possibility; he further reported that such thoughts usually occurred when events were going well in his life and his affective state was decidedly nonnegative—the setpoint had been exceeded.

Evidence to support the notion of the emotional setpoint comes from three sources. Schwartz (1986) reviewed literature concerning cognitive and affective balance (ratio of positive to negative cognitions within the internal dialogue); a typical ratio can be restored by seeking and/or interpreting events in a negative fashion whether or not the facts fit the interpretation. Andrews (1989) reviewed an extensive literature on self-confirmation theory and individuals' nonconscious attempts to evoke predictable responses from others. Nathanson (1987) reported clinical observations of patients provoking responses from others that serve the purpose of returning them to their accustomed emotional states following positive experiences.

No fundamental affect, for example, anxiety, is postulated, but shame is singled out for special attention in cognitive-appraisal therapy. Shame is implicated in one's self-image and arises from the exposure of one's inadequacies, shortcomings, and failure to conform to one's own rules. Self-image arises out of and is validated through interpersonal processes; psychological security also arises out of interpersonal processes—one knows who one is and one's status in one's social system. Ellis (1979) emphasized the importance of shame in neurotic disturbance, and Lewis (1987) researched shame, finding it ubiquitous and implicated in the very process of therapy that requires people to reveal their shameful secrets.

Shame is a feature of several disorders of personality: dependent (easily hurt by criticism or disapproval), avoidant (fear of negative evaluation), narcissistic (hypersensitivity to evalutions of others, reacts to criticism with feelings of rage, shame, or humiliation), and paranoid (sees people as deliberately demeaning). The rage observed in narcissistic and borderline-personality disorders is a reaction to being or feeling shamed. Shame seems particularly easy to infer in self-defeating patterns of behavior if it is assumed that shame is nonconsciously sought, while consciously avoided by persons for whom it is a familiar, security-providing feeling.

In cognitive-appraisal therapy, the analysis of PRLs, SMs, and justifying cognitions is central to the treatment of anxiety, depression, and anger and to the treatment of personality disorders that shore up negative affect, particularly shame. Insight is needed to overcome inertia that prevents change, both by gaining an understanding of the role of nonconscious needs to reexperience certain negative feelings and then by acting in opposition to the usual security-seeking pattern. The changing of self-hypotheses is no easy matter as SMs insure that long-held beliefs and images will not be threatened. The process of change requires a therapist who facilitates insights, offers support as new patterns are attempted, and, most importantly, never shames the patient.

REFERENCES

Abelson, R. P. (1963). Computer simulation of "hot cognitions." In S. Tompkins & S. Messick (Eds.), *Computer simulations of personality*. New York: Wiley.

Andrews, J. D. W. (1989). *The active self in psychotherapy*. Boston: Allyn & Bacon.

Arnold, M. B. (1960). *Emotion and personality*. New York: Columbia University Press.

Bandura, A. (1977). *Social learning theory*. Englewood Cliffs, NJ: Prentice-Hall.

Bandura, A. (1986). *Social foundations of thought and action: A social cognitive theory*. Englewood Cliffs, NJ: Prentice-Hall.

Beck, A. T. (1976). *Cognitive therapy and the emotional disorders*. New York: International Universities Press.

Carson, R. C. (1969). *Interaction concepts of personality*. Chicago, IL: Aldine.

Dryden, W., & Ellis, A. (1986). Rational-emotive therapy (RET). In W. Dryden & W. Golden (Eds.), *Cognitive-behavioural approaches to psychotherapy*. London: Harper & Row.

Ellis, A. (1962). *Reason and emotion in psychotherapy*. New York: Lyle Stuart.

Ellis, A. (1979). Toward a new theory of personality. In A. Ellis & J. M. Whitely (Eds.), *Theoretical and empirical foundations of rational-emotive therapy*. Monterey, CA: Brooks/Cole.

Epstein, S. (1973). The self-concept revisited: Or a theory of a theory. *American Psychologist, 28,* 404–416.

Försterling, F. (1985). Attributional retraining. A review. *Psychological Bulletin,* **98,** 495–512.

Försterling, F. (1986). Attributional conceptions in clinical psychology. *American Psychologist,* **41,** 275–285.

Fromm, E. (1977). *The anatomy of human destructiveness*. London: Penguin Books.

Greenberg, L. S., & Safran, J. D. (1984). Integrating affect and cognition: A perspective on the process of therapeutic change. *Cognitive Therapy and Research,* **8,** 559–578.

Guidano, V. F., & Liotti, G. (1983). *Cognitive processes and the emotional disorders*. New York: Guilford Press.

Heider, F. (1958). *The psychology of interpersonal relations*. New York: Wiley.

Hogan, R. (1973). Moral conduct and moral character: A psychological perspective. *Psychological Bulletin,* **79,** 217–232.

Isen, A. M. (1984). Toward understanding the role of affect in cognition. In R. S. Wyer, Jr. & T. K. Srull, *Handbook of social cognition* (Vol. 3). HIllsdale, NJ: Erlbaum.

Kelly, G. A. (1955). *The psychology of personal constructs*. New York: Norton.

Kihlstrom, J. F. (1984). Conscious, subconscious, unconscious: A cognitive perspective. In K. S. Bowers & D. Meichenbaum (Eds.), *The unconscious reconsidered*. New York: Wiley.

Lazarus, A. A. (1981) *The practice of multimodal therapy*. New York: McGraw-Hill.

Lazarus, R. S. (1984). On the primacy of cognition. *American Psychologist,* **39,** 124–129.

Lazarus, R. S., & Folkman, S. (1984). *Stress, appraisal, and coping*. New York: Springer.

Leventhal, H. (1979). A perceptual-motor processing model of emotion. In P. Pliner, K. R. Blankstein, & I. M. Spigel (Eds.), *Advances in the study of communication and affect: Vol. 5. Perception of emotion in self and others*. New York: Plenum.

Lewicki, P. (1986). *Nonconscious social information processing.* Orlando, FL: Academic Press.

Lewis, H. B. (1987). Shame—the "sleeper" in psychopathology. In H. B. Lewis (Ed.), *The role of shame in symptom formation.* Hillsdale, NJ: Erlbaum.

Liotti, G. (1986). Structural cognitive therapy. In W. Dryden & W. Golden (Eds.), *Cognitive-behavioural approaches to psychotherapy.* London: Harper & Row.

Mahoney, M. J. (1977). Reflections on the cognitive-learning trend in psychotherapy. *American Psychologist,* **32,** 5–13.

Mandler, G. (1984). *Mind and body: Psychology of emotion and stress.* New York: Norton

Meichenbaum, D. (1977). *Cognitive behavior modification.* New York: Plenum.

Mcichenbaum, D., & Gilmore, J. B. (1984). The nature of unconscious processes: A cognitive-behavioral perspective. In K. S. Bowers & D. Meichenbaum (Eds.), *The unconscious reconsidered.* New York: Wiley.

Nathanson, D. L. (1987). The shame/pride axis. In H. B. Lewis (Ed.), *The role of shame in symptom formation.* Hillsdale, NJ: Erlbaum.

Neisser, U. (1976). *Cognition and reality.* San Francisco, CA: Freeman.

Nisbett, R. E., & Ross, L. (1980). *Human inference: Strategies and shortcomings of social judgment.* Englewood Cliffs, NJ: Prentice-Hall.

Plutchik, R. (1980). *Emotion: A psychoevolutionary synthesis.* New York: Harper & Row.

Raimy, V. (1975). *Misunderstandings of the self.* San Francisco, CA: Jossey-Bass.

Rotter, J. B. (1954). *Social learning and clinical psychology.* Englewood Cliffs, NJ: Prentice-Hall.

Schwartz, R. M. (1986). The internal dialogue: On the asymmetry between positive and negative coping thoughts. *Cognitive Therapy and Research,* **10,** 591–605.

Sommers, S. (1981). Emotionality reconsidered: The role of cognition in emotional responsiveness. *Journal of Personality and Social Psychology,* **41,** 553–561.

Tversky, A., & Kahnemann, D. (1981). The framing of decisions and the psychology of choice. *Science,* **211,** 453–458.

Wessler, R. A., & Wessler, R. L. (1980). *The principles and practice of rational-emotive therapy.* San Francisco, CA: Jossey-Bass.

Wessler, R. L. (1984). Alternative conceptions of rational-emotive therapy: Toward a philosophically neutral psychotherapy. In M. Reda & M. J. Mahoney (Eds.), *Cognitive psychotherapies: Recent developments in theory, research, and practice.* Cambridge, MA: Ballinger.

Wessler, R. L. (1986a). Conceptualising cognitions in the cognitive behavioural therapies. In W. Dryden & W. Golden (Eds.), *Cognitive-behavioural approaches to psychotherapy.* London: Harper & Row.

Wessler, R. L. (1986b). Varieties of cognitions in the cognitively-oriented therapies. In A. Ellis & R. Grieger (Eds.), *Handbook of rational-emotive therapy* (Vol. 2). New York: Springer.

Wessler, R. L., & Hankin-Wessler, S. W. R. (1986). Cognitive appraisal therapy (CAT). In W. Dryden & W. Golden (Eds.), *Cognitive-behavioural approaches to psychotherapy.* London: Harper & Row.

Woods, P. J. (1974). A taxonomy of instrumental conditioning. *American Psychologist* **29,** 584–597.

Woods, P J. (1985). Learning paradigms, expectancies, and behavioural control: An expanded classification for learned behaviour. *British Journal of Cognitive Psychotherapy,* **3,** 43–58.

Zajonc, R. B. (1984). On the primacy of affect. *American Psychologist,* **39,** 117–123.

AUTHOR INDEX

SUBJECT INDEX

A

Acceptance, group psychotherapy and, 152, 155, 157
Achievement, psychotherapy and, 189
Acknowledgment
 change processes in psychotherapy and, 60, 65–68, 74
 primary process and, 110
Action, rules of living and, 238
Adaptation
 change processes in psychotherapy and, 60, 61
  acknowledging, 67
  affective assessment, 63, 64
  affective-change processes, 65
  anxiety, 81–83
 group psychotherapy and, 153
 primary process and, 92, 98, 100, 101
 psychoanalytic affect theory and, 126
 psychoevolutionary perspective of
  psychotherapy and, 5, 14, 19–21, 27, 36
 rules of living and, 242, 247
Adjectives, psychotherapy and, 180, 181, 191

Affect
 cathartic model and, 210, 223, 225, 227, 228
 change processes in psychotherapy and, 62–72, 74
  anxiety, 80, 81, 83
  core beliefs, 80
 cognitive approaches to psychotherapy and, 178, 180, 188
 group psychotherapy and, 162, 163, 165
 multimodal therapy and, 197–199, 201–205
 psychoanalytic theory, see Psychoanalytic
  affect theory
 psychoevolutionary perspective of
  psychotherapy and, 8
 rules of living and, 237, 238, 247–251
 time and, 134
Affective assessment, psychotherapy and, 62–64
Affiliation
 cathartic model and, 218
 group psychotherapy and, 153, 154, 161, 165
Affirmation, psychotherapy and, 73
Age, psychotherapy and, 11, 15, 21

261

272

SUBJECT INDEX

Psychopathology (*cont.*)
  cognitive approaches to psychotherapy and,
    178, 191
  psychoanalytic affect theory and, 128
  rules of living and, 231, 233, 234, 238,
    250–252
  time and, 133, 140
Psychosis, time and, 141
Psychotherapy
  cathartic model and, 210, 221, 227
  change processes in, 59, 60, 83, 84
    acknowledgment, 67, 68
    affective assessment, 62–64
    affective-change processes, 65, 66
    anxiety, 80–83
    arousing affect, 69–71
    core beliefs, 79, 80
    creation of meaning, 68, 69
    emotion as adaptive, 60, 61
    emotion as synthesis, 61, 62
    events, 74
    expression, 72–74
    interrupted expression, 76–79
    maladaptive affective process, 72
    painful emotion, 74–76
    primary emotion, 64, 65
    taking responsibility, 71, 72
  cognitive approaches to, 177
    depressogenic assumptions, 182, 183
    future directions, 190–192
    future schemas, 181, 182
    model of depression, 178, 179
    operations, 184, 185
    products, 186, 187
    propositions, 183, 184
    self-schemas, 180, 181
    structures, 179, 180
    vulnerability, 187–190
  group, *see* Group psychotherapy
  multimodal therapy and, 198–200
  psychoevolutionary perspective of, 3, 4, 19–
    21, 37
    adult ethogram, 13, 14
    biology, 16, 17
    causation, 10, 11
    change, 27–30
    cognitions, 17–19
    compromises, 14
    coping, 26, 27
    deception, 15, 16
    evolutionary theory, 8, 10, 19–21
    existential crises, 25, 26
    hierarchy, 21, 22
    identity, 22, 23
    psychoevolutionary theory, 4–9, 21, 24
    tactics, 32, 34–37
    temporality, 23, 25
    territoriality, 22
    therapeutic communication, 30–33
    traits, 11–13
  rules of living and, 232–234, 237, 240,
    246–250

R

Rational-emotive therapy
  multimodal therapy and, 199
  rules of living and, 232–234
Reaction formation
  primary process and, 108, 109
  psychotherapy and, 8
Recall
  cathartic model and, 221
  psychotherapy and, 180, 181, 185
Reciprocity
  anger and, 47
  cognitive approaches to psychotherapy and,
    178
  group psychotherapy and, 157
  multimodal therapy and, 199, 200, 202, 205
  psychoevolutionary perspective of
    psychotherapy and, 14, 16, 31
Regression
  primary process and, 90, 91, 106, 108
  psychoanalytic affect theory and, 123
  time and, 142
Reinforcement
  cathartic model and, 223
  cognitive approaches to psychotherapy and,
    185, 187
  group psychotherapy and, 163, 164, 168
  multimodal therapy and, 202
  primary process and, 103
  psychoevolutionary perspective of
    psychotherapy and, 29
  rules of living and, 234, 236, 238–241, 248
Reintegration, primary process and, 110, 111
Reinterpretation, psychotherapy and, 37
Rejection
  cathartic model and, 224

CONTENTS OF PREVIOUS VOLUMES

277

VOLUME 3: BIOLOGICAL FOUNDATIONS OF EMOTION

Part I General Models of Brain Functioning

Part II Ethological and Evolutionary Considerations